Social Security and Pension Reform

Social Security and Pension Reform

International Perspectives

Marek Szczepański
John A. Turner
Editors

2014

W.E. Upjohn Institute for Employment Research
Kalamazoo, Michigan

Library of Congress Cataloging-in-Publication Data

Social security and pension reform international perspectives / Marek Szczepanski, John A. Turner, editors.
    pages cm
    "This book is based largely on the 2012 conference of the European Network for Research on Supplementary Pensions (ENRSP), held at Poznan University of Technology, Poznan, Poland, on September 13-14, 2012"—Preface.
    Includes index.
    ISBN 978-0-88099-467-5 (pbk. : alk. paper) — ISBN 0-88099-467-3 (pbk. : alk. paper) — ISBN 978-0-88099-468-2 (hardcover : alk. paper) — ISBN 0-88099-468-1 (hardcover : alk. paper)
    1. Social security. 2. Pensions. 3. Pensions—Government policy. I. Szczepanski, Marek, 1959- II. Turner, John A. (John Andrew), 1949 July 9-
    HD7091.S5865 2014
    331.25'22—dc23
                                  2013043011

The facts presented in this study and the observations and viewpoints expressed are the sole responsibility of the authors. They do not necessarily represent positions of the W.E. Upjohn Institute for Employment Research.

Cover design by Alcorn Publication Design.
Index prepared by Diane Worden.
Printed in the United States of America.
Printed on recycled paper.

Contents

Part 3: Reforms in Australia, Asia, Africa, and the Americas

Part 4: Reform Issues

Preface

This book is based largely on the 2012 conference of the European Network for Research on Supplementary Pensions (ENRSP), held at Poznań University of Technology, Poznań, Poland, on September 13–14, 2012. The ENRSP is a research network for independent researchers in the field of private pensions. Marek Szczepański, chair of Economic Sciences at Poznań University of Technology, organized the conference. It was the first conference of the network held in Eastern Europe. Financial support for the conference was provided by ENRSP and by the PZU Pension Society in Poland.

Szczepański has edited a conference volume for that conference, which is published in English in Poland under the title *Old-Age Crisis and Pension Reform: Where Do We Stand?* This volume differs from that in that it is oriented toward pension policy experts in the United States. It does not include all the papers from the conference, while it does include several papers not presented at the conference. The volume published in Poland has more of a focus on Central and Eastern Europe, while this volume, through the addition of several papers, has more of a global focus. In addition, all of the papers have been edited so that they use U.S. pension terminology.

Part 1

Overview

1

Social Security and Pension Reform

The Views of 16 Authors

Marek Szczepański
Poznań University of Technology

John A. Turner
Pension Policy Center

Countries around the world are reforming their social security and pension systems. International studies often focus on social security reforms in Europe and North America, and may include Latin America. Reforms, however, are also occurring in Asia and Africa, and include reforms of voluntary and employer-provided pensions as well as social security programs. This book discusses both social security and employer-provided pension reforms, as well as reforms in most regions of the world.

This chapter provides an overview of the book. Many of the chapters were originally presented at a conference of the European Network for Research on Supplementary Pensions (ENRSP) in Poznań, Poland, in 2012, that was organized by Marek Szczepański. Other chapters have been added to expand the range of countries covered.

OVERVIEW

Part 1 of the book contains this introduction and a chapter written by John A. Turner and David Rajnes that examines social security and pension reforms around the world. It includes a survey of some of the main points of chapters of this book, but has a considerably broader focus in terms of countries and issues. For example, an issue not touched on elsewhere is the trend in some countries toward adopting automatic adjustment mechanisms as a way of maintaining the solvency of their social security systems. In some countries, the level of social security benefits at retirement is automatically adjusted downward to reflect improvements over time in life expectancy. Turner and Rajnes's chapter also discusses the policy that a number of countries have adopted, which is raising the earliest age at which social security benefits can be received, and other policies to encourage workers to postpone retirement, which are ways of dealing with the added costs to pension systems due to increased life expectancy.

Turner and Rajnes discuss in Chapter 2 issues of concern in high-income countries, and also the problem that most workers around the world are not covered by social security or pension programs. Countries such as China and Kenya have developed innovative programs to attempt to deal with that issue. The programs in those two countries are discussed in greater depth in Chapters 10 and 11.

REFORMS IN EUROPE

Part 2, which focuses on reforms of social security and pensions in Europe, is the largest section of the book. The authors discuss reforms in Ireland, Sweden, Norway, Portugal, Poland, and other countries in Central and Eastern Europe.

Chapter 3, by Gerard Hughes, discusses the reform in Ireland mandating that employers provide their employees the option to participate in an employer-provided pension plan, called a Personal Retirement Savings Account (PRSA). Although the reform requires employers who do not provide a pension plan for all their employees to designate a personal pension provider for their employees, less than half of the firms have done so. This may be in part because employees have shown limited interest, as no one is contributing to a PRSA in four-fifths of the firms that have designated a PRSA provider. Thus, the hopes that policy analysts had for this approach to extend pension coverage have not been realized. Requiring employers to offer pensions, but making the take-up by employees voluntary, has not succeeded in significantly raising pension coverage in Ireland.

By comparison, the United Kingdom has adopted a policy that goes further: all private employers will be required to offer retirement plans meeting minimum requirements for their employees. Those plans can be defined benefit plans or defined contribution plans. In addition, going beyond the requirements in Ireland, employers will be required to automatically enroll their employees in the new system, with the employees having the option to withdraw. It is anticipated that this change will increase pension participation in the United Kingdom by 5–9 million workers (Segars 2012). An additional requirement is that mandatory contributions in the case of defined contribution plans will be made by employers, employees, and the government. When fully phased in, contributions will be 4 percent of pay for employees, 3 percent for employers, and a 1 percent government subsidy, making a total contribution of 8 percent of pay. Initially, contributions will start at a total of 2 percent of pay, reaching 8 percent by 2018.

The requirements apply to workers who earn more than minimum wage and are at least 22 years old; the maximum age for men is 65, with the maximum of 65 being phased in for women. The requirement for automatic enrollment into a qualifying pension plan was initially phased in on October 1, 2012, and will continue to be phased in through 2016. It will apply first to large companies, and over time to all others. Eventually automatic enrollment will apply to all employees who do not have another plan.

For companies that do not offer a qualifying plan, all money contributed to pension plans for employees will go into the National Employment Savings Trust (NEST), a jointly trusteed investment vehicle that will offer a number of funds. Employees who use the NEST plan will have the option to choose investments or have a default investment chosen for them, which will be a retirement date fund based on what the employee indicates is his or her expected retirement date.

Chapter 4, by Gabriella Sjögren Lindquist and Eskil Wadensjö, focuses on low-income retirees in Sweden. The chapter begins with an outline of the Swedish system, which some countries have considered as a possible model for reform. The system includes a notional defined contribution system as the primary source of benefits and a mandatory individual account system, neither of which contain redistributive elements. Redistribution toward low-income pensioners occurs through other government programs, such as the guarantee pension, which is based on the level of other pension income a person receives, and a housing allowance. Women, the self-employed, immigrants, and persons at advanced ages are more likely to have low income in retirement than other groups.

Nonetheless, poverty in Sweden is low compared to other European Union (EU) countries. It is defined on a relative basis as having an income below 60 percent of median income. Because Sweden is a high-income country, if poverty were defined alternatively as being below 60 percent of median income in the EU, the poverty rate would be even lower.

Chapter 5, by Maria Clara Murteira, discusses social security reform in Portugal and how the EU has affected it. The demand for macroeconomic budgetary reform has put pressure on countries to reform their social security programs. In addition, demand for fiscal austerity has put further pressure on pay-as-you-go (PAYG) financing of social security because of increased unemployment.

Murteira argues that while the social security reform of 2007 was presented as a technical reform, it in fact involved a fundamental change in principles and objectives for the social security program. By means of parametric changes, a structural reform was achieved. She criticizes the reform because it focused on the means of social policy (financing) and not on its goals (providing adequate retirement income). While PAYG financing was not replaced by funding, the overall logic of the system was changed. The goal of social security retirement pensions in Portugal is no longer to provide income maintenance. Instead, the goal now is to provide a modest level of income protection against old-age poverty. Murteira concludes that ultimately social security policy is about political choices, as it is influenced by the beliefs and ideas about the role of government in society.

Chapter 6, by Magdalena Mosionek-Schweda, describes the Norwegian Government Pension Fund, which is a sovereign wealth fund and is one of the largest pension funds in the world. The fund has two parts: one that is (Norway) is entirely invested in Scandinavia and another part (Global) that is entirely invested outside Norway. She focuses on the Global fund, which is financed by revenues from the extraction of oil in Norway. It currently is worth about $120,000 per person in

Norway, and is expected to grow on a per capita basis before it is drawn on to help pay for retirement benefits. The fund does not have a legal liability for future pension benefits, but it is designed to be used for the purpose of helping to pay for these benefits. As discussed in Chapters 2 and 10, Ireland, China, and several other countries have similar funds. If the United States were to return to an era of budget surpluses, as it did during the Clinton administration, it could establish a similar fund.

Chapter 7, by Maciej Żukowski, describes social security reform in Central and Eastern Europe. This chapter provides a survey of a number of countries in Central and Eastern Europe, with a more detailed discussion of the reforms in Poland. While many aspects of the socialist economies in this region were not functioning well before the breakup of the Soviet Union in 1991, they did have functioning social security systems. However, starting in 1998, most of the countries in the region have had major reforms to their social security systems, introducing funded individual accounts as part of the systems. Of the 10 Central and Eastern European countries that are now members of the EU, all but Slovenia have adopted mandatory funded individual accounts as part of their social security systems, along with a reduced PAYG social security program (U.S. Social Security Administration 2012).

Because of the global financial crisis, since 2010, some of these countries have reduced the contributions to the funded individual accounts. They have encountered the double payment problem, which is needing to finance the PAYG systems while at the same time also contributing to a funded system. These countries did not adequately take into account this problem when they established their individual account systems. The European Union Stability and Growth Pact, which sets target limits on government debt and deficits, has influenced them to cut back on their individual account plan contributions. This issue is also discussed in Chapter 5, where EU policies are seen to have led to a reduction in the PAYG system in Portugal.

Chapter 8, by Marek Szczepański and Tomasz Brzęczek, discusses the risks in employer-provided pension plans in Poland. Like Sweden, Poland has a mandatory notional defined contribution system and a mandatory individual account system. However, unlike Sweden it has relatively few voluntary employer-provided pensions. Those pensions in Sweden cover most workers, in part due to widespread collective bargaining agreements. Szczepański and Brzęczek survey representatives of businesses that provide pension plans, who indicate that the two most important risks facing pension plans are financial market risk and economic market risk. They find a high degree of mistrust by employers sponsoring pension plans of the advice provided by the pension plan managers. They also find that pension plans in Poland have invested in low-risk, low-return portfolios.

REFORMS IN AUSTRALIA, CHINA, EAST AFRICA, AND THE AMERICAS

The following four chapters comprise Part 3 of the book and discuss pension and social security reform in Australia, China, East Africa, and the Americas.

Chapter 9, by Ross Clare, discusses the retirement income system in Australia and issues of equity or fairness. Recent reforms in Australia have reduced the extent of tax preferences going to high earners. He finds that less than 15 percent of the government assistance for pension contributions flows to those paying the top marginal tax rate. Government assistance includes tax preferences and a government matching contribution for low earners. This compares to the approximately 30 percent of aggregate personal income tax collections that is paid by that group of taxpayers. Thus, a far smaller percentage of tax preferences and government contribution assistance in Australia goes to upper-income persons than in the United States. A study in the United States finds that two-thirds of the benefits from pension tax preferences accrue to the top 20 percent of the income distribution (Orszag 2000).

To further limit the tax benefits accruing to high earners in Australia, a proposal is being considered that would reduce the amount of tax-preferenced contributions that could be made by persons with a pension account of A$500,000 or more. (Australian dollars are roughly equal in value to U.S. dollars at 2013 exchange rates, although exchange rates fluctuate over time.) When viewing the Australian retirement income system in a broader framework, also taking into account the Age Pension, which is received by most persons but whose value declines with increases in personal income, the amount of government subsidy to the retirement income system is fairly equal across deciles of the income distribution.

Chapter 10, by Tianhong Chen and John A. Turner, describes social security reform in China, which has roughly one-fifth of the world's population aged 60 and older. Also adding to the importance of understanding China's retirement income system, China is undergoing a period of important changes in its provision of old-age benefits. At the start of 2009, less than 30 percent of the adult population in China was covered by a social security old-age benefits program, but by 2012 that number had increased to 55 percent. Affecting its ability to provide old-age benefits, China is also undergoing important labor force changes—because of its one-child policy, the labor force declined in 2012 for the first time, and declines are projected to continue for many years.

China has a decentralized system of social security, where the central government establishes general guidelines, but subprovincial governments (county governments) have some discretion in establishing the programs, for example, in setting contribution rates. This feature alone would make the system complex. However, within that framework, there are separate systems for urban workers, rural workers, and rural workers working in urban areas. Each of these three systems has two parts—an individual account portion and a PAYG system. In addition, government employees have separate systems, and Hong Kong has a separate system.

An unusual feature of social security provision in China is that its new program for rural workers, which is voluntary, has been highly successful in attracting participants. Because voluntary programs generally fail to cover more than half of the eligible population in high-income countries, and a much lower portion in middle- and low-income countries, China's program may provide a model for other countries.

Chapter 11, by John A. Turner, describes social security and pension reform in the five countries of the East African Community—Kenya, Tanzania, Uganda, Burundi, and Rwanda. The chapter discusses social security and employer-provided pensions for both private and public sector workers. Many of the issues these countries face are similar to retirement income issues in other countries in sub-Saharan Africa. A different aspect, however, is that these five countries are attempting to move toward greater economic integration, with the possibility of eventually having a single currency and a common market.

Most workers in the region and throughout sub-Saharan Africa—and in most middle- and lower-income countries—are not participating in social security or in another pension program. Therefore, extending social security or pension coverage to rural and informal sector workers is arguably the most important issue facing social security programs in most countries around the world.

Kenya has recently developed an innovative voluntary pension program that may hold promise for extending pension coverage to low-income workers in other parts of the world. In this system, workers can contribute small amounts, as little as $0.25, using their cell phones and a mobile money system. Advances in cell phone technology have greatly reduced the cost of cell phones and usage rates so that even poor people in Kenya have cell phones, and so that small transactions are economically feasible. Many more people have cell phones than have bank accounts. This program is a promising development for extending pension coverage to poor people in other countries.

Chapter 12, by Denise Gómez-Hernández and Alberto M. Ramírez de Jurado Frías, analyzes defined contributions in a sample of countries from North, Central, and South America. Instead of using a replacement rate to measure the effectiveness of the defined contribution systems, they compare projected pension benefits to a measure of the basic market basket of goods. They find that differences in the level of fees charged to pensions across countries have an important effect on the outcomes of the pension systems.

REFORM ISSUES

Part 4 contains the final two chapters, which discuss particular issues in social security and pension reform rather than focus on particular countries. Chapter 13, by Adam Samborski, discusses issues in pension fund governance, focusing on principal-agent problems in pension fund governance. In agency theory, agency relationships are understood as contracts under which a principal engages a third-party (agent) to perform certain actions on its behalf in dealing with a second party, which is the provider of the service. The agent provides a managerial or advisory role. In pension arrangements, the plan participant is the principal, the plan sponsor is the agent, and the financial institution managing the pension funds is the second party. This implies the need for the principal to delegate specific powers to the agent to make certain decisions. However, both the agent and the second party may have conflicts of interest so that they are motivated to not act in the best interests of the pension participant.

Chapter 14, by John A. Turner and Dana M. Muir, discusses issues in financial literacy, financial education, and financial advice. A lack of financial literacy is widespread in countries around the world. This is particularly a problem in countries that rely on mandatory individual accounts and defined contribution pensions, where workers have added responsibility for financial decision making. Financial education has been considered as a remedy, but studies have shown that many workers lack interest in gaining the required knowledge. Financial education may be more successful if it is incorporated into school education programs for students. Financial advice has been recognized as another way of dealing with financial illiteracy. However, many financial advisers have conflicts of interest that cause the advice they provide to not be in the best interest of their clients. Because of the way financial advisers are compensated, the advice that provides them the highest income may also lead to pension participants and plan sponsors paying higher fees, but with no improvement in investment outcomes. Surveys have documented that persons receiving financial advice may receive lower rates of return net of fees than those not receiving advice.

CONCLUSION

Many countries around the world are undertaking social security and pension reforms. These reforms are motivated in part by population aging, but they also are occurring in response to economic development in Africa, China, and elsewhere, and are due to changing views about how retirement income should be provided. Countries often look to international experience when considering reform options, and this book discusses social security and pension reform issues in different parts of the world.

References

Orszag, Peter R. 2000. "How the 'Cross-Testing' Pension Loophole Harms Low- and Moderate-Income Earners." Washington, DC: Center on Budget and Policy Priorities. http://www.cbpp.org/cms/index.cfm?fa=view&id=1736 (accessed April 2, 2013).

Segars, Joanne. 2012. "Motherhood, Apple Pie, and Risk Sharing." In *Defining Ambition: Views from the Industry on Achieving Risk Sharing*. London: National Association of Pension Funds, pp. 14–23. http://www.napf.co.uk/PolicyandResearch/DocumentLibrary/~/media/Policy/Documents/0266_Defining_Ambition_Views_from_the_industry_on_achieving_risk_sharing.ashx (accessed April 2, 2013).

U.S. Social Security Administration. 2012. "Focus on Central and Eastern Europe: An Inventory of Pension Reforms, 2008 to Present." *International Update*. March. http://www.ssa.gov/policy/docs/progdesc/intl_update/2012-03/index.html (accessed April 2, 2013).

2

Social Security and Pension Trends around the World

John A. Turner
Pension Policy Center

David Rajnes
Social Security Administration

Retirement income systems are in a state of change. Increasing longevity and declining birth rates cause population aging and put pressure on retirement income financing. For this reason, countries around the world are reforming their retirement income systems of pensions and social security old-age benefits. Changing views about the provision of retirement income and innovations in program design are also influencing the trends.

This chapter surveys trends in social security and pension programs around the world. It first discusses social security reforms and mandatory individual account programs, and then discusses reforms of employer-provided pension plans.

SOCIAL SECURITY AND MANDATORY INDIVIDUAL ACCOUNT PROGRAMS

Social security programs and mandatory individual account programs are considered together as part of government mandated provision for retirement.

Raising Retirement Ages

With people living longer in many parts of the world, the cost of providing social security and pension benefits in traditional pension systems is increasing because those benefits are being provided for more years. To offset this cost increase, many countries in Europe, Eastern Europe, and elsewhere have legislated increases in the early retirement age for social security benefits, sometimes called the eligibility age or minimum age for retirement. That is the earliest age at which social security retirement benefits can be received. Often those increases are legislated to occur a number of years into the future, or are phased in over a number of years. In some countries, changes have also occurred in the age at which the worker can receive a full benefit, but those changes are more aptly described as changes in benefit generosity, rather than changes in retirement ages.

Japan is raising the eligibility age for both of its social security programs (Rajnes 2007). Japan passed legislation in 1995 that raised the eligibility age for its flat rate pension (National Pension) by one year every three years, with it increasing from age 60 to 61 in 2001 and reaching 65 in 2014. Based on legislation passed in 2000, Japan is raising the eligibility age for its earnings-related pension (Employees' Pension Insurance) by one year every three years starting in 2013. With these changes, men born after 1960 and women born after 1965 have a retirement age for both programs of 65 by 2025 for men and 2030 for women.

New Zealand raised its eligibility age from 60 in 1991 to 65 in 2001. Those workers who turned 60 before March 31, 1992, were eligible for a social security benefit at age 60. The legislation, which passed August 1, 1991, took effect the following April, when eligibility increased from age 60 to 61. Beginning July 1, 1993, eligibility rose by three months for each six-month period until April 1, 2001, when the eligibility age reached 65. Thus, a five-year increase in the eligibility age phased in over nine years. A Transitional Retirement Benefit was paid over this period to those affected by the changes, with the age of eligibility for this benefit also rising until it was phased out on April 1, 2001.

Some Organisation for Economic Co-operation and Development (OECD) countries have had a longstanding eligibility age of 65, and some are raising the eligibility age even higher. In Australia, Austria, Germany, Switzerland, and the United Kingdom, the eligibility age for men has been 65 since at least 1949. In 2012, the Netherlands passed a law that will raise the retirement age in 2020 from 65 to 66. In Ireland, starting in 2014, the age of entitlement for social security benefits will be raised from 65 to 66. In Australia, it will be gradually rising to 67 from 2017 to 2023 for both men and women.

Some countries have had a higher eligibility age in social security in the past than they do currently. In 1913, when social security was introduced in Sweden, the eligibility age was 67 (Lindquist and Wadensjö, this volume). The eligibility age in the United States was 65 in 1940 but now is 62.

In Central and Eastern Europe, a number of countries—Bulgaria, Croatia, the Czech Republic, Estonia, Latvia, Hungary, and Poland— are increasing their retirement eligibility ages as a move toward insuring the solvency of their social security systems. In 2012, Latvia enacted legislation raising the eligibility age for social security benefits from 62 to 65, rising by three months a year, and reaching 65 in 2025 (U.S. Social Security Administration 2012).

Some low-income countries in Africa retain low benefit eligibility ages for social security benefits. For example, the early retirement age is 50 in Swaziland. However, some high-income countries also have low eligibility ages. In Kuwait, the retirement age is 50, but it is increasing to 55 by 2020.

Equalizing Benefit Eligibility Ages for Men and Women

Many countries historically have had lower early retirement ages for women than for men. However, many of these countries have equalized the ages for men and women by raising over time the early retirement age of women so that it reaches the level for men. China, Cuba, Vietnam, and the former communist country of Russia are among the countries that maintain lower early retirement ages for women than men.

Changes to Encourage Later Retirement

Many countries have enacted changes other than increases in early retirement ages to encourage later retirement. Among OECD countries, the Czech Republic, Denmark, Finland, France, Greece, Hungary, Poland, and Spain have enacted tighter requirements to qualify for early retirement benefits (Whitehouse and Antolin 2012). In Canada in 2012, an earlier enacted change took effect, raising benefits for workers who postpone taking benefits past age 65, cutting them for workers who retire before age 65, and introducing a new benefit for workers who are still working. Bulgaria in 2012 also raised benefits for workers postponing retirement. In 2012, Denmark scaled back its government-subsidized program providing early retirement benefits. Sweden has instituted income tax credits for workers aged 65 and older. Portugal has reduced social security contributions for workers aged 65 and older. France has increased the actuarial reduction of benefits for early retirement. In Kenya, pension benefits received at age 65 or older are tax free, in order to encourage postponement of receipt of those benefits.

In raising the retirement age, one option is to provide for early retirement for workers who have worked for many years. Some countries with special early retirement benefits have raised the number of years required to be eligible for those benefits. France has raised the number of years from 37.5 to 40, while Belgium has raised the number of years from 20 to 35 (U.S. Government Accountability Office 2005).

In 2011, Spain passed a law that increased incentives for older workers to remain in the labor force. An innovative aspect of this reform is that the incentives are greater for workers with more years of service. For workers with less than 25 years of service, for every year an individual continues working beyond the full retirement age, the incentive will remain at 2 percent; from 25 to 36 years, 2.75 percent; and 37 or more years, 4 percent. Some countries encourage work at older ages by reducing the social security contribution rate. In Portugal, the rate the employee pays has dropped from 11 percent to 8 percent since 2009.

Retrenchment in Traditional Social Security Programs

A number of countries have cut back on the generosity of their social security benefits, resulting in falling income replacement rates in old age. These countries include France, Japan, Sweden, Greece, South Korea, and the United States. Among OECD countries, cutbacks in benefit generosity have typically reduced future benefits between one-fifth and one-quarter (Whitehoues and Antolin 2012).

Sometimes the cutback is expressed in another way, perhaps to reduce the political reaction to the change. For example, one way to cut benefits is to postpone access to full benefits to a later age, coupled with actuarial reductions in benefits received at an earlier age. This approach has been used by Germany, Italy, Japan, Switzerland, and the United States. The United States has reduced benefits at the eligibility age by raising the Normal Retirement Age from 65 to 67 over the period 2000–2022.

Many countries have reduced benefits in traditional social insurance old-age benefits programs by increasing the years used in the earnings averaging period for calculating benefits. Spain has done so, resulting in more years of relatively low earnings being included, lowering average earnings in the benefit calculation. Finland, Austria, France, Italy, Greece, and the United Kingdom have also increased the number of years used in benefit calculation. In Italy, the increase was from the worker's last five years of earnings to lifetime earnings. Portugal increased the number of years from 10 years to all years of work. However, it also defined a transitional period, from 2002 to 2016, during which the most favorable method of calculation—the former, the latter, or a weighted average of both—could be applied in order to guarantee beneficiaries the most favorable rule to determine the pension level. In 2007, it subsequently passed a law that shortened the transitional period (See Murteira, this volume).

Benefits can be reduced by changing the calculation of cost-of-living adjustments. Germany and Japan have both moved from basing postretirement benefit adjustments on the growth of net wages rather than gross wages. With the growth of taxes and social security contribution rates, net wages grow less rapidly than gross wages. Reductions in cost-of-living adjustments reduce benefits more at older ages than at younger ages because for each retiree, the effect of the cuts is cumulative over the time period since retirement.

Countries with traditional benefit formulas have a parameter in those formulas that determines the generosity of the rate at which future benefits accrue with additional work. Japan, Norway, and Portugal have cut future benefits by reducing the benefit accrual rate in the benefit formula. For example, Japan cut the accrual rate from 1 percent per year of work to 0.7125 percent (U.S. Government Accountability Office 2005). Austria has reduced the accrual rates used to calculate the initial benefit from an annual rate of 2 percent to 1.78 percent starting in 2009.

Benefit Reductions That Affect Current Retirees

Traditionally, social security benefit cuts have been targeted so that they did not affect people who were already receiving benefits because those people were considered to be particularly vulnerable. Because of their age, for many returning to work to offset the benefit cuts was not an option. That policy of protecting current beneficiaries has changed in some countries.

In most countries, benefits in payment are indexed so that they at least keep pace with the rate of inflation and thus maintain their real (inflation-corrected) value during retirement. Greece and Norway have cut benefits by reducing the indexing of benefits in payment. Sweden's automatic adjustment mechanism can involve a reduction in indexing of benefits in payment so that it is less than the rate of inflation.

Increasing Contribution Rates

Some countries have raised contribution rates, particularly countries that have relatively low contribution rates, but increases are not limited to those countries. Kenya is an example (Turner, this volume). Contribution rates have been increased in many OECD countries, including Denmark, Finland, France, and Sweden. They have also increased in some countries with mandatory individual accounts and mandatory pensions, such as Mexico, Singapore, and Australia. Australia is raising further its contribution rate for its mandatory pension system from 9 percent to 12 percent (Clare, this volume).

Increasing the Contribution Base

Social security contributions can be increased by raising the contribution base rather than raising the contribution rate. Countries that have completely eliminated the ceiling on taxable earnings for social security financing include Finland and Norway. In 2001, Ireland eliminated the ceiling on taxable earnings for social security for employer contributions. The United Kingdom also requires employers to pay social security taxes on employee earnings without a ceiling on those earnings. Some countries have expanded the range of earnings included in taxable earnings. Japan, for example, included the twice-yearly bonuses in taxable earnings. France, in addition to raising the contribution rate, increased the contribution base to include employer contributions to occupational pension plans.

New Revenue Sources

Some countries have decided that they cannot raise the payroll tax any further. For example, Japan has been concerned about the effects of increases in the payroll tax, which would raise labor costs, on the international competitiveness of its workforce. By comparison, however, China, which has large trade surpluses, has a social security tax rate that varies across provinces but averages 28 percent (Chen and Turner, this volume), substantially higher than in Japan.

In 2012, Japan legislated an increase of its value added tax (VAT) from 5 to 10 percent, starting in 2014, with the increased revenue being used to finance its social security program. Although all OECD countries use contributions from employers and employees to finance social security old age benefits, nearly all those countries also use general revenue funding. France has levied a tax of 1 percent on all income that is dedicated to financing old-age benefits (U.S. Government Accountability Office 2005). More recently, Portugal in 2012 levied a tax on pensions of more than 1,500 euros per month.

Unification of National Social Security Systems

When social security systems were started they often excluded certain groups, such as government workers, workers in particular industries that already had good pensions, or workers in industries with low wages, such as agriculture. Some countries developed multiple pension systems to cover different workers. Reforms in the United States, Chile, Nigeria, and Greece have expanded the coverage of national social security systems to include more groups of workers, in the process unifying. Part of this movement has been a trend to include government workers in the national social security program. Thailand is currently phasing out some special programs for government workers. In 2011, China established a national unified social security system for urban workers, which facilitates workers moving between different parts of the country (Chen and Turner, this volume). In Africa, Cape

Verde, Sierra Leone, Ghana, Nigeria, and Zambia have all consolidated their social security programs for formal sector workers (Republic of Kenya 2012).

Ending Provident Funds

Provident funds are defined contribution plans that typically provide lump sum benefits and have a single investment pool for all participants. These types of plans were established in many countries that were formerly British colonies or British protectorates, in part because of their simplicity. Provident funds were established in most of the former British colonies or protectorates in Africa—Gambia, Ghana, Kenya, Nigeria, Seychelles, Swaziland, Tanzania, Uganda, and Zambia. Swaziland retains such a plan; however, many countries, including Ghana, Nigeria, and Tanzania, have ended those plans and switched to social insurance types of plans. Kenya and Uganda in 2012 were considering converting their provident funds to defined contribution pensions, rather than to a defined benefit social insurance pension (Turner, this volume). Nigeria subsequently switched to a mandatory individual account system. In the Caribbean, the Bahamas, Saint Kitts and Nevis, and Saint Vincent and the Grenadines are among countries that converted a provident fund to a traditional defined benefit social security program (Gillion et al. 2000).

Social Security Privatization with Mandatory Funded Individual Accounts

Most countries provide social security benefits through traditional defined benefit pay-as-you-go systems (PAYG) based on principles of social insurance. However, many countries in Latin America, Central and Eastern Europe, and elsewhere have added mandatory individual accounts as a component of their social security programs. One of the motivations for social security privatization was the belief that this innovation would lead to a closer connection between contributions and benefits, which would lead to less distortion of incentives in labor markets.

In 1981, Chile was the first country to privatize its social security program with mandatory individual accounts. Chile completely ended its PAYG system for private sector workers, replacing it with an individual account system, while most other countries that followed it cut back on the PAYG system and combined it with a mandatory individual account system. Since 1990, 10 other countries in Latin America have followed Chile (Kritzer, Kay, and Sinha 2011). The first countries following Chile to switch to individual accounts (with the year implemented) were Peru (1993), Colombia (1993), Argentina (1994), Uruguay (1996), and Mexico (1997). These were followed by two of the poorest countries in the region, Bolivia (1997) and El Salvador (1998). In 2008, Panama added mandatory individual accounts as part of social security for new entrants into the social security system.

Beginning in the late 1990s, following the fall of the Soviet Union, a number of countries that were part of the Soviet Union or that were in Central and Eastern Europe added mandatory individual accounts as part of their social security systems. Kazakhstan (1997), Hungary (1998), and Poland (1999) were early leaders, but they were followed by Bulgaria (2000), Latvia (2001), Croatia (2002), and Estonia (2002) (Szczepański and Brzęczek, this volume). Other countries include Bulgaria (2002), the former Yugoslav Republic of Macedonia (2003), Slovakia (2005), and Romania (2008) (Żukowski, this volume). In addition, Lithuania, the Czech Republic, Slovenia, and Russia have enacted reforms.

Mandatory defined contribution plans have also been introduced in countries in other regions, either in addition to or in replacement of existing traditional social security programs. In 2011, Thailand introduced the National Pension Fund as a mandatory defined contribution plan to supplement its traditional social security plan. In 2010, Egypt passed a law replacing its PAYG system with a system of mandatory individual accounts. In 2010, Brunei added mandatory individual accounts to its existing mandatory social security system. Between 1988 and 2008, 29 countries followed Chile and established a funded first pillar social security system (Holzmann 2012).

Retrenchment on Privatization

Some countries that enacted reforms privatizing social security by adding individual accounts have later cut back on those reforms, reducing or eliminating the contributions to privatized individual accounts. Argentina ended its system of privatized individual accounts in 2008, while Bolivia nationalized its system of individual accounts in late 2010. Retrenchment has been more common in Central and Eastern Europe than in South America, in part because of the financial crisis there and the subsequent economic downturn. In Central and Eastern Europe, Poland, Latvia, Lithuania, Estonia, Romania, and Slovakia all retrenched their privatized systems in some way since 2010 (Fultz 2012). Starting in 2010, Hungary ceased funding for its second-tier program and returned most of the accumulated funds to the participants.

Retrenchment has occurred in part because of the double payment problem, where payments are being made into the new individual accounts, while payments are still required into the traditional PAYG system to pay the benefits promised from that system. Some governments have found that it was too expensive to pay for the existing PAYG system and for the new individual accounts, particularly in an economic downturn. In 2012, the Slovak Republic reduced the contributions to the mandatory individual accounts and transferred those contributions to the PAYG system. It also temporarily permitted workers to withdraw from the system.

In 1997, China established a multipillar reform, adding funded individual accounts to a PAYG system. However, it later decided not to fully fund those accounts, taking some of the money originally designated for the individual accounts and using it to finance the PAYG benefits. Those accounts now are more like notional accounts, with an unfunded liability arising due to their total liabilities exceeding their total assets (Chen and Turner, this volume).

It was initially thought that competition among service providers would reduce high fees in mandatory individual account systems, but that has not proved to be the case. The reason may be that participants are not sensitive to fees when choosing among service providers, perhaps because they do not understand how much fees can reduce future account balances.

Chile and Mexico have taken steps to reduce fees. In Chile, every two years a bidding process determines the lowest-fee pension fund provider. All new entrants must use that provider. Mexico has taken steps to increase competition among pension fund providers as a way to reduce fees. The United Kingdom has limited the maximum fees that can be charged on stakeholder pensions, which are a form of voluntary individual account pension. Australia has introduced a low-cost fund as an alternative in its mandatory employer-provided pension system. The United States and the United Kingdom have taken steps to have more disclosure of fee information to pension participants.

Defaults to Deal with Decision-Making Problems

Defaults have been used in mandatory individual account systems for workers who do not wish to make an investment choice. For example, in the Swedish Premium Pension system, which is a mandatory individual account system, if a worker fails to choose an investment, the worker is placed in the default investment. In 2010, Sweden changed that default so that the risk of the portfolio varies by the age of the participant, with the percent invested in low-risk assets increasing as the participant ages. In Australia in the mandatory pension fund system, if an employer does not wish to choose a pension fund for its employees, it can use the default fund for employers in its industry. In New Zealand in the KiwiSaver program, workers who do not choose a pension provider are automatically enrolled in the employer's preferred plan, but if the employer has not chosen a plan they are randomly assigned to one of six default plans. In Peru, recent reform measures encourage more competition among AFPs (Pension Fund Associations) by assigning new labor force entrants to the AFP with the lowest administrative fee. From October through December 2012, all new entrants to the system of individual accounts were assigned to Prima, the pension fund management company (AFP) that offered the lowest administrative fee in the tender held in September.

Raising Limits on International Investments

Some countries have raised the limits on international investments allowed both for mandatory pension plans and for voluntary pension plans. A few countries have no limits on these investments. In 2008, Uruguay raised from 0 to 15 percent the limit on international investments in its mandatory individual account system, and Colombia raised its limit to 40 percent. In 2009, Brazil raised to 10 percent the limits on international investments for certain pension funds provided voluntarily by employers. In 2010 and 2011, Chile raised the limits on the percentage of a pension fund's assets in its mandatory system that can be invested in international investments, with the limit reaching 80 percent in 2011. Peru raised the limit in its mandatory system to 30 percent in 2010. In Sweden in mandatory individual accounts, and in the United States in voluntary individual account defined contribution plans, individuals can invest entirely in international investments.

Notional Account Plans

In notional account or notional defined contribution systems (or nonfinancial defined contribution systems), each worker has an account, but the account is not fully funded, generally only having limited funding. Rather, it has a notional or accounting value for each participant. This system is essentially a PAYG system, though there may also be a reserve fund. A notional rate of return is assigned to each account. One of the motivations for this type of plan is that it attempts to make a closer connection between contributions and benefits, based on the view that such a connection may encourage workers to view the contribution not as a tax but as a payment for a future benefit. When Sweden reformed its social security system by enacting a notional account system, it extended the years taken into account in calculating benefits from 15 years to all years of work (Lindquist and Wadensjö, this volume).

Sweden, Poland, Latvia, Norway, and Italy—a diverse set of countries—have adopted this type of system. Egypt adopted this type of system in 2010, with implementation expected in 2013 (Holzmann 2012).

Automatic Adjustment Mechanisms

At least 12 countries have adopted automatic adjustment mechanisms as a way to maintain the solvency of their PAYG social security programs. In 1998, Brazil adopted life expectancy indexing of its social security benefits for private sector workers. At retirement age, the calculation of social security benefits takes into account the average life expectancy for the population at that age, with an annual updating of life expectancy at retirement age. Life expectancy is officially estimated by the annual household survey of the Brazilian Institute of Geography and Statistics.

Finland, Portugal, and Norway adjust the generosity of benefits received at retirement automatically for changes in life expectancy. Portugal passed legislation in 2007, introducing a sustainability coefficient in the benefit formula for calculating pensions. This coefficient equals the ratio between life expectancy in 2006 and life expectancy in the year preceding retirement. The level of statutory pension is multiplied by the coefficient, reducing the benefit level as life expectancy increases (Murteira, this volume). The August 2011 pension reform law in Spain required that a sustainability factor be introduced to the system in 2027 that will adjust the relevant parameters of the system to changes in life expectancy every five years.

In Sweden, life expectancy indexing of benefits is done by using an annuity divisor that reflects improvements in life expectancy at age 65. No further reductions in benefits for improvements in mortality occur after age 65. Thus, the life expectancy adjustment does not take into account life expectancy improvements that occur after age 65. It is expected that the failure to adjust for life expectancy improvements after retirement will be expensive, costing about 1 percent of payroll in contributions (Palmer 2000). The initial generation in the system will benefit from this feature, but subsequent generations will pay for it through the automatic adjustment process required to maintain solvency.

In Sweden, mortality experience is averaged over the previous five years to avoid year-to-year fluctuations that do not reflect longer-term trends. The Swedish system uses, as do the other systems, period mortality tables, which are mortality tables based on the experience of the cross section of older persons. For each birth cohort in Sweden, the annuity divisor adjustment is established at age 65, with a provisional adjustment made for retirements starting at age 61, which is the benefit entitlement age.

In addition to the automatic adjustment of benefits for longevity improvement, every year the Swedish government tests whether the system is in balance. If it falls out of balance, adjustments are automatically made to decrease benefits, without the intervention of elected government officials needing to decide what to do. Thus, automatic adjustment mechanisms reduce the political risk that no action will be taken until a crisis—rather, actions will be taken automatically, without the intervention of politicians.

In 2012, Greece adopted a pension system with a notional rate of return and an automatic adjustment mechanism to maintain solvency. Italy, Poland, and Latvia also have automatic life expectancy indexing in a notional account system. France in 2003 legislated an increase in the number of years of earnings required to receive a full pension from 40 to 41, rising by one quarter per year from 2009 to 2012. Thereafter, through 2020, the contribution period for full benefits will increase automatically as needed to keep the ratio of the contribution period to the average retirement period equal to its ratio in 2003, which is approximately two to one. This adjustment mechanism effectively results in a reduction in benefits that is tied to increases in life expectancy. The French government retains the right to not make these adjustments if labor market conditions, such as high unemployment, do not support the extra years of work.

In 2012, the Netherlands passed a law that will automatically adjust its normal retirement age for increases in life expectancy, starting in 2020. This provides an alternative approach for indexing benefits to improvements in life expectancy. Every five years, the government will assess whether life expectancy improvements have been sufficient to warrant an increase in the retirement age. According to projections, the retirement age will increase from 66 to 67 in 2025 and from 67 to 68 in 2040. Workers will still be able to receive benefits at age 65, but these changes in the normal retirement age result in a cut in benefits at that age by 6.5 percent for every one-year increase in the normal retirement age.

Japan, Germany, and Canada have also adopted different types of automatic adjustment mechanisms. While in many countries with automatic adjustment mechanisms the adjustments occur annually, in Canada, because of the stability of its long-term financing, it is expected that its automatic adjustment mechanism will be used rarely, if at all.

One issue with these mechanisms has been how automatic they actually were in practice, with Sweden, Germany, and Italy making changes to the adjustment mechanism when unpopular adjustments were required. In 2009, Germany passed a law that for the second consecutive year overrode the automatic adjustment mechanism.

National Savings Funds for Retirement Financing

Ireland, France, China, and New Zealand have introduced separate national savings funds, separate from their social security programs, for the purpose of prefinancing future social security benefits. Subsequently, however, some of these countries ended up drawing down these funds earlier than expected (Whitehouse and Antolin 2012). In Ireland, for example, the National Pension Reserve Fund was used to help bail out Irish banks in 2011 because of the financial crisis. In 2007, Argentina established a national social security sustainability fund to help guarantee the payment of future social security benefits. In 2008, Russia established the National Welfare Fund to help pay for future public pension benefits. Norway has a large national savings fund, one of the largest pension funds in the world (Mosionek-Schweda, this volume).

Extending Coverage to More Workers

The majority of workers around the world, particularly outside of the high-income countries, lack social security coverage. This is one of the key problems facing social security programs, particularly for middle- and lower-income countries. On average, social security programs in Africa only cover 10 percent of workers (Gillion et al. 2000), partly because many workers are employed in the informal sector, which many social security programs do not cover. Part of the reason also is that many workers who should be covered by law are not participating because of contribution evasion, which is the failure of employers and workers to make mandatory social security contributions.

Many countries are attempting to extend coverage to more workers. Burundi has an innovative system where motorcycle taxi cab drivers are covered through contributions to their national association (Turner, this volume). To encourage coverage among agricultural workers, who are typically more difficult to bring into the social security system, Tanzania has a public relations campaign to encourage more people to participate in the social security system. Tunisia charges agricultural workers a lower contribution rate than urban workers. Egypt allows self-employed workers to declare their level of income, with the minimum level varying by occupation. Vietnam has a program that allows agricultural workers to make contributions in kilos of rice, and later receive benefits in rice. Thailand, China, and India also have a matching contribution for voluntary programs for informal sector or rural workers. In 2010, the Indian government introduced a new pension initiative, which runs from 2010 through 2014, to increase participation in the national New Pension Scheme, aimed particularly at the 300 million workers in the unorganized sector who are generally excluded from formal pension provisions. The initiative includes a partial contribution match to encourage participation in the plan.

In 2012, Peru enacted a law extending mandatory coverage to self-employed workers earning more than 1.5 times the minimum wage. Chile is also extending coverage of its mandatory individual accounts to self-employed workers earning above a minimum amount, but with the choice to opt out during a five-year transition period. In 2010, Malaysia extended coverage to part-time workers. That same year, South Korea extended coverage of its mandatory employer-sponsored pension system to small employers having four or fewer employees.

Some countries in Africa have not had social security programs for private sector workers, only for workers in government and government-controlled enterprises. In 2011, Ethiopia extended social security coverage to private sector workers.

It was initially thought that individual account systems would succeed in extending coverage to more workers because of the link between contributions and account balances and thus benefits. In fact, the link is quite variable. It is variable because of financial market risk, which affects both the link between contributions and account balances at retirement and the link between account balances and annuitized benefits. Perhaps for other reasons as well, the extension of coverage in countries adopting individual accounts has not occurred. Reforms with individual account plans did not increase coverage in any of the reforming countries in Latin America (Kritzer, Kay, and Sinha 2011).

Some countries have extended coverage to uncovered workers on a voluntary basis. China has a voluntary pension system for rural workers (Chen and Turner, this volume). Kenya in 2011 launched a voluntary individual account system, called the Mbao Pension Plan (Kwena and Turner 2013; Turner, this volume), where poor workers can contribute small amounts (as little as $0.25) using mobile phone technology. This system is feasible because mobile phone costs have decreased to the extent that they are available in Kenya for as little as $5 or $10.

Noncontributory Social Security Pensions

A number of middle- and lower-income countries have established noncontributory means-tested old-age pensions to provide benefits to poor people in old age and to extend the coverage of social security programs (International Labour Office 2007). This trend has been motivated by an attempt to reduce poverty in old age and appears to be gaining greater acceptance around the world. These programs are sometimes called social pensions. Countries with social pensions include Brazil, India, Nepal, Lesotho, Botswana, Namibia, South Africa, and Mauritius. Swaziland and Lesotho have tax-financed programs that provide cash transfers to older persons (Vincent and Cull 2011). Chile adopted such a program in 2008, and also established a minimum benefit for participants who had contributed to the mandatory individual accounts and met certain other requirements. In 2008, Belize extended to indigent older men its noncontributory poverty program that already applied for indigent older women. The Maldives adopted a program in 2010. Peru and the Philippines both adopted programs in 2011.

International Agreements to Facilitate Work and Retirement in Other Countries

Although for many years countries have had international agreements concerning social security benefits for workers moving between countries, there is an increased interest in global collaboration to provide these benefits. Mercosur—the Southern Common Market—signed an agreement in 2007 whereby retirees could receive their social security benefits in any country in the region without charge. The benefits are wired from the social security agency in the home country to the social security agency in the new country of residence. Formerly, the benefits were wired to a bank in the residence country, which charged money transfer and foreign exchange fees. In addition, all documentation is sent electronically, rather than by mail, which expedites the process of workers receiving benefits from other countries. In 2007, 22 countries signed the Ibero-American Multilateral Social Security Agreement, which will facilitate the provision of social security benefits to international workers in Hispanic countries. In 2011, a new Ibero multilateral agreement provides social security benefits to migrant workers and their families in eight countries: Bolivia, Brazil, Chile, Ecuador, El Salvador, Spain, Paraguay, and Portugal.

The EU has regulations regarding the coordination of social security in EU countries. The East African Community is considering this issue (Turner, this volume). As well as these multilateral agreements, increasingly countries have bilateral agreements, sometimes called totalization agreements. New Zealand and Australia are also discussing the portability of pension benefits between those two countries as part of an effort to move those countries to a single economic market.

EMPLOYER-PROVIDED PENSION PLANS

Unisex Pensions from Defined Contribution Plans

Because women on average live longer than men, life insurance companies selling annuities generally charge a higher price to women than men for an annuity paying an equal annual benefit. Gender-based benefit calculations when annuitizing defined contribution accounts, which results in equal expected lifetime benefits for men and women the same age, is viewed as discriminatory against women by some people because it provides lower annual benefits to women than men. In 1983, the U.S. Supreme Court outlawed gender-based pensions for employer-provided defined contribution plans on the grounds that it constituted discrimination in compensation against women. In 2012, the EU outlawed that practice for all annuities, including annuities both provided through pension plans and purchased individually.

Extending Voluntary Pension Coverage

Extending voluntary pension coverage, as a supplement to mandatory pension coverage, has long been a goal for many countries. Ireland mandated that by 2003 all employers were required to provide their employees the option to participate in a Personal Retirement Savings Account, but many employers have failed to comply with this requirement, and among those that have, some have no participants in the plans provided (Hughes, this volume). In 2008, the Philippine Congress passed a law creating private voluntary retirement accounts as a supplement to the country's public PAYG system. Under the law, public- and private-sector employees and the self-employed may set up Personal Equity and Retirement Accounts (PERAs). In 2009, a program took effect in Israel through an agreement between labor unions and manufacturing associations to extend pension coverage to workers not already having such coverage. In 2011, Chile established new rules to encourage employers to voluntarily provide pension plans. In 2012, India extended a defined contribution system designed for government workers so as to make it available to private sector workers, and Malaysia established a voluntary pension system to supplement its mandatory system.

Some countries, however, provide voluntary pension systems to workers who do not participate in social security as a substitute for social security. In 2007, Pakistan introduced a new voluntary pension system. In 2009, China extended voluntary pension coverage to 650 million rural workers by establishing the National Rural Pension Scheme. By 2011, there were more than 258 million contributors and 100 million beneficiaries (Turner and Chen, this volume).

Pension Regulators

As employer-provided pensions are increasing, many more countries gradually are adopting pension regulators. With the growing importance of defined contribution plans, pension regulators more often are not part of Labor Departments but are part of government departments focusing on financial market regulation. Kenya, Uganda, and Tanzania have all instituted pension regulatory authorities. Burundi, however, does not have a pension regulator (Turner, this volume).

The Decline in Defined Benefit Plans and the Trend toward Defined Contribution Plans

In countries with established pension systems, defined benefit plans were traditionally the primary plans in the private sector but have since declined in importance, being supplanted by defined contribution plans. Generally, the decline has been considerably less in the public sector, where defined benefit plans still predominate. These countries include the United Kingdom, Ireland, the United States, and Kenya. In the

United States, a type of defined contribution plan called the 401(k) plan has replaced defined benefit plans as the most important type of plan in the private sector, but Individual Retirement Accounts, which are defined contribution plans established by individuals without reference to a particular employer, have since replaced 401(k) plans as the most important type of retirement plan in terms of assets. The decline in private sector defined benefit plans has not occurred in all countries where they have been prevalent. For example, it has not occurred in Germany or Japan. There has also been a movement away from defined benefit plans for public sector employees, with Kenya and Brazil taking steps to end those plans for public sector employees.

Automatic Enrollment to Extend Coverage

To solve the problem of workers not participating in voluntary employer-provided pension plans when they have the opportunity to do so, there has been a trend toward automatic enrollment. In traditional plans, workers need to actively enroll in employer-provided defined contribution plans. If they do nothing, they are not enrolled. Thus, traditionally the default is nonenrollment.

A number of employers sponsoring defined contribution pension plans in the United States have adopted automatic enrollment. In the KiwiSaver program in New Zealand, starting in 2007, workers are placed in the system by default but can opt out. In the United Kingdom, starting in October 2012, all employers are required to offer a pension plan to their employees, and they are required to automatically enroll their employees (Szczepański and Turner, this volume). The requirement starts with large firms and is being phased in over four years so that it will eventually apply to all employers. The mandatory contribution rate to the plan is 8 percent, also being phased in, with 1 percent of that provided by a government subsidy.

Defaults

Along with automatic enrollment, which is a form of default, defaults have been used for investment options. Many participants are uncertain as to what a good investment choice would be. With defaults, if they take no action they automatically are signed up for the default investment. Initially, in the United States that investment was a low-risk option, but there has been a move toward higher-risk defaults because low-risk defaults resulted in small accounts due to low returns. The defaults now generally being used are ones that reduce the portfolio risk as the participant approached retirement. These are sometimes called target-date funds, or retirement date funds.

In 2012, the United Kingdom established a nationwide default, known as the National Employment Savings Trust (NEST), which provides retirement date funds for workers whose employers do not offer a plan and who do not choose one of the other funds offered by NEST (Szczepański and Turner, this volume). This system is largely based on the KiwiSaver system in New Zealand.

Financial Education

Financial education has been a response to the problem of financial illiteracy for participants in defined contribution systems, both in mandatory and voluntary defined contribution systems (Turner and Muir, this volume). The increase in financial education provided by governments and employers is a direct result of the growing importance of defined contribution plans as voluntary or mandatory parts of retirement income systems. Financial education can cover such topics as investment terminology, asset allocation, risk tolerance, and retirement goal setting. Using financial education to address the lack of financial literacy of pension participants is not a quick fix but needs to be a long-term, sustained, and costly effort.

Several international organizations, such as the OECD and the International Organisation of Pension Supervisors (IOPS), have taken an interest in financial education for pension participants in individual account pension systems. In 2008, the OECD created the International Network on Financial Education. A survey by IOPS found that 16 out of 19 financial supervisors of pension systems provided some type of financial education (IOPS 2011). The pension supervisors not providing financial education tended to be fairly young, with intentions of providing financial education in the future.

Chile, the United Kingdom, Mexico, and the United States have all developed financial education programs. In 2009, Colombia enacted a law providing incentives for organizations to establish low-cost programs for financial education.

Greater Transparency

With some countries moving to defined contribution plans, they also are leaning toward providing greater transparency, particularly concerning fees. The United States in 2012 released regulations requiring greater disclosure to private sector pension participants of information concerning fees. Transparency is also an issue in terms of conflicts of interest that financial advisers may have. The issue of transparency is being considered in a number of other countries, as well. In the UK, private pension companies will be forced to reveal fees and charges taken from employees' retirement savings under an agreement with the Association of British Insurers. The requirement will be implemented in 2014 for autoenrollment pension plans, and in 2015 for all other workplace pension plans.

Hybrid Plans

Traditionally, pension plans have been divided into either defined benefit plans or defined contribution plans, but hybrid plans do not fit neatly into either category. These include defined contribution plans with rate of return guarantees, such as the Riester plans in Germany. Hybrid plans developed in the Netherlands include collective defined contribution plans, which have a defined benefit plan formula but with the workers collectively bearing the investment risk. The most common hybrid plan in the United States is the cash balance plan.

CONCLUSION

This chapter has surveyed trends in social security and employer-provided pensions around the world. Many countries have reformed their social security and employer-provided pension systems. Reforms of social security programs include raising the benefit entitlement age, adopting automatic adjustment mechanisms, and raising contribution rates. While most countries have retained traditional social insurance–type social security systems, there have been two other significant trends relating to plan type. First, countries with provident funds have been converting those funds to social insurance–type social security systems. Second, some countries with traditional social security systems have added mandatory individual accounts, but more recently a number of countries have cut back on the contributions to those accounts. An additional trend is that low-income countries have continued to look for ways to include more of their workers in their social security systems, with some countries adopting innovative programs targeted at groups who have not participated in or been covered by social security.

Trends in employer-provided pensions include a shift toward defined contributions and away from defined benefit plans, increased use of hybrid plans, and a greater usage of unisex mortality tables in calculating annuities.

Note

We have received valuable comments from Dalmer Hoskins of the U.S. Social Security Administration. This chapter draws heavily on the Social Security Administration's monthly newsletter, *International Update: Recent Developments in Foreign Public and Private Pensions*.

References

Fultz, Elaine. 2012. "The Retrenchment of Second-Tier Pensions in Hungary and Poland: A Precautionary Tale." *International Social Security Review* 65(2): 1–26.

Gillion, Colin, John A. Turner, Clive Bailey, and Denis Latulippe. 2000. *Social Security Pensions: Development and Reform*. Geneva: International Labour Office.

Holzmann, Robert. 2012. "Global Pensions Systems and Their Reform: Worldwide Drivers, Trends, and Challenges." IZA Discussion Paper No. 6800. Bonn: IZA. http://ftp.iza.org/dp6800.pdf (accessed April 2, 2013).

International Labour Office. 2007. "Global Update on Trends in Income Security in Old Age." Briefing paper, presented at the AARP and United Nations Programme on Ageing, held in New York City, February 7–9. http://www.globalaging.org/pension/world/2007/iloaarp.pdf (accessed April 2, 2013).

International Organisation of Pension Supervisors (IOPS). 2011. "Pension Supervisory Authorities and Financial Education: Lessons Learnt." Paris: IOPS Information Paper 1. http://www.iopsweb.org/dataoecd/3/41/49009719.pdf (accessed April 2, 2013).

Kritzer, Barbara E., Stephen J. Kay, and Tapen Sinha. 2011. "Next Generation of Individual Account Pension Reforms in Latin America." *Social Security Bulletin* 70(1): 35–76. http://mwww.ba.ssa.gov/policy/docs/ssb/v71n1/v71n1p35.pdf (accessed April 2, 2013).

Kwena, Rose Musonye, and John A. Turner. 2013. "Extending Pension and Savings Plan Coverage to the Informal Sector: Kenya's Mbao Program." *International Social Security Review* 66(2): 79–99.

Palmer, Edward. 2000. *The Swedish Pension Reform Model: Framework and Issues.* Social Protection Discussion Paper No. 0012. Washington, DC: World Bank. http://siteresources.worldbank.org/SOCIALPROTECTION/Resources/SP-Discussion-papers/Pensions-DP/0012.pdf (accessed April 2, 2013).

Rajnes, David. 2007. "The Evolution of Japanese Employer-Sponsored Retirement Plans." *Social Security Bulletin* 67(3): 89–104. http://www.ssa.gov/policy/docs/ssb/v67n3/v67n3p89.html (accessed April 2, 2013).

Republic of Kenya, Ministry of Planning. 2012. "Kenya Social Protection Sector Review: Executive Report." June. http://www.vision2030.go.ke/cms/vds/SP_Executive_Report_FINAL1.pdf (accessed April 2, 2013).

U.S. Government Accountability Office. 2005. "Social Security Reform: Other Countries' Experiences Provide Lessons for the United States." October. GAO-06-126. Washington, DC: USGAO. http://www.gao.gov/new.items/d06126.pdf (accessed April 2, 2013).

U.S. Social Security Administration. 2012. "Focus on Central and Eastern Europe: An Inventory of Pension Reforms, 2008 to Present." *International Update.* Washington, DC: SSA. March: 1–6. http://www.ssa.gov/policy/docs/progdesc/intl_update/2012-03/index.html (accessed April 2, 2013).

Vincent, Katherine, and Tracy Cull. 2011. "Cell Phones, Electronic Delivery Systems, and Social Cash Transfers: Recent Evidence and Experiences from Africa." *International Social Security Review* 64(1): 37–51.

Whitehouse, Edward, and Pablo Antolin. 2012. *OECD Pensions Outlook 2012.* Paris: OECD. http://www.aafp.cl/wp-content/uploads/2012/10/OECD-Pensions-Outlook.pdf (accessed April 2, 2013).

Part 2

Reforms in Europe

3

Have Personal Retirement Savings Accounts Achieved Their Objectives in Ireland?

Gerard Hughes
Trinity College Dublin

In its report *Averting the Old Age Crisis,* the World Bank (1994) argued that OECD and Eastern European economies and several Latin American economies faced imminent problems with their retirement income systems. It said that the public pillars of national social security pension systems should not be relied on to solve these problems, as high tax rates are required to finance them and they inhibit growth and reduce rates of return to workers. Believing that the social security pillar of retirement income would become more costly in the future, the report recommended that these countries make the transition to a multipillar system, which would include a privately managed, mandatory personal retirement savings plan.

In Ireland, the publication of the World Bank report coincided with a survey of occupational and personal pension coverage. The results of this survey were published in 1996 (Hughes and Whelan 1996). The report revealed that less than half of those in employment and less than one-tenth of those not economically active were covered by a pension plan. Following publication of the survey results, the Pensions Board and the Department of Social, Community and Family affairs jointly sponsored a National Pensions Policy Initiative. The purpose of this initiative was to facilitate a national debate on how to develop the national pension system. In its report *Securing Retirement Income*, the Pensions Board (1998) recommended that a legal framework be put in place that would encourage private sector financial institutions to introduce on a voluntary basis a new type of pension product, the Personal Retirement Savings Account (PRSA). The retirement income system in Ireland consists now of a mandatory social security program, a means-tested social assistance program, voluntary occupational pensions provided by employers, PRSAs provided by employers mandatorily but with voluntary participation by workers, and voluntary personal pensions.

OBJECTIVES SET FOR PRSAs

The primary objective set for the PRSA was to increase coverage of private pension plans for those aged 30 and over from 54 percent to 70 percent within 10 years of their introduction. In terms of all those at work, this objective can be expressed as a requirement to increase the coverage rate from less than half to 60 percent in a 10-year period.

A wide range of other objectives were set for PRSAs, but no systematic effort has been made to publish information that would facilitate evaluation of how successful they are in achieving these objectives. However, a number of key objectives of PRSAs for which enough information is published facilitate an evaluation of how well PRSAs have performed since their introduction. There are six key objectives set for the PRSA product:

1) It should be a lower-cost product than was available in the past.

2) In addition to traditional providers of pensions, the PRSA should be supplied by the post office and other retail outlets, such as supermarkets.

3) It should have a flexible retirement age.

4) Owners of PRSAs should eventually buy an annuity for life.

5) It should be mandatory for all employers, except those with occupational plans for all employees, to provide access for all their employees to a PRSA provider.

6) The primary market for the PRSA should be employees in nonpensionable employment, and individuals who change or lose their jobs should be able to continue contributing to their pensions.[1]

Some of the key objectives set for PRSAs can be evaluated on the basis of the terms and conditions on which the new pension saving product was introduced after negotiations between the government and pension providers, while others require data stretching back to September 2003 when the new product was introduced. We begin our evaluation by considering objectives 1–4 in the list above and then proceeding to consider objectives 5–6 together with the primary objective of increasing pension coverage from less than half to 60 percent within a 10-year period.

PRSA FEES AND PROVIDERS

The terms and conditions on which PRSA products were issued by pension providers differed in important respects from those envisaged by the Pensions Board in its report *Securing Retirement Income* (1998). Instead of one PRSA product with government certification to indicate that it met certain quality requirements, two products were introduced—the standard PRSA and the nonstandard PRSA. The difference between the two is that the fees for a standard PRSA are capped at 5 percent of PRSA contributions and 1 percent of PRSA assets, and it can invest only in unit funds, whereas a nonstandard PRSA has no cap on fees and it can invest in a wide choice of assets. Far from being a lower-cost product than personal pension products previously available, the standard PRSA turned out to have higher fees than was usual for existing personal pension products.

Table 3.1 shows how fees for a standard PRSA compare with those for an Additional Voluntary Contribution (AVC) plan for teachers operated by Cornmarket Group Financial Services, an off-the-shelf personal pension marketed by one of the largest providers of pensions in Ireland, the Irish Life Assurance Company, and fees for existing personal pension products. For an Irish Life personal pension, a flat rate fee of €3.81 per contribution was charged, whereas 5 percent of each contribution was deducted for the standard PRSA, and the annual management fee for the Irish Life pension was 0.9 percent compared with 1 percent for the PRSA. The capped fee for a standard PRSA of 5 percent of each contribution is the same as the usual fee for a personal pension contract,

Table 3.1 Maximum Charges for a Standard PRSA in 2003 and Personal Pensions in the UK, Hungary, and Poland

	Standard PRSA Maximum fees	Irish life personal pension	Personal pension contract	Cornmarket group fees for AVC for a teacher	UK stakeholder pension (2001)	Hungary mandatory and voluntary private account (2011)	Poland mandatory private account (2010)
Charge for each contribution	5%	€3.81	5%	5%	0	0.9%	3.5%
Annual management charge (%)	1	0.9	0.75	1.25	1	0.2	0.45[a]
Once off charge	0	0	0	€732	0	0	

[a] An increment of 0.05 percent can be added for the best performing funds.

SOURCE: Brady (2001a), Fultz (2012), and O'Quigley (2003).

but the annual 1 percent fee levied on the value of the fund is higher than the usual annual fee of 0.75 percent of the value of the fund for a personal pension contract. The note by O'Quigley (2003), which provides the information on the usual fees for personal pension contracts, points out that the fees for a standard PRSA are "not particularly low" and that fees per contribution for personal pensions are "frequently less" than 5 percent. Although the annual fee of 1.25 percent of the value of the fund by Cornmarket Group for an AVC for a teacher is higher than the annual fee for a standard PRSA, the source of the information for this group, Brady (2001a, p. 12), points out that they were charging "at the top end of what is normal practice in the pensions business." Fees for a standard PRSA were also higher than fees for a Stakeholder Pension in the UK, which was introduced in 2001, two years earlier than the PRSA. The only fee for a Stakeholder Pension was the 1 percent annual management fee.[2] PRSA fees are also higher than the revised maximum fees imposed in 2010 in Hungary on mandatory and voluntary private pension investment accounts and on mandatory accounts in Poland in 2012. The deductions from contributions in Ireland are nearly 40 percent greater than in Poland while the annual management fees are two-thirds greater. Both sets of fees are five times greater in Ireland than in Hungary.

Why did the standard PRSA turn out to be a higher-cost product than envisaged by the Pensions Board? The main reason appears to be that the pension providers were not prepared to offer a PRSA at a much lower cost than they previously charged for a personal pension, and they were able to insist on this because the government was not willing to offer the PRSA product without their cooperation

During the negotiations between pension providers and the government on the terms and conditions that would be attached to the new PRSA product, financial journalists discovered from their own sources that the providers were opposed to both a government certification and any cap on their fees. For example, Kerby (2001, p. 52) reports in *Business and Finance* magazine that "the pension companies lobbied hard against a kite-mark or a maximum charge (they certainly didn't want anything like the total 1 percent limit imposed on Stakeholder, the UK version of the PRSA)."

What emerged eventually from the negotiations was a compromise under which the providers would offer a standard PRSA, with fees generally higher than usual for previous personal pension products, and they would offer a nonstandard PRSA, which allowed the providers to levy higher fees than previous personal pension products. In the same article, Kerby (2001, p. 52) points out that "the non-standard PRSA is certainly a compromise—a way for the pension companies (who have had this market to themselves up to now) to earn higher margins and to reward their commission-paid brokers."

Subsequently, another journalist (Brady 2001b) investigating the negotiations between pension providers and the government, found a letter under the Freedom of Information Act from the Irish Insurance Federation that warned that "if the eventual regime does not give sufficient scope for profitability" there is a danger that "only a limited number of providers [will] choose to enter the market."

Very little additional information has emerged about the negotiations between pension providers and the government, but it is likely that the traditional pension providers were also opposed to new providers entering the pensions market. Neither the post office nor other retail outlets, such as national supermarket chain stores, entered the pensions market. The traditional providers may also have been opposed to a flexible retirement age for the PRSA product, as when it was introduced it was stipulated that owners of PRSA products could not retire before age 60. The providers also appear to have been opposed to owners of PRSAs being obliged to take out an annuity. This was a requirement when the PRSA was introduced but the pensions industry frequently insisted that owners of PRSAs should be able to avail of the Approved Retirement Fund (ARF) and Approved Minimum Retirement Fund (AMRF) options in the same way as the self-employed. This objective was achieved in 2011 when the ARF and AMRF options were extended to owners of PRSAs.[3]

The hope, expressed by the Pensions Board and others, that promoting the PRSA would help to simplify the pension system was not realized. Instead, it greatly increased the complexity of the choices that ordinary savers faced. One professional advisor, Gilhawley (2003), argued that what eventually emerged from the negotiations "isn't a pretty sight" and that it "ensured that the PRSA market will be a jungle for the ordinary saver" (p. 7).

PRSA ACCESS AND COVERAGE

Following agreement with pension providers on the terms and conditions on which a standard PRSA could be offered in the market, providers were accredited by the Pensions Board. Accredited providers started to advertise their PRSAs in April 2003 so that they would be ready to be nominated by employers as designated providers by September 2003. This was the date set by the Pensions Board by which the great majority of employers would be required by law to have nominated at least one provider to supply a PRSA to their employees.

In June 2003, a few months before that date, the Irish Financial Services Regulatory Authority (IFSRA), which was jointly responsible with the Pensions Board for regulating PRSAs, issued instructions to PRSA providers that suggested the regulators were concerned to avoid a repetition in Ireland of practices by personal pension providers, which led to the pensions misselling scandal in the UK in the 1990s (Ward 2000). These instructions required providers at the point of sale to

- inform prospective clients about the difference between a standard and a nonstandard PRSA,

- have a statement signed by both parties that all risks have been pointed out and that all relevant information has been provided, and

- give clients the IFSRA consumer fact sheet about PRSAs to help them assess which type of PRSA would best suit their needs.

Kerby (2003) reports that the reason the IFSRA stipulated what information should be available to prospective purchasers of PRSAs was that the director of the consumer division of the IFSRA had said, "We do not want consumers encouraged to purchase a nonstandard PRSA when it is not required, simply to generate additional revenue for the financial institutions."

The objective that all employers, except the 4 percent or so with occupational plans for all employees (Hughes and Whelan 1996), should designate a PRSA provider has fallen well short of target. Figures 3.1 and 3.2 show, starting in September 2003, the cumulative number and percentage of employers who have designated a PRSA provider and

Figure 3.1 Number of Employers Designating a PRSA Provider and Number of Employer Designations Where Employees Have Taken Out a PRSA Contract, 2003–2012

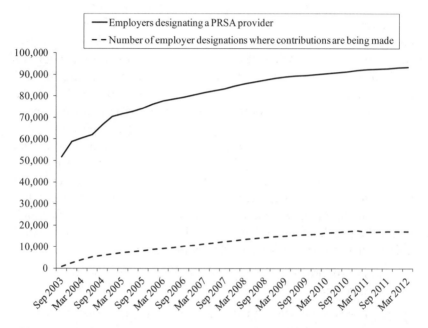

SOURCE: Pensions Board Web site: http://www.pensionsboard.ie/en/Regulation/ PRSAs (accessed November 14, 2013).

the cumulative number and percentage of firms in which employees have taken out PRSA contracts. It should be noted that we do not know how many employees continue to make PRSA contributions because the Pensions Board does not publish this information. Experience in the UK shows that about half of contributors to personal pensions have ceased to make contributions within four years of taking out a contract (Financial Services Authority 2006).

By the end of 2003, when all employers were legally obliged to designate a PRSA provider, only 58,770, or less than half of all the firms listed in the Companies Registration Office, had nominated a provider. In those firms that had a designated provider, only 2,502, or less than 2 percent of all firms, had employees who had taken out a PRSA contract. This outcome of the long planning stage for the designation

Figure 3.2 Percentage of Firms Designating a PRSA Provider and Percentage of Firms Whose Employees Have Taken Out a PRSA Contract, 2004–2011

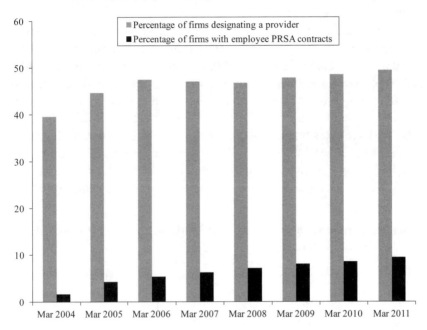

SOURCE: Pensions Board Web site: http://www.pensionsboard.ie/en/Regulation/PRSAs (accessed November 14, 2013).

of PRSA providers was so abysmal that in September 2004, a year after the launch, the Pensions Board contacted 64,000 firms to remind them of their legal obligation to designate a PRSA provider for their employees. In the period up to March 2012, about a decade after the launch of PRSAs, there has been an increase in the number of employers designating a provider and in the number of these firms in which employees have taken out a PRSA contract to 93,401 and 17,209, respectively. However, after an initial spurt in the number of employers designating a provider up to December 2005, the percentage of employers designating a provider has remained fairly stable at less than 50 percent, while the percentage of firms in which employees have taken out a PRSA contract has increased from less than 2 percent to around 10 percent. Looking at the figures in terms of employers who have designated a PRSA provider, they show that 81 percent of employer-designated plans have no one contributing to them. Where employers do have employees who have taken out a PRSA contract, the average number of employees with contracts is about four.

Figure 3.3 shows the cumulative number of standard, nonstandard, and total PRSAs sold. Sales were slow at first but they increased rapidly so that by December 2012 over 200,000 PRSA contracts had been sold, of which over 150,000, or three-quarters, were standard, and almost 50,000, or one-quarter, were nonstandard. On the face of it, this looks like a satisfactory outcome. That is what the Pensions Board implies in its quarterly press releases about the sales figures. However, the group for which PRSAs were originally intended are employees in nonpensionable employment. But this is not the group to which most PRSAs have been sold. Figures 3.4 and 3.5 show the number of employees and

Figure 3.3 Number of Standard, Nonstandard, and Total PRSAs Sold, 2003–2012

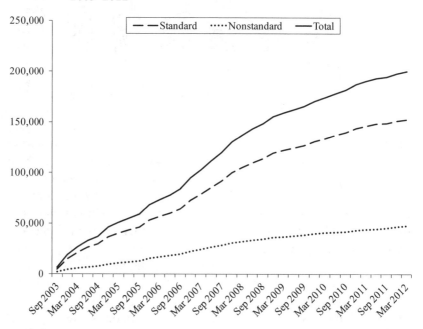

SOURCE: Pensions Board Web site: http://www.pensionsboard.ie/en/Regulation/ PRSAs (accessed November 14, 2013).

Figure 3.4 Number of Employees and Self-Employed and Those Not in the Labor Force Who Have Taken Out a PRSA Contract, 2003–2012

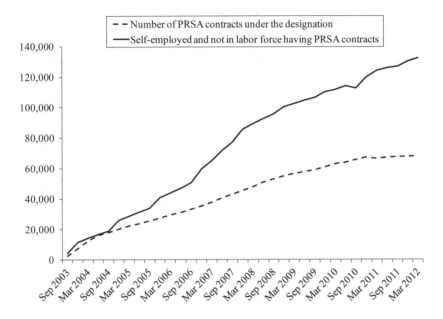

SOURCE: Pensions Board Web site: http://www.pensionsboard.ie/en/Regulation/ PRSAs (accessed November 14, 2013).

self-employed and other individuals not in the labor force who have taken out PRSA contracts.

In the first year following their introduction, the number and percentage of employees and self-employed and those not in the labor force taking out a PRSA contract were about the same. After September 2004, the number and percentage of self-employed and purchasers not in the labor force began to increase much more rapidly than employees. By March 2012, the cumulative number of purchasers of PRSA contracts who were self-employed or not in the labor force was double the number of employees who had taken out contracts—132,345 versus 67,973—while the percentage of self-employed and purchasers not in the labor force relative to all those not in the labor force was three times greater, 9.4 percent versus 3.2 percent.

**Figure 3.5 Percentage of Employees and Self-Employed and Those Not
in the Labor Force Who Have Taken Out a PRSA Contract,
2003–2012**

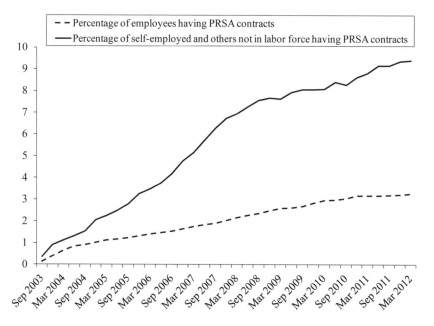

SOURCE: Pensions Board Web site: http://www.pensionsboard.ie/en/Regulation/
PRSAs (accessed November 14, 2013).

Gilhawley (2007) has identified four separate markets where PRSAs
are being sold: 1) employees in nonpensionable employment—the target group for which PRSAs were originally intended; 2) self-employed
individuals who can contribute to a Retirement Annuity Contract or a
PRSA or both; 3) employees who are already in pensionable employment who have an AVC plan; and 4) employees and the self-employed
who already have either an occupational pension or a Retirement Annuity Contract who can transfer their pension funds to a PRSA. The
Pensions Board has not published sufficient information to identify how
many PRSA contracts have been taken out by each of these groups or
by those not in the labor force who can also contribute to a PRSA.
However, as employer-designated plans are obliged to offer at least one
standard PRSA, it is reasonable to assume, as Gilhawley (2007) does,

that all PRSAs purchased through an employer-designated plan are standard PRSAs. This assumption also enables us to identify how many standard and nonstandard PRSAs have been sold to the self-employed and other individuals not in the labor force.

Figure 3.6 shows that when the PRSA product was launched in September 2003, about one-third of all PRSA contracts were taken out by employees for whom they were intended, and about two-thirds were taken out by self-employed and others who were not in the labor force. In the first two years of operation, there was a significant increase in the percentage of all contracts bought by employees and a significant decrease for the other group to almost 50 percent in each case. Thereafter, the percentage of all PRSA contracts sold to employees gradually

Figure 3.6 Standard PRSA Contracts Taken Out by Employees and PRSA Contracts Taken Out by Self-Employed and Those Not in the Labor Force as Percentage of All PRSA Contracts, 2003–2012

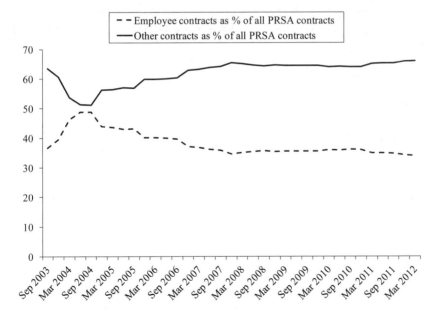

SOURCE: Pensions Board Web site: http://www.pensionsboard.ie/en/Regulation/ PRSAs (accessed November 14, 2013).

decreased to around one-third, while the percentage sold to the self-employed and others gradually increased to about two-thirds. In December 2011, the cumulative figures for PRSA contracts sold indicated that only one-third of the contracts have been sold into the target market, while two-thirds have been bought by individuals for whom the PRSA product was not intended.

Figure 3.7 shows the percentage of PRSA contracts purchased by the self-employed and individuals outside the labor force that are standard and nonstandard. In September 2003, when the PRSA was launched, about 54 percent of the contracts bought by people who were not working were standard PRSAs, while 46 percent were nonstandard. However, in the next quarter ending in December 2003, about two-thirds of the PRSA products bought by the self-employed and others

Figure 3.7 Percentage of PRSA Contracts Sold to Self-Employed and Those Not in the Labor Force That Are Standard and Nonstandard, 2003–2012

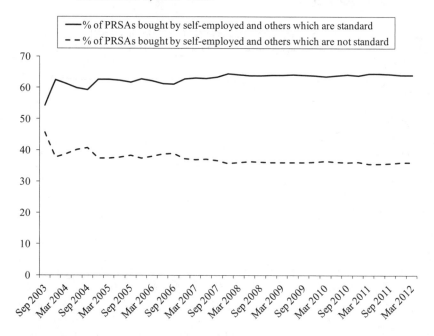

SOURCE: Pensions Board Web site: http://www.pensionsboard.ie/en/Regulation/ PRSAs (accessed November 14, 2013).

not in the labor force were standard PRSAs while one-third were non-standard. Subsequently, these proportions did not change much, so that by December 2011, about two-thirds of the PRSAs bought by the self-employed and those not in the labor force were standard PRSAs, while one-third were nonstandard.

The influence of the self-employed on sales of PRSAs can be seen, as Gilhawley (2007) has noted, from the spikes in the quarterly figures for nonemployer designated sales, which occur in the last quarter of the year (Figure 3.8). These spikes are related to the October 31 tax deadline for backdating pension contributions by the self-employed to the previous tax year.

Before the property bubble burst in Ireland in 2007, sales in the first three quarters averaged around 3,000 per quarter, but this figure jumped to around 7,000 in the last quarter. After the property collapse, sales in

Figure 3.8 Quarterly Sales of PRSA Contracts to Self-Employed and Those Not in the Labor Force, 2003–2012

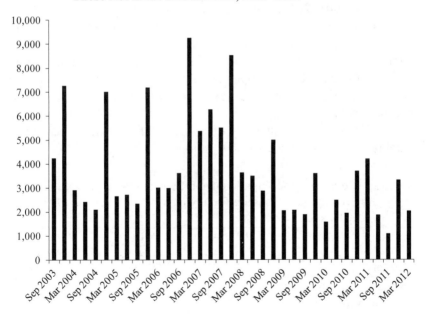

SOURCE: Pensions Board Web site: http://www.pensionsboard.ie/en/Regulation/ PRSAs (accessed November 14, 2013).

the first three quarters of the year fell back to around 2,000, while sales in the last quarter were about double this at around 4,000.

Almost 10 years after their introduction, sales of PRSAs to employees in nonpensionable employment, who are the target market, have been and continue to be low. On the other hand, sales to the self-employed and others not in the labor force, for whom they were not intended, account for the significant growth in sales of PRSAs.

EFFECT OF PRSAs ON PENSION COVERAGE

The primary objective that was set for PRSAs by the Pensions Board was that within 10 years of their introduction they would help to increase the coverage rate of private pension plans to 60 percent of those in employment. Special surveys of pension coverage in 2002, 2005, and 2009 have been undertaken by the Central Statistics Office (2004, 2006, 2011). These surveys enable us to evaluate whether PRSAs have helped to increase the coverage rate of private pension plans in a way that will lead to the achievement of the 60 percent target by the end of 2013. Table 3.2 shows that, contrary to expectations, there was no increase in the coverage rate of personal pension plans between 2002 and 2005, whereas there was an increase in the coverage rate of occupational plans.

We know from the quarterly PRSA sales figures that 1.3 percent of employees had taken out a PRSA contract by the end of 2005, which

Table 3.2 Coverage of Occupational and Personal Pension Plans as a Percentage of Those in Employment (ILO) Aged 20–69, 2002, 2005, and 2009

Category	Pension coverage Q1 2002	Pension coverage Q4 2005	Pension coverage Q4 2009
Occupational pension only	35.4	40.1	38.9
Personal pension only	12.9	12.1	9.6
Both	2.9	2.8	2.5
Total pension coverage	51.2	55.0	51.0

SOURCE: Central Statistics Office (2004, 2011) and author's calculations.

should have resulted in an increase in the personal pension coverage rate. The fact that the Central Statistics Office survey did not pick up such an increase but instead recorded a much bigger increase in the occupational pension coverage rate suggests that the coverage of occupational pensions increased independently of the introduction of PRSAs. It may also indicate that many respondents to the survey who purchase a personal pension through an employer-designated plan may identify it as an occupational rather than a personal pension.

In 2007, the Irish property market collapsed, and a year later the global financial crisis began. Both of these events resulted in massive financial and job losses across the Irish economy. For example, total employment fell by over 300,000, or by 15 percent, between the beginning of 2008 and the end of 2010, and the real value of pension fund assets fell by 37.5 percent in 2008 compared with 22.3 percent in Hungary, 17.7 percent in Poland, and a weighted average of 23.7 percent in the OECD as a whole (OECD 2011). The effect of these losses was that the gains made in private pension coverage between 2002 and 2005 were lost so that the coverage of occupational and personal pension plans fell from 40 percent to 39 percent and from 12 percent to 10 percent, respectively. Overall the private pension coverage rate fell from 55 percent in 2005 to 51 percent in 2009. This brought the coverage rate in 2009 back to its level in 2002 before PRSAs were introduced.

PRSAs HAVE REINFORCED EXISTING INEQUITIES

In order to promote PRSAs, the government gave them entitlements similar to other pension plans to tax reliefs (preferential tax treatment) on employer and employee contributions and investment income and capital gains, and made the PRSA pension taxable on payment. Table 3.3 shows estimates of the cost of tax relief on PRSA contributions since 2004 together with the number of contributors who claimed tax relief. These figures do not include contributions made by employers or by employees through their employer-designated PRSA for reasons explained in the note to Table 3.3. As employees contributing to a PRSA through an employer-designated plan are excluded from these figures, they refer to the cost of tax reliefs for contributors who are self-

Table 3.3 Cost of Tax Relief on PRSA Contributions and Number of Beneficiaries, 2006

Year	Cost of tax relief (€million)	No. of beneficiaries
2004	13.7	6,300
2005	42.2	32,900
2006	56.4	45,200
2007	61.1	46,600
2008	73.8	53,900
2009	77.0	56,200

NOTE: The figures do not include contributions made by employees through employers' payroll systems and in respect of which tax relief is provided on the net pay basis. Information on such contributions is not captured in such a way as to make it possible to provide disaggregated figures.
SOURCE: Revenue Commissioners Statistical Reports 2007–2010.

employed or not in the labor force. An estimate of the extent to which the figures in Table 3.3 are underestimated can be derived from additional information that the Revenue Commissioners sought in 2006 from employers about employer and employee contributions to PRSA and other pension plans. The improved data for 2006 show that the cost of tax reliefs for PRSA contributions amounted to €120 million and that there were 71,500 beneficiaries (Government of Ireland 2007, Table 7.2). In 2006, therefore, the cost of tax reliefs for PRSAs appears to have been twice as great as the figure published in the Revenue Commissioners' report, and the number of beneficiaries appears to have been nearly 60 percent greater.

Table 3.3 shows that between 2004 and 2009, the Exchequer (the government treasury) has subsidized PRSAs by at least €320 million in the form of foregone tax. PRSA employer and employee contributions in 2006 amounted to €330 million, so in that year the Exchequer subsidy for PRSAs of €120 million amounted to 36 percent of total contributions.

In Ireland, government subsidies (through tax preferences) for private pensions overwhelmingly accrue to taxpayers with the largest incomes (Callan, Keane, and Walsh 2009; Hughes 2000; Hughes and Sinfield 2004), and some commentators (Hughes and Sinfield 2004) warned that the introduction of personal pension accounts would reinforce the existing inequalities. This warning has proved to be well founded.

Using data from the Revenue Commissioners, Figure 3.9 shows the distribution of the cost of tax reliefs by income decile for the self-employed and others not in the labor force in 2006. Nearly 36 percent of the tax reliefs were captured by the top income decile, and over half of them accrued to the top income quintile. In sharp contrast, the bottom income decile received about 1.5 percent of the tax reliefs, and the bottom income quintile received less than 3 percent of them.

CONCLUSION

The great hopes that advocates of private personal pensions in Ireland had for a new voluntary pension product, the Personal Retirement

Figure 3.9 Percentage of Tax Relief on PRSA Contributions by Self-Employed and Others Not in Labor Force Accruing to Each Income Decile of PRSA Contributors, 2006

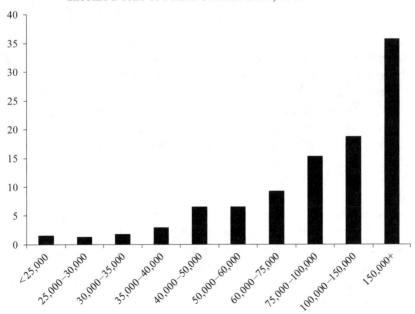

SOURCE: Houses of the Oireachtas Web site: http://www.debates.oireachtas.ie/dail/2009/06/30/00120.asp (accessed November 14, 2013).

Savings Account, have not been realized. Few of the key objectives set by the government regulator of private pension plans have been attained. The fees for a standard PRSA have generally been higher than the usual fees for personal pension products available before PRSAs were introduced. Neither the post office nor other retail outlets, such as supermarket chain stores, entered the new market for personal pensions. Standard PRSAs do not have a flexible retirement age, as owners cannot receive their benefits until they are age 60. Owners of PRSAs are not obliged to buy an annuity if they can satisfy the conditions for transferring their PRSA pension fund into an ARF or an AMRF pension fund. While it was made mandatory that all employers who did not provide an occupational pension for all their employees should designate a personal pension provider for their employees, less than half of the firms registered with the Companies Office have actually designated a PRSA provider. Employees in nonpensionable employment have shown limited interest in the PRSA product, as no one is contributing to a PRSA in four-fifths of the firms that have designated a PRSA provider.

Up to the beginning of 2012, the take-up of PRSAs by employees has been very poor, with only 3 percent of employees deciding to buy a PRSA. The take-up has been much greater by a group for whom PRSAs were not intended—the self-employed and those not in the labor force. Approximately 9 percent of these have taken out PRSA contracts, and this group is now the largest market for personal pension products in Ireland. Up to the end of 2009, the introduction of PRSAs had failed to make any progress toward their primary objective of increasing pension coverage of the employed population to 60 percent—indeed, the coverage rate was slightly lower in 2009 than it was in 2002. Given the lack of trust in the private pension system's ability to deliver on its promises, it is most unlikely that the coverage rate will reach anywhere near the 60 percent figure by the end of 2013.

In addition to failing to meet the objectives set by the government and the Pensions Board, PRSAs have reinforced inequities in the private pension system that existed before PRSAs were introduced. As with previous private pension products, PRSAs have predominantly been bought by taxpayers in the top half of the income distribution. The benefits of government subsidies for PRSAs have been captured mainly by high-income earners, with over half of the tax reliefs for PRSAs accruing to the top 20 percent of those who have claimed tax relief on their PRSA contributions.

Ireland has spent the last 15 years trying to shift the public/private balance of pension provision toward private pensions on a voluntary basis. This policy has failed; the pension coverage rate now is no greater than it was before the new personal pensions were introduced in 2003. Some advocates of private pensions argue that coverage should be made mandatory, as it is in some other countries like Poland, Hungary, and Australia. Consideration was given to mandatory approaches in the Pensions Board's (2005) *National Pensions Review* in 2005 and in a report by Fitzpatrick Associates (2006) commissioned by the Pensions Board in 2006. The Fitzpatrick report considered a number of different mandatory models and concluded that " . . . in general it would seem that the implementation of a mandatory scheme would generate similar effects to those of any new national tax. The extent of the negative impact on growth rates will be determined by . . . design and delivery issues . . ." (p. 23).

In addition to this negative assessment of mandatory plans, the experience of countries with mandatory private pensions suggests that this approach suffers from the same problems of high costs, lost tax revenue, and uncertain benefits as the voluntary approach (Fultz 2012). These problems could be avoided if Ireland were to adopt another approach that members of the Pension Policy Research Group at Trinity College Dublin have advocated for many years (Hughes and Stewart 2007; Stewart 2005).

They argue that it would be more equitable if tax relief for private pension saving was given only at the standard rate of tax and that the additional tax revenue that this would generate should be used to increase the basic state pension to above the poverty level. As the great majority of employees in nonpensionable employment will be dependent in their retirement on the state pension, this solution has a number of merits.

It would give them an assurance that they could look forward to a modest defined benefit pension related to the average industrial wage rather than having to bear all the risks of a voluntary, soft mandatory, or mandatory PRSA defined contribution plan. If the state pension were increased to around 40 percent of the average industrial wage it could significantly reduce pensioner poverty. New Zealand has a flat-rate pension benefit similar to Ireland's, but at a higher level relative to the average wage, and it has one of the lowest rates of pensioner poverty in the OECD. It would reduce the cost of tax reliefs on private pensions in Ireland, which comparative research suggests are among the highest in the OECD (Yoo and de Serres 2004). It would provide the revenue needed to maintain the state pension at a time of economic crisis when there are calls to reduce it. Finally, it would introduce a greater measure of fairness into Ireland's pension system by redistributing resources from the top 20 percent of households which receive nearly 80 percent of the pension tax reliefs to the 80 percent of households whose main source of retirement income is the state pension.

Notes

I am grateful to Jim Stewart of Trinity College Dublin and Elaine Fultz of JMF Research Associates, Philadelphia, for comments on an earlier draft.

1. Previously, individuals who changed or lost their jobs had to cease contributing to their pension arrangement.
2. In 2005, the annual management fee for a Stakeholder Pension was increased to 1.5 percent for the first 10 years, after which it falls back to 1 percent.
3. An Approved Retirement Fund (ARF) option is an alternative to an annuity purchase. On retirement, the self-employed owner of a Retirement Annuity Contract or an owner of a PRSA can decide to invest the pension fund into a fund administered by a qualifying fund manager and take one-fourth of the value of the fund as a tax free lump sum. Income and gains from an ARF are tax free within the fund whereas drawdowns from the fund are subject to income tax. If the individual has a guaranteed retirement income less than 1.5 times the state Old Age Contributory Pension, the pension fund has to be invested in an Approved Minimum Retirement Fund (AMRF) until the person reaches age 75 when the AMRF can be transferred into an ARF.

References

Brady, N. 2001a. "Teacher's Pension Lesson." *Sunday Tribune*, June 24, p. 12.
———. 2001b. "Insurers Attack Government Charge Controls on Pensions." *Sunday Tribune,* August 12.
Callan, Tim, Claire Keane, and John R. Walsh. 2009. *Pension Policy: New Evidence on Key Issues*. Research Series No. 14. Dublin: Economic and Social Research Institute.
Central Statistics Office. 2004. *Quarterly National Household Survey: Pensions Update Quarter 1, 2004*. Dublin: Central Statistics Office.
———. 2006. *Quarterly National Household Survey: Pensions Update Quarter 1, 2005*. Dublin: Central Statistics Office.
———. 2011. *Quarterly National Household Survey: Pensions Update Quarter 1, 2009*. Dublin: Central Statistics Office.
Financial Services Authority. 2006. *Survey of Persistency of Life and Pensions Policies*. London: Financial Services Authority.
Fitzpatrick Associates. 2006. *The Economic Impact of Mandatory Pensions*. Dublin: Fitzpatrick Associates Economic Consultants.
Fultz, Elaine. 2012. "The Rentrenchment of Second-Tier Pensions in Hungary and Poland: A Precautionary Tale." *International Social Security Review* 65(3): 1–25.
Gilhawley, Tony. 2003. "PRSAs—The Real Picture Emerges, and It Isn't a Pretty Sight." *Irish Pensions* (Summer): 7–9.
———. 2007. "PRSA Sales . . . Only about 1/3rd Relate to Target Market." Dublin: Technical Guidance Ltd.
Government of Ireland. 2007. *Green Paper on Pensions*. Dublin: Stationery Office.
Hughes, Gerard. 2000. "The Cost and Distribution of Tax Expenditure on Occupational Pensions in Ireland." In *Economic Problems of Ireland in Europe*: *The Thirty-First Geary Lecture*. Dublin: Economic and Social Research Institute.
Hughes, Gerard, and Adrian Sinfield. 2004. "Financing Pensions by Stealth: The Anglo-American Model and the Cost and Distribution of Tax Benefits for Private Pensions." In *Reforming Pensions in Europe: Evolution of Pension Financing and Sources of Retirement Income*, Gerard Hughes and Jim Stewart, eds. Cheltenham, UK: Edward Elgar, pp. 163–192.
Hughes, Gerard, and Jim Stewart, eds. 2007. *Choosing Your Future: How to Reform Ireland's Pension System*. Dublin: Tasc at New Island.
Hughes, Gerard, and Brendan J. Whelan. 1996. *Occupational and Personal Pension Coverage 1995*. Dublin: Economic and Social Research Institute.

Kerby, Jill. 2001. "Hatching Your Own Nest Egg." *Business and Finance*, April 19, p. 52.

———. 2003. "Regulator Right to Target Non-Standard PRSAs." *Sunday Times*, June 29.

O'Quigley, J. 2003. "When It Comes to PRSAs—Caveat Emptor." Dublin: Deloitte and Touche.

Organisation for Economic Co-operation and Development (OECD). 2011. *Pensions at a Glance: Retirement-Income Systems in OECD and G20 Countries*. Paris: OECD.

Pensions Board. 1998. *Securing Retirement Income: National Pensions Policy Initiative Report of the Pensions Board*. Dublin: Pensions Board.

———. 2005. *National Pensions Review: Report of the Pensions Board*. Dublin: Pensions Board.

Stewart, Jim, ed. 2005. *For Richer, For Poorer: An Investigation of the Irish Pension System.* Dublin: Tasc at New Island.

Ward, Sue. 2000. "Personal Pensions in the UK, the Mis-selling Scandal and the Lessons to be Learned." In *Pensions in the European Union: Adapting to Economic and Social Change*, G. Hughes and J. Stewart, eds. Dordrecht: Kluwer Academic Publishers, pp. 139–146.

World Bank. 1994. *Averting the Old Age Crisis: Policies to Protect the Old and Promote Growth*. Oxford: Oxford University Press.

Yoo, K-Y., and A. de Serres. 2004. "Tax Treatment of Private Pension Savings in OECD Countries and the Net Tax Cost per Unit of Contribution to Tax-Favoured Schemes." OECD Working Paper No. 406. Paris: OECD. http:// dx.doi.org/10.2139/ssrn.607185 (accessed April 2, 2013).

4

Social Security and Pension Income in Sweden

Gabriella Sjögren Lindquist
Swedish Institute for Social Research, Stockholm University

Eskil Wadensjö
*Swedish Institute for Social Research, Stockholm University, and
Stockholm University Linnaeus Center for Integration Studies*

From an international perspective, the poverty rate among pensioners in Sweden is low. This is explained by both the pension system, especially by the guarantee pension, and housing allowance for pensioners, as well as other parts of the Swedish welfare system. According to a comparative study of 15 European countries (van Vliet et al. 2011), Sweden has the lowest proportion of poor among the elderly, along with Luxembourg and the Netherlands. However, in Sweden many retirees have a vulnerable position with a standard only slightly above the guidelines for when social assistance may be granted. The disposable income at the 20th percentile is only slightly above the norm for social assistance. Mainly older retirees (aged 75 and older) are in this group. In the first half of the 1990s, more and more people were under the poverty line, which is defined as those who have an income of below 60 percent of the median income, but since 1998, poverty measured in this way has decreased (Gustafsson, Johansson, and Palmer 2009).

Thus, even though pensioner poverty is rare, there are good reasons for investigating who the poor pensioners are, why they are poor, and how they are likely to do in the future. The future development of pensions depends strongly on the transition that Sweden, like many other countries, has gone through from defined benefit to defined contribution pensions in both the social security pension system and the occupational pension system. This means that pensions depend on an individual's work and labor income history to a greater extent than before. To be able to receive a high pension, working in Sweden for many years is required. Concern for future pensions is also due to the fact that economic growth affects defined contribution pensions in different ways. Not least, there is concern about the fate of pensions that are based on individuals' choices of pension funds. In some other countries, this has led to a considerable reduction of the pensions for people who have already left the workforce for retirement, and some people have returned to work because of economic necessity.

In this chapter, we outline the Swedish pension system, the changes in employment among those aged 60 years and older, definitions of retirement, the data used, and the measures we use to study income differences. We then examine how the income distribution differs between pensioners and those of working age, and whether and how the difference has changed over time, and we discuss the differences in pensioner income distribution among different cohorts and men and women, and why the income gaps between pensioner groups have increased. Pension income is the main source of income for those aged 65 and older, but many also have substantial income from labor or capital, and many have assets primarily in their homes, which we also report. We then study how the level of pension income is influenced by the individual's work history, record of self-employment, and number of years in Sweden. In the last sections, we study in more detail some groups with low pension incomes. We end with a summary and offer some conclusions.

THE SWEDISH PENSION SYSTEM

To understand the income differences and their changes over time among retired people in Sweden, we give a short introduction to the structure of the Swedish pension system.[1] The Swedish pension system is a three-tier system consisting of social security pensions, occupational pensions, and personal pensions. As the system has changed a great deal since the 1990s, different cohorts belong to different pension systems, and some cohorts have pensions from different generations of pensions systems.

Social security pensions were introduced in Sweden 100 years ago in 1913. The retirement age when benefits first could be received was

67. After some minor changes to the system in the 1920s and 1930s, a major change followed in 1948, when a non-income-tested and non-income-dependent pension was introduced. This basic pension (*folkpension*) was the same for everyone except that married pensioners got a lower pension than those who were not married. An earnings-related additional pension (ATP), a defined benefit system, was introduced in 1960 and was based on the 15 years with the highest income. There was a ceiling regarding the income included for the calculation of the pension per year in the ATP system. The ATP pension required that a person work for at least 30 years in order to obtain a full pension; with fewer years of work, the pension was proportionally reduced. The normal pension age was lowered from 67 to 65 in 1976, but it was possible to take a reduced pension earlier or postpone the take-up and receive an enhanced pension at an older age. The pension benefits were price indexed.

A new social security pension system—a defined contribution system—was decided on in two steps by the parliament in 1994 and 1998 and implemented from 1999 onward. The pension contribution rate is 18.5 percent of the worker's income up to a ceiling, 16 percent of which is allocated to a notional defined contribution system, and 2.5 percent of which is for an individual account system (called the premium pension), where each individual can choose between many investment funds. The pension derived from the notional defined contribution is income indexed. Pension benefits from the notional defined contribution system can be received starting at age 61 but are higher the later they are taken (it is an actuarially fair system with respect to benefit receipt at different ages).

For those who have had no income or a low income, there is a guarantee pension. Qualification to receive this pension is based on the benefit levels from the income-related social security pension. To receive a full guarantee pension, 40 years of residence in Sweden is necessary, otherwise it is proportionally reduced. The guarantee pension is price indexed. Those aged 65 or older who have a low pension or other low levels of income and have taken up their entire social security pension may be eligible for a housing allowance.

There has been a gradual change from the old to the new social security pension system. Those born in 1937 or earlier are completely in the old system. Those born in 1938 are to 4/20 in the new system, those born in 1944 are to 10/20 in the new system and those born in 1954 are totally in the new system.[2]

When the ATP system was introduced, those employed in the public sector and white-collar workers in the private sector were already covered by occupational pension plans. These plans deliver additional income replacement for income under the ceiling and a high replacement for income over the ceiling in the social security pension system. Blue-collar workers in the private sector achieved an agreement concerning occupational pensions in the 1970s. After the pension reforms in the 1990s, the occupational pension plans were changed so that many are defined contribution plans, but there are still important defined benefit elements in all systems, with the exception of blue-collar workers in the private sector. Sweden has high occupational pension coverage of its workforce, as around 90 percent of all wage-earners are employed at workplaces with collective agreements and thus are covered by occupational pension plans.

Many people also have personal pensions. There are tax reductions for savings for personal pensions, but the maximum tax reduction has gradually been reduced.

The Law of Employment Security (LAS) covers people up to age 67. Mandatory retirement under age 67 has not been allowed since 2003 (before 2003, this age was 65). In some sectors, 67 is becoming the normal age of retirement.

CHANGES IN EMPLOYMENT AMONG OLDER PEOPLE IN SWEDEN

In Sweden, it is possible to follow labor force participation and employment in labor force surveys for over 50 years. Statistics Sweden carried out its first labor force survey in 1961, after the Labor Market Board (AMS) had conducted pilot studies in 1959 and 1960. In 1961, the male employment rate was high for those aged 60–69, but this gradually declined in the mid-1990s for those aged 60 and older. The male employment rate has increased since the mid-1990s for those aged 60–64, and since 2003 for those aged 65–66. It is, however, still much lower than it was in the early 1960s (Figure 4.1).

Figure 4.1 Employment Rate for Men, 1961–2011

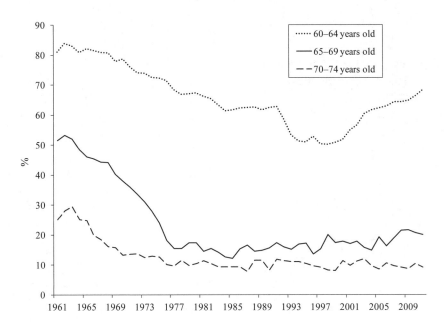

SOURCE: Updated from Wadensjö (2011).

The female employment rate was low in the early 1960s, when it was common for women to be housewives, but for those under age 65 it has gradually increased since then with some business cycle variations (Figure 4.2). The employment rate is still higher among men than women in all age groups, but the difference has gradually decreased with new cohorts and also within each cohort.

WHO HAS RETIRED?

This study deals with income distribution among pensioners. The line between being retired and being in the labor force, however, is in many cases unclear, and retirement age varies widely among individuals. Taking a pension and retiring is not the same thing. When someone

Figure 4.2 Employment Rate for Women, 1961–2011

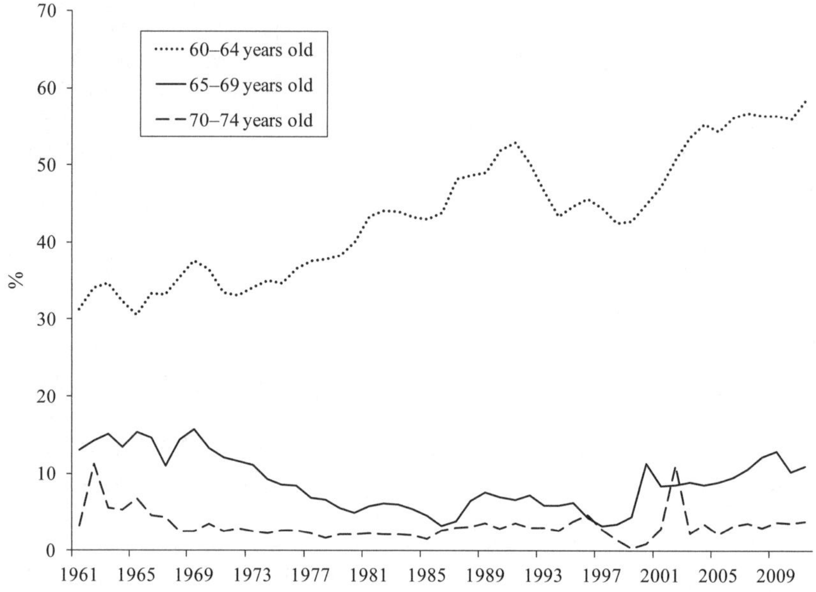

SOURCE: Updated from Wadensjö (2011).

takes a pension it does not mean that he or she leaves the labor force—a pension from the social security system can be taken while working, and the pension is not means-tested against other pension, other income, or wealth. One definition is that someone is retired when his or her pension income exceeds the sum of labor income and unemployment benefit or other social insurance benefits.

The Swedish Pensions Agency uses four different measures of retirement in its analysis (Karlsson and Olsson 2012). The first measure is the Average Exit Age, which is the age that a person leaves the workforce, given that he or she was working at age 50. The other three measures are different average pension age measures. Average Pension Age I is the average age for taking an old-age pension (not only the individual account premium pension), Average Pension Age II includes those who receive a disability pension (taken up from age 30 or older), and Average Pension Age III also includes those receiving a disability pension, but only when they are 50 or older. Average Pension Age III is more in line with the definition of the Average Exit Age, which also has 50 as an age limit. Occupational and personal pensions are not included in the definition of pension income.

According to the Swedish Pensions Agency, in 2011 the Average Pension Ages I, II, and III were 64.6, 62.5, and 63.9, respectively.

Age limits in the pension system and in the Employment Protection Act (LAS) influence when someone leaves the workforce. The social security pension can be claimed at age 61, but the guarantee pension cannot be taken before age 65. In the next few years, it is expected that about 25 percent of new retirees will receive the guarantee pension. In 2008, 778,000 individuals had a guarantee pension, of which 180,000 (15 percent) had a full one. Of those who received a guarantee pension, 80 percent were women (Olsson 2011). Nearly half of female pensioners aged 65–69 received a guarantee pension in 2008. Housing allowances for older persons may be granted from age 65 if the full social security pension is drawn. The Employment Protection Act, on the other hand, covers employees up to age 67.

In addition to these age limits, occupational and personal pension plans have different age limits. Personal pensions and occupational pensions from the private sector (ITP and SAF-LO) and the defined contribution component of the pensions for municipal and county employees (KAP-KL) can be claimed from age 55. Employees in the public sector can take their pensions from age 61. Occupational pensions should, according to collective agreements, be taken out for retirement purposes.

In our analysis of patterns of income receipt among older persons, we chose to draw the line at age 65 for several reasons: the majority take their pensions at age 65, a guarantee pension can first be granted at age 65, the age limit for unemployment insurance and disability pension is 65, and special rules apply to those 65 years and older regarding sickness benefit and compensation from work injury insurance. In the labor market policy programs, there are no formal age limits, but those aged 65 and older are in practice not assigned to labor market programs. In addition, many (wrongly) think that the retirement age in the social security pension system is 65.

MEASURING INCOME DISTRIBUTION

When studying the income distribution and how it changes, we can use several different kinds of income measures. The most common one is the household's disposable income, that is, household market income minus taxes plus transfers (see, for example, Björklund and Jäntti [2011]). When we compare the income distribution for those who are under 65 with the incomes of those who are older, we can use both the disposable income per individual in the household and the individual household member's own disposable income. When we look more closely at the income distribution for those aged 65 and older, we can analyze different types of income and the distribution of those incomes. Here, in addition to average disposable income per person in a household, we analyze individual disposable income, pension income from the social security and occupational pension systems, and income from capital. We also study the distribution of wealth. The information on disposable income, pensions, and capital income is derived from the Longitudinal Income Database (LINDA) for the years 1982–2009 (see Kruse [2010]). LINDA consists of register data of a representative sample of the population, including information regarding the person's family. The data on wealth come from HEK (the incomes of the households), which is an annual telephone survey of a representative sample of the population (see Rosén Karlsson [2011]).

In this study, we use percentile ratios when we look at income inequality and how it has changed over time. We chose this measure rather than the often used Gini coefficient because of its simple interpretation, and because by using percentile ratios, we can investigate both the lower and the upper sections of income distribution.[3]

The ratio between the 90th percentile and the 10th percentile (P90/P10) shows how many times higher the income of a person with the 90th percentile income is compared to the income of a person who has the 10th percentile income. If the ratio is 2, the person with the 90th percentile income has twice as much in income as the person with the 10th percentile income.[4]

In order to investigate those with high incomes and those with low incomes, we compare the 90th and 10th percentiles with the median, P90/P50 and P50/P10, respectively. By using percentile ratios as a measurement of wage dispersion, one can examine whether income inequality increases or decreases from year to year. The measure is not influenced by general income growth.

DOES THE INCOME DISTRIBUTION DIFFER BETWEEN OLDER AND YOUNGER PERSONS?

Disposable incomes are lower for those aged 65 and older than for those aged 55–64. Those aged 75 and older have particularly low incomes. Figure 4.3 shows household disposable income per person for different income groups. Income inequality has increased for those aged 50–64 and 65–74. For those aged 75 and older, the income differences have been more or less the same until the last few years. Many in this age group only receive the basic pension from the old pension system, which leads to a compressed income structure. Over the past

Figure 4.3   Development in Disposable Income per Person in the Household, 1991–2009

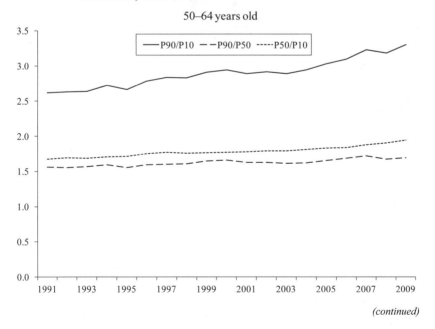

50–64 years old

(continued)

Figure 4.3 (continued)

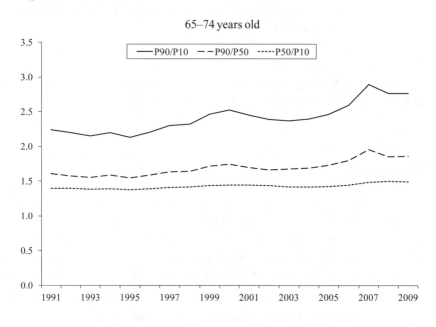

65–74 years old

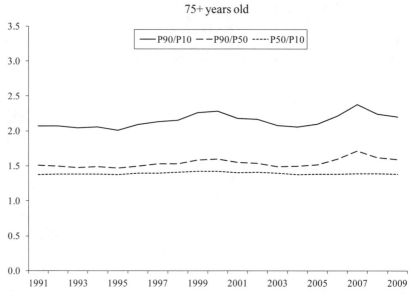

75+ years old

SOURCE: LINDA.

few years, however, income inequality has first increased and then decreased slightly. The share of this age group with income-related social security pensions and occupational pension systems has increased.

Having already demonstrated the changes over time in income inequality among households, Figures 4.4 and 4.5 show the disposable incomes of men and women. Income inequality for men aged 50–64 and 65–74 has increased sharply. In recent years, the trend has been particularly pronounced among those who are aged 50–64. For those aged 65–75, the income gap has mainly grown in the upper part of the distribution (P90/P50).

Figure 4.5 shows that income inequality among women aged 50–64 was high in the beginning of the 1980s. Many women were not employed, and many of those employed worked part time, often short part time. As women gradually entered the labor market, income inequality among women aged 50–64 decreased strongly. Among women 65 and older, in contrast, income inequality increased, especially in the upper part of the distribution. More women now have income-related

Figure 4.4 Development in Disposable Income for Men, 1982–2009

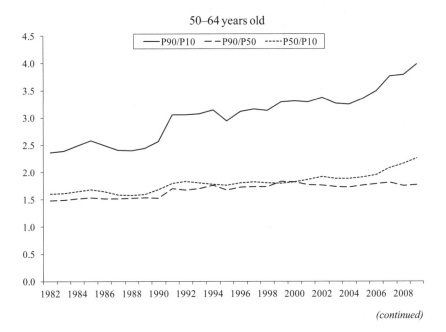

(continued)

Figure 4.4 (continued)

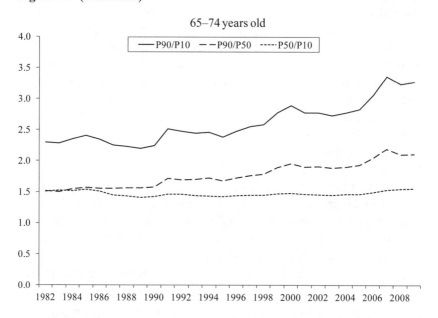

65–74 years old

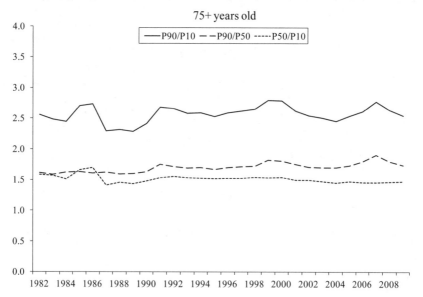

75+ years old

SOURCE: LINDA.

Figure 4.5 Development in Disposable Income for Women, 1982–2009

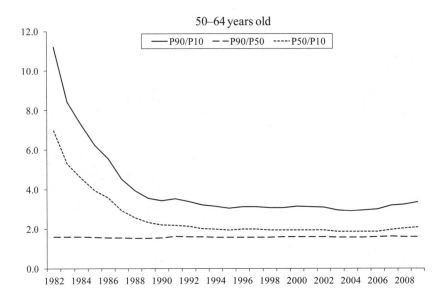

50–64 years old

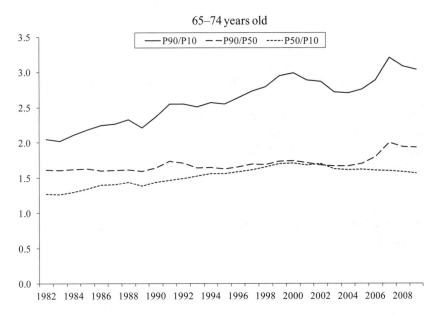

65–74 years old

(continued)

Figure 4.5 (continued)

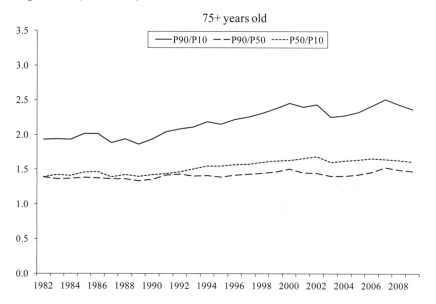

SOURCE: LINDA.

pensions, but many still have a guarantee pension only or one that is combined with a low-income pension.

Has income inequality increased or decreased? The main tendency is that it has increased significantly among both men and women aged 65–74 and also among women 75 and older. This applies particularly to those with high incomes (P90), who now have much higher incomes than those in the same age with low incomes (P10). In the lower part of the income distribution, the changes are much smaller (P50/P10).

THE DISTRIBUTION OF INCOME AMONG OLDER PEOPLE IN SWEDEN

We now compare further the incomes of men and women and foreign born and native people, respectively. Here, we estimate the percentile distribution separately of each of those four groups and then compare them. There are a number of reasons for conducting these two comparisons. Women have had and still have a weaker labor market attachment than men, and pensions are based on earned income over the years. In the old pension system, 30 years of earnings were required for a full pension, and the best 15 years counted for the calculation of the pension. In the new system, the income for all years is counted. Women more often have had career breaks and are more likely than men to have worked part time. This leads to lower pensions for women than for men in the new system. This means that women often receive a guarantee pension, which, unlike the income pension, is not indexed to income growth in the economy but is price indexed. This situation will probably lead to a gradual reduction of the average economic standard for women compared to that of men.

The foreign born in many cases have a weak labor market attachment. They often are not in the labor force or unemployed, more so than natives, and many of those who are employed have low incomes. Coming to Sweden as an adult can also lead to a low pension—it is often difficult to enter the labor market, and therefore many have few years with a contribution to the pension system. Those who immigrate after age 25 cannot reach the 40 years' residence in Sweden needed to receive a full guarantee pension at age 65.

The foreign born in Sweden are a heterogeneous group. Those who come from other Nordic countries and other countries in Western Europe have generally had a much better situation on the labor market before their retirement than those from countries outside Europe. The rules for pensions also differ depending on country of origin due to the existence of various international agreements. The rules are different for those coming from other Nordic countries, other EU/EEA countries, other countries with which Sweden has a pension agreement, and countries with which Sweden has no agreement regarding social security pensions.

COMPARING THE INCOMES OF WOMEN AND MEN

Figure 4.6 shows that women's disposable incomes are lower than men's. This applies to all three age groups—50–64, 65–74, and 75 and

Figure 4.6   Disposable Incomes for Women as a Share of the Disposable Incomes for Men at the 10th, 50th, and 90th percentiles, 1982–2009

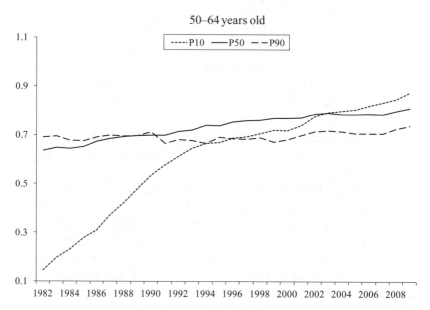

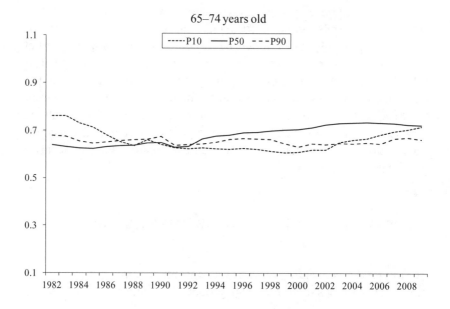

Figure 4.6 (continued)

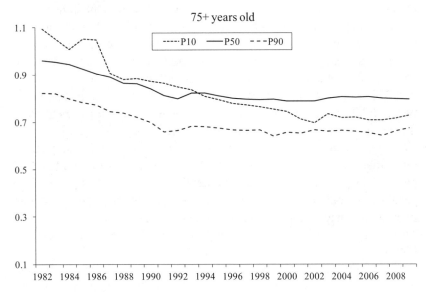

SOURCE: LINDA.

older—and all three percentiles that we report—P10, P50, and P90. However, there are some differences. Women aged 50–64 in the 10th percentile had low incomes at the beginning of the period compared to men in the same percentile. It was a period when many women were not employed; housewives were common. Women's relative earnings later increased among those in the 10th percentile. Since the mid-1990s, women's disposable incomes have been 70–80 percent of men's incomes in all three percentiles for those aged 50–64. For those aged 65–74, women's incomes have fluctuated between 65 and 75 percent of men's incomes for the three percentiles over the past 27 years.

Among those 75 and older, women's incomes declined relative to those of men throughout the period. During the 1980s, income differences were small in this age group. Among those with the lowest incomes (P10), women even had slightly higher incomes than men. This is explained by the fact that women more often than men are not married (including widows) in this age group, and that a single person received a slightly higher pension than a married person according to the rules of the basic social security pension. In the late 2000s, the income differences between men and women were large in all three percentile groups. The difference was largest for those with high incomes (P90), where women's incomes were only about 65 percent of men's.

The next step is to compare the pensions of women and men aged 65–74 and 75 and older in the same percentiles as before—P10, P50, and P90 (Figure 4.7). There was a large sudden change in pensions between 2002 and 2003. This is explained by the fact that payment from the new pension system started in 2003. The basic pension and the pension supplement were replaced by the guarantee pension in that year. In the statistics for 2002 and earlier, only the basic pension and the ATP pension, but not the pension supplement, were included as parts of the pension income. The graphs in Figure 3.1 outline disposable income, including pension supplements and housing allowances for pensioners. This explains why we do not see large sudden changes in the graphs in Figure 3.1.

We finally show the pension income distribution for women and men aged 65–74 and 75 and older (Figure 4.8). Pension income inequality increased for female pensioners, both for those 65–74 and for those 75 and older, but the differences in pensions are slightly lower for the older group. For women aged 65–74, income inequality decreased in the upper part of the distribution.

For the oldest women, pension income inequality increased. At the beginning of the 1980s, a large majority of the oldest women only had a basic pension. Therefore the pension income distribution was compressed. As more women in that age group received income-related social security pensions and occupational pensions, they pulled away from those with only a basic pension, and pension income inequality increased.

For men aged 65–74, pension income inequality has remained fairly constant. The exception is the P90/P10 ratio. This ratio first declined for some years and then rose for several years. However, there are larger changes for those aged 75 and over for P90/P10 and P50/P10. A marked rise in the ratio P90/P10, and to a lesser extent P50/P10 is followed by a jump down and then stabilization.

Figure 4.7 Pension (Social Security and Occupational) Incomes of Women as a Share of the Pension Incomes of Men at the 10th, 50th, and 90th Percentiles, 1982–2009

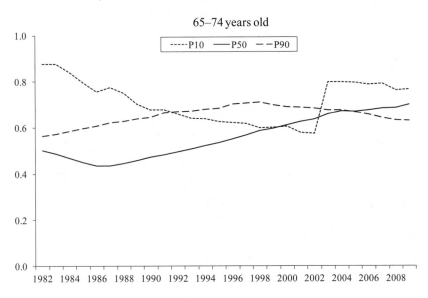

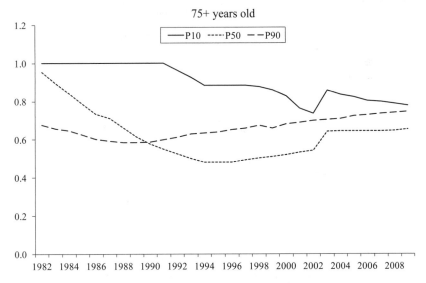

NOTE: Only those with a social security pension are included.
SOURCE: LINDA.

Figure 4.8 Changes in Pension Incomes (Social and Occupational) for Women with a Pension in Different Age Groups, 1982–2009

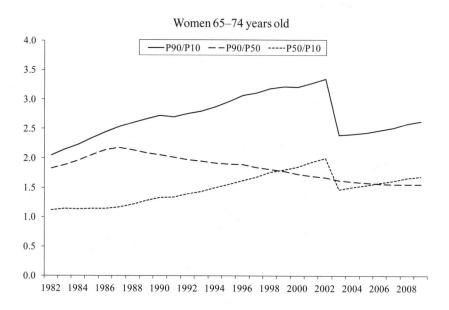

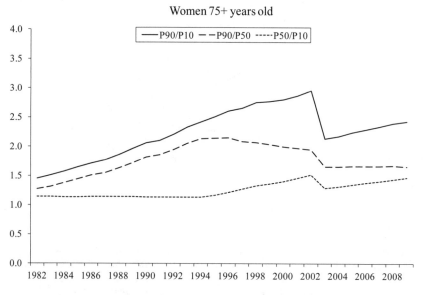

SOURCE: LINDA.

INCOME FROM CAPITAL

Income from capital has become an increasingly important part of pensioners' income and now represents one-fifth of the income of those aged 65 and older. It is unevenly distributed between pensioners, and mainly concentrated on those with the highest incomes. The fact that capital income has risen sharply for those with the highest incomes has contributed the most to increased income inequality among pensioners (Gustafsson, Zaid, and Franzén 2007).

Those who are 65 and older have on average about the same financial assets but lower debt and higher real assets (property) compared to those under 65 (Flood 2004). This means that their net wealth is high, especially when compared to those below age 50. On average, the net wealth is SEK 1.2 million for those 65 and older, and slightly lower for those 75 and older. The net wealth of men 65 and older is on average half a million SEK higher than for women the same age.

Flood (2004) examines the total net assets in different age groups in 2000 and establishes that wealth is greatest at age 56 and remains at a high level to about age 65. Those 65 and older had less wealth, and their levels of wealth declined even more as they got older. This corresponds with the theory of redistribution of income over the life cycle—you save when you are of working age and use the savings when you have retired. The differences could also be partly explained by differences in the cohorts' wealth positions when they reach retirement age. It is important to note that the data in Flood's study are from a cross-section, and individuals are not followed over several years.

Many banks provide "senior loans" with the home of the retirees as security. Homeownership can thus contribute to increased consumption. The share of those who owned a house was almost as great among those aged 65–74 (41 percent) as among those aged 30–65 (46–49 percent) (Table 4.1). A quarter of those 75 and older owned a house. On average, the value of the house was slightly higher for those 65 and older than for younger age groups. The share of those 65 and older who owned a house was higher among men compared to women. The houses men own are also somewhat more valuable than the houses women own.

Table 4.1 Average Real Assets for Women and Men in Different Age Groups, 2007

Gender/age	Mean value for those with a value		House[a]		Building society flat		Summer house	
	Share with value (%)	(thousand SEK)	Share with value (%)	Mean value for those with a value (thousand SEK)	Share with value (%)	Mean value for those with a value (thousand SEK)	Share with value (%)	Mean value for those with a value (thousand SEK)
Women and men	44.0	1,381	29.0	1,165	12.0	944	7.0	761
0–19	0.4	697	0.1	677	0.2	641	0.1	429
20–29	24.0	950	8.0	730	14.0	1,017	2.0	572
30–49	63.0	1,297	46.0	1,128	15.0	1,035	8.0	718
50–64	69.0	1,559	49.0	1,206	16.0	951	15.0	785
65–74	64.0	1,507	41.0	1,262	18.0	811	14.0	785
75 +	49.0	1,287	24.0	1,245	21.0	787	7.0	804
Women	42.0	1,260	26.0	1,132	13.0	951	7.0	757
0–19	0.4	676	0.1	660	0.2	615	0.1	424
20–29	24.0	940	9.0	720	14.0	1,063	1.0	561
30–49	62.0	1,218	45.0	1,112	14.0	1,028	7.0	703
50–64	66.0	1,396	44.0	1,173	17.0	966	15.0	781
65–74	56.0	1,316	31.0	1,202	20.0	828	13.0	791
75 +	41.0	1,173	17.0	1,228	21.0	824	5.0	816
Men	46.0	1,492	31.0	1,193	12.0	937	8.0	765
0–19	0.4	721	0.1	694	0.2	676	0.1	434
20–29	24.0	959	7.0	741	15.0	978	2.0	582

30–49	64.0	1,370	46.0	1,143	15.0	1,041	8.0	732
50–64	73.0	1,705	54.0	1,233	15.0	935	15.0	789
65–74	73.0	1,665	51.0	1,300	16.0	790	16.0	780
75 +	61.0	1,407	36.0	1,257	20.0	726	10.0	795

[a] A house with one or two (semidetached house) homes.
SOURCE: Statistics Sweden's wealth statistics.

WHAT CAUSED THE INCOME GAP BETWEEN PENSIONERS?

Pension income is the main income of those aged 65 and older. In this section, we examine the importance of labor income, labor market attachment, disability pension, the sector they retired from, self-employment, marital status, sex, country of birth (grouped level), and the age for retirement with regard to the probability of belonging to the groups of low- and high-income pensioners. We investigate the probability of belonging to the 10 and 20 percent group with the lowest pension income and the 20 or 10 percent group with the highest pension incomes for those who retired between 2005 and 2008. Our measure of pension income includes social security and occupational pensions. Being retired is defined here as receiving a pension income (social security and occupational pension) that exceeds labor income. We use the pension income for the year after retirement when we examine the likelihood of persons being low- or high-income pensioners. The analysis includes only those whom we have information for at least five years before retirement.

Table 4.2 summarizes the results of probit estimates. Marginal effects are reported. Men are less likely to belong to the group of pensioners with the lowest pensions and more likely to belong to the group with the highest pensions. Being married has no effect on the pension income group to which a pensioner belongs.

The later persons retire, the lower the probability of their belonging to the group of pensioners with low incomes. However, the retirement age does not matter for the probability of belonging to those with the highest pension incomes. This is a result of effects working in different directions. Those with high pensions can better afford to take their pensions early, so that many with high pensions leave the workforce early. On the other hand, the pensions for those who leave the workforce late will be higher given their earlier incomes, as pensions are based on previous incomes, and the incomes will be higher if the pension is taken up at a higher age (fewer years with a pension are expected). The estimates show that the higher the income is five years before retirement, the lower the probability is of being among those with a low pension.

One group with low pensions, which we return to later, is the self-employed. Those who were self-employed five years before retirement belong more often to the group with the lowest pension incomes and are less likely to belong to the group with the highest pensions. Those leaving the labor force with a disability pension are another group with low pensions.

We have also included a variable for those who have a weak labor market attachment five years before retirement. This group includes those who did not have any income from work (either as an employee or as self-employed). Among those who belong to this group, some have low pensions and others have high pensions. These mixed results suggest that this group includes both those with a poor labor market attachment, due to difficulties in getting a job, and the wealthy who choose to not work but five years later receive a good pension.

The risk of being one of those with the 10 percent lowest incomes is higher for those born outside Sweden. Being born in another Nordic country has a negative effect on the probability of belonging to those with the highest pension incomes. However, there is no difference between natives and those born outside the Nordic countries with regard to the probability of being in the group with the highest pensions.

Even if pension income is the main income for pensioners, other sources such as other income transfers, labor income, and capital income are important parts of the retirees' incomes.[5] The share belonging to the group with the 10 percent lowest pension incomes who belongs to the group with the 10 percent lowest disposable incomes is 43 percent. Of those with the 20 percent lowest pension incomes, 57 percent belong to the group with the 20 percent lowest disposable income. We see a similar pattern for those with the highest pensions. Of those with the 20 percent highest pensions, 61 percent belong to the group with the 20 percent highest disposable incomes, and of those with the 10 percent highest pensions, 53 percent belong to those with the 10 percent highest disposable incomes. In Table 4.3 we show probit estimates for the probability of belonging to the group of those with the lowest and highest disposable incomes.

Those who have a weak labor market attachment five years before retirement more often belong to the group of those with the lowest pensions but less often to the group of those with the lowest disposable incomes. One explanation may be that those who have had a weak labor market attachment receive other income transfers, and that the group

Table 4.2 The Probability of Belonging to the Group with 10 or 20 Percent Lowest and Highest Incomes from Pensions (Social Security and Occupational Pensions), among Those 65 and Older

	10% lowest pension	20% lowest pension	20% highest pension	10% highest pension
Men	-0.018***	-0.099***	0.103***	0.036***
	0.003	0.006	0.007	0.004
Married	-0.003	0.006	0.012	0.009
	0.003	0.006	0.008	0.004
Age at retirement	-0.013***	-0.021***	0.001	0.001
	0.001	0.001	0.001	0.001
Annual labor income/10,000 five years before retirement	-0.002***	-0.007***	0.013***	0.004***
	0.000	0.000	0.000	0.000
Self-employed five years before retirement	0.058***	0.270***	-0.110***	-0.046***
	0.010	0.019	0.009	0.003
Disability pension	0.061***	0.074***	-0.081***	-0.024***
	0.006	0.008	0.008	0.004
Weak labor market attachment five years before retirement	0.063***	0.086***	0.357***	0.217***
	0.011	0.015	0.030	0.027
Born in Sweden	Ref.[a]	Ref.[a]	Ref.[a]	Ref.[a]
Born in another Nordic country	0.017**	0.004	-0.064***	-0.015*
	0.009	0.013	0.012	0.007
Born in EU15 and OECD6	0.037***	0.028	-0.032	-0.014
	0.017	0.023	0.021	0.010
Born in other countries	0.076***	0.166***	-0.030	-0.008
	0.017	0.028	0.019	0.010

| Number of observations | 13,286 | 13,286 | 13,286 | 13,286 |
| LR chi2(10) | 2,097.65 | 3,331.56 | 5,064.41 | 2,050.18 |

[a] Reference category.

NOTE: *significantly different from zero at the 0.10 level; **significantly different from zero at the 0.05 level; ***significantly different from zero at the 0.01 level. The EU15 and OECD6 countries are Australia, Austria, Belgium, Canada, France, Germany, Greece, Ireland, Italy, Japan, Luxembourg, Netherlands, New Zealand, Portugal, Spain, Switzerland, UK, and the United States. The annual labor income is divided by 10,000 to facilitate the reporting of the estimates.

SOURCE: LINDA.

Table 4.3 The Probability of Belonging to Different Deciles of Disposable Incomes among Those 65 and Older

	10% lowest income	20% lowest income	20% highest income	10% highest income
Men	-0.052***	-0.117***	0.074***	0.023***
	0.004	0.006	0.007	0.005
Married	0.018***	0.032***	-0.015*	-0.009
	0.003	0.005	0.009	0.006
Age at retirement	-0.002***	-0.003***	0.000	0.000
	0.000	0.001	0.001	0.001
Annual labor income/10 000 five years before retirement	-0.004***	-0.010***	0.011***	0.005***
	0.000	0.000	0.000	0.000
Self-employed five years before retirement	0.030***	0.019**	0.115***	0.054***
	0.007	0.011	0.019	0.014
Weak labor market attachment five years before retirement	-0.007***	-0.058***	0.318***	0.187***
	0.004	0.006	0.026	0.024
Disability pension	-0.015***	-0.018***	-0.038***	-0.016**
	0.003	0.006	0.010	0.006
Born in Sweden	Ref.[a]	Ref.[a]	Ref.[a]	Ref.[a]
Born in another Nordic country	0.005	0.025*	-0.052***	-0.029***
	0.007	0.014	0.015	0.009
Born in EU15 and OECD6	0.017	0.033	-0.006	0.001
	0.013	0.023	0.026	0.017
Born in other countries	0.076***	0.131***	-0.046**	-0.008
	0.017	0.025	0.020	0.014

| Number of observations | 13,286 | 13,286 | 13,286 | 13,286 |
| LR chi2(10) | 2,040.15 | 3,240.44 | 3,238.41 | 2,050.18 |

[a] Reference category.

NOTE: *significantly different from zero at the 0.10 level; **significantly different from zero at the 0.05 level; ***significantly different from zero at the 0.01 level. The EU15 and OECD6 countries are Australia, Austria, Belgium, Canada, France, Germany, Greece, Ireland, Italy, Japan, Luxembourg, Netherlands, New Zealand, Portugal, Spain, Switzerland, UK and the United States. The annual labor income is divided by 10,000 to facilitate the reporting of the estimates.

SOURCE: LINDA.

may also contain some of those with a strong economic position who have chosen to stop working early.

Many of those with low and high pensions have low and high disposable incomes, respectively, but there are some differences. The self-employed have low pensions on average, but a higher probability of belonging to the groups of those with the lowest and highest disposable incomes. This reflects the heterogeneity among the self-employed. While some people have been able to save for old age, others have not.

GROUPS AT RISK FOR LOW PENSIONS AND LOW INCOME

Self-employed

The income differences among self-employed workers are large. Many have low incomes, and many do not have a supplementary pension of the same type employees tend to have. The number of self-employed is large and growing, making it important to study this group. Many of the self-employed are foreign born.

Employees who become self-employed have different backgrounds. Those who take into account characteristics such as education have low labor income as employees and those who have a high labor income as employees are overrepresented among those becoming self-employed (Andersson Joona and Wadensjö 2013). The latter group is doing considerably better than the first one in being self-employed, which indicates that the conditions for being self-employed vary greatly, as do the opportunities and knowledge of how best to prepare financially for life as a pensioner.

More than half of small business owners pay into pensions for themselves, but a quarter of the self-employed have no retirement savings; they save neither privately nor through their firms. Of the self-employed who save, 45 percent save less than 2,000 SEK per month. In order to receive the same pension that their employees receive from occupational pensions, the self-employed have to save 5 percent of their gross incomes from age 25 until retirement. If they start to save later, the annual savings required are higher (Svärdman 2011). The main reason the self-employed give when asked why they are not saving for a pension for themselves is that they cannot afford it. Other reasons are that they do not see any need, as their incomes as retirees are guaranteed by other means; they do not know how it works with occupational pensions; and they do not have time to gain an understanding of pension issues (Burreau 2011).

Today's retirees who have been self-employed have significantly lower pensions than those who have been wage earners. Both men and women who were self-employed five years before retirement had on average a total pension (social security, occupational, and personal) corresponding to about 70 percent of the average total pension for those who were wage earners five years before retirement in the period 2005–2009.[6]

Figures 4.9 and 4.10 show how much the average social security, occupational and personal pensions are for those who were wage earners or self-employed. Those who were wage earners had higher social security and occupational pensions but lower personal pensions than those who were self-employed. The social security pensions of the self-employed were about 75–80 percent of the social security pensions of wage earners for both men and women. For self-employed women, the occupational and personal pensions together constitute about 45–55 percent of the pensions of women who are wage earners, with an exception for self-employed women aged 75 and older who had occupational and personal pensions that were higher than those for wage earners. The corresponding figures for men are between 40 and 50 percent.

Guarantee Pensioners, Those without Occupational Pensions, and the Foreign Born

Some groups other than the self-employed have low pensions, such as those who have had low or irregular earnings and therefore receive a guarantee pension. The guarantee pension is only price indexed and not income indexed like the income pension. The group may therefore lag behind in income growth compared to those receiving an income pension. For the next few years it is expected that about 25 percent of new retirees will receive a guarantee pension. In 2008, 778,000 individuals received a guarantee pension, of which 180,000 (15 percent) received a full one. Of those who received a guarantee pension, 80 percent were

Figure 4.9 Pension Incomes for Men, 2005–2009

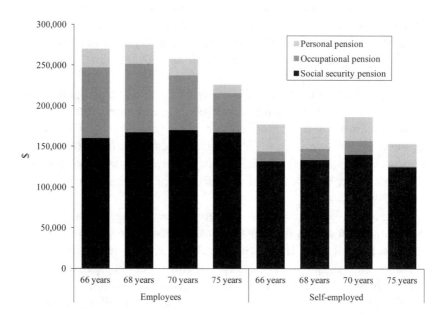

NOTE: Employees are defined as those who had their main incomes from employment five years before retirement. Self-employed are those with their main income from self-employment five years before retirement. Someone is defined as retired when pension income from social security and occupational pension exceed labor income.
SOURCE: LINDA.

women (Olsson 2011). Nearly half of female pensioners aged 65–70 received a guarantee pension in 2008. Among women aged 70 and older, it is even more common to receive a guarantee pension, as the older cohorts have had low labor force participation. For example, just less than 60 percent of women aged 70–75, over 80 percent of those aged 80–85, and over 90 percent of those aged 90 and older receive a guarantee pension. The proportion of men who receive a guarantee pension is much lower. In the age group 65–70, only slightly more than 10 percent receive a guarantee pension. Among men aged 80–85, a quarter receive a guarantee pension, and among those 90 and older, half receive a guarantee pension.

Figure 4.10 Pension Incomes for Women, 2005–2009

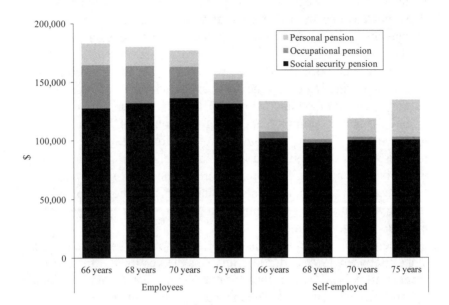

NOTE: Employees are defined as those who had their main income from employment five years before retirement. Self-employed are those with their main income from self-employment five years before retirement. Someone is defined as retired when pension income from social security and occupational pension exceed labor income.
SOURCE: LINDA.

Employees not covered by collective bargaining labor agreements are a second group at risk for low pensions. Occupational pension is most important for those who have had incomes above the ceiling in the income pension system, but it is important not just for them. Most receive their occupational pensions through a collective agreement. Over 90 percent of employees are employed in workplaces covered by collective bargaining agreements and thus have occupational pensions. Those who lack an occupational pension are primarily those who work in firms with few employees, those with the highest and lowest wages, and the self-employed and unemployed. Only a third of small business owners have signed up for an occupational pension. Employers without a collective agreement may pay for an occupational pension plan for their employees and at the same time for themselves. Of businesses without a collective agreement, 40 percent have a pension plan. Among those not covered by a collective agreement pension, approximately 60 percent have signed up for a separate personal pension (Svärdman 2011).

The foreign born are a third group at risk for low pensions. This is a group with large income differences and includes many low-income earners. Flood and Mitrut (2010) have written a report for the Social Council on immigrants coming from non-OECD countries and their pensions. The pensions of this group of foreign born are predicted to be low. Between 1992 and 2007, the foreign-born men's earnings were about 75 percent, and foreign-born women's earnings were about 60 percent of native-born men's earnings. This can be compared with the native-born women's earnings, which were about 70 percent of the earnings of native-born men.

The growth of earnings has important implications for future pensions. Between 1992 and 2007, this was slower for the foreign born from non-OECD countries than for natives. As an example we take the cohort born in 1960–1964. The income growth (among those who had earned income) was 62 percent for native men, 72 percent for native women, 47 percent for foreign-born men, and 49 percent for foreign-born women.

Labor force participation among the foreign born is lower than among natives even after taking into account differences in education, age, gender, etc. This leads to lower pensions for the foreign born than for natives. It should be emphasized that there are significant differences depending on country of origin. Low wages, low labor force participation, high unemployment, and fewer years in Sweden lead to lower pensions. Probably only a few foreign born from non-OECD countries have pension rights from their country of origin that can be transferred.

Forecasts of future social security pensions show that foreign-born people from non-OECD countries will have much lower pensions than natives. Foreign-born men born between 1946 and 1970 will receive about 60–65 percent of the native men's social security pension. The corresponding figure for foreign-born women is about 55 percent of the native men's social security pension.

The foreign born from non-OECD countries have significantly lower incomes and wealth than natives. Native-born men had in 2007 three to four times higher real assets than foreign-born men. The same relationship applies to the wealth of native- and foreign-born women.

Also, assets in personal pension savings are much smaller for the foreign born from non-OECD countries than for natives. For the cohort born 1945–1949, this amounted to one-third for both men and women compared to native men in the same cohort. For younger cohorts, the difference was even greater. For example, for the cohort born 1960–1964, the foreign-born personal pension wealth was 18 percent of that of native men in the same cohort, and for the cohort born 1970–1974 it was only 11 percent.

CONCLUSION

In this section, we summarize our results and mention some areas where we lack essential knowledge.

One important result is that some groups aged 65 and older have low pensions and other low incomes compared to others the same age. Women 65 and older on average have lower incomes and pensions than men the same age. The main reason for this is that working-age women have had a greater responsibility for unpaid housework than men. This does not mean that all of them live in households with low incomes as they get older. Many are married to men who have high pensions or other forms of income, but older women are often single. Women live longer than men, and women are on average younger than the men they marry. This means that women are more likely to be widowed than men. In addition, divorce is common, and pension wealth is not distributed in full upon divorce. Many women thus become single with a low pension. The long-run solution is a more equal division of labor between men and women both in the household and in the market. However, it can take a long time before such a change takes effect. Pensions are based on earnings over a lifetime or for many years (some of the occupational pensions). There are good reasons for reviewing the rules on pension plans.

The foreign born are another group that on average has low pensions. This is because many have a weak labor market attachment and many have lived for less than the 40 years in Sweden required at 65 for a full guarantee pension. The long-term solution is a stronger labor market attachment, but there are good reasons to review the rules for pension plans, particularly the rule about the number of years of residence required for a full guarantee pension.

The self-employed is a third group that often has low pensions. One explanation is that they have not paid for a pension corresponding to the occupational pensions for employees; another is that many of the self-employed have low incomes. A solution may be that more information could be given about the pension plans for self-employed, but there may be other ways of bringing this about.

A fourth group, which largely coincides with the three previously mentioned, consists of those who for various reasons have had a weak attachment to the labor market over a number of years. Also, after age 65 they usually have a weak attachment to the labor market, and they receive a low social security income–based pension and a price-indexed guarantee pension.

It is important to investigate different ways to improve the situation for those four mentioned groups who often have low incomes and pensions after age 65, that is, to improve the conditions for women, foreign born, self-employed, and those who for prolonged periods have had a weak attachment to the labor market. Different types of solutions may be required for the various groups.

Notes

We thank participants at the TrefF seminar in Oslo on May 31, 2012; the Swedish Fiscal Policy Council conference in Stockholm on June 18, 2012; and the ENRSP Conference in Poznan on September 13–14, 2012. We also thank Christer Gerdes for helpful comments on an earlier version.

1. See Sjögren Lindquist and Wadensjö (2011) for a more detailed presentation.
2. There is a gradual change from one system to another. For those who are born in 1938, 4 parts of 20 are calculated according to the new system (and 16 parts of 20 according to the old system). In 1944, 10 parts of 20 are calculated according to the new system (and 10 parts of 20 according to the old system).
3. For a discussion of different measures of income inequality among pensioners, see Johnson and Stears (1999).
4. van Vliet et al. (2011) use P80/P20 to measure the income distribution among older people in 15 European countries. They find that the ratio is lowest in the

four Nordic countries included in their study—Denmark, Finland, Norway, and Sweden.
5. See also Sjöström and Örnhall Ljung (2011) and Klevmarken (2010) for an analysis of who is working after 65.
6. Retirement is defined here as the first-year pension income from social security and occupational pension exceed labor income.

References

Andersson Joona, Pernilla, and Eskil Wadensjö. 2013. "The Best and the Brightest or the Least Successful? Self-Employment Entry among Male Wage-Earners in Sweden." *Small Business Economics* 40(1): 155–172.

Björklund, Anders, and Markus Jäntti. 2011. *Inkomstfördelningen i Sverige.* Stockholm: SNS Förlag.

Burreau, Britta. 2011. *Småföretagarna väljer bort tjänstepensionen.* Stockholm: Nordea.

Flood, Lennart. 2004. "Vilka pensioner får framtidens pensionärer?" *Ekonomisk Debatt* 32(3): 16–30.

Flood, Lennart, and Andreea Mitrut. 2010. *Ålderspension för invandrare från länder utanför OECD-området.* SOU 2010:105.

Gustafsson, Björn, Mats Johansson, and Edward Palmer. 2009. "The Welfare of Sweden's Old-Age Pensioners in Times of Bust and Boom from 1990." *Ageing and Society* 29(4): 539–561.

Gustafsson, Björn, Asghar Zaid, and Eva Franzén. 2007. "Financial Poverty." *International Journal of Social Welfare* 16(suppl. 1): 67–90.

Johnson, Paul, and Gary Stears. 1999. "Pensioner Income Inequality." *Fiscal Studies* 16(4): 69–93.

Karlsson, Hans, and Hans Olsson. 2012. *Medelpensioneringsålder och utträdesålder 2011.* Stockholm: Pensionsmyndigheten.

Klevmarken, Anders. 2010. *Vem arbetar efter 65 års ålder? En statistisk analys.* SOU 2010:85.

Kruse, Daniel. 2010. Longitudinell individatabas (LINDA). Beskrivning av statistiken, BV/EV. 2010-08-18. Stockholm: SCB.

Olsson, Hans. 2011. *Pensionsåldern.* Statistik och utvärdering. Stockholm: Pensionsmyndigheten.

Rosén Karlsson, Karin. 2011. Hushållens ekonomi (HEK), Beskrivning av statistiken, BV/EV, 2011-10-28. Stockholm: SCB.

Sjögren Lindquist, Gabriella, and Eskil Wadensjö. 2011. "A Viable Public-Private Pension System." In *Varieties of Pension Governance: Pension Privatization in Europe*, Bernhard Ebbinghaus, ed. Oxford: Oxford University Press, pp. 240–261.

Sjöström, Magnus, and Sara Örnhall Ljungh. 2011. *Efter 65 – inte bara pension. En analys av de äldres ekonomiska situation*, Ds 2011:42.

Svärdman, Håkan. 2011. *Småföretagande = små pensioner?* Stockholm: Folksam.

van Vliet, Olaf, Jim Been, Koen Caminada, and Kees Goudswaard. 2011. "Pension Reform and Income Inequality among the Elderly in 15 European Countries." Research Memorandum 2011.3. Leiden, Netherlands: Department of Economics, Leiden University.

Wadensjö, Eskil. 2011. "De äldres återkomst till arbetsmarknaden – ett långsiktigt perspektiv." In SCB, *Arbetskraftsundersökningarna (AKU) 50 år. Fyra forskarperspektiv på arbetsmarknaden*. Bakgrundsfakta 2011:3. Stockholm: SCB.

5

The Reform of Social Security Pensions in Portugal

A Critical Assessment

Maria Clara Murteira
University of Coimbra

This chapter provides a critical perspective on the policy direction followed in Portugal after the reform of social security pensions in 2007. First, it examines and assesses the main legislative changes introduced in that year by the former socialist government. The reform has been presented to the public as unavoidable, intended to improve financial sustainability while preserving the overall logic of the system. The chapter argues that it did not have a limited impact in the structure of the pension system, as it has introduced a fundamental change of perspective regarding the objectives and principles of pension policy. It also tries to show how the Portuguese process of reform has been influenced by political decisions from the EU, by focusing on restrictive rules that guide economic policy and the EU strategy for pensions. Economic policies inspired by the New Classical Economics paradigm and an agenda for pensions aligned with supply-side oriented economic policies have been important features in national pension policy. A particular emphasis is attributed to the critical influence of economic performance on pension systems' budgetary equilibrium, arguing that economic failures explain, to a great extent, much of the problems identified in Portugal.

The chapter is organized as follows. The first section describes the main measures introduced by the reform program of the social security pension system introduced in 2007. The second section develops a critical analysis of that reform. It examines its adverse effects regarding pensioners' well-being and its methodological incoherence. Next, it describes the path change introduced in the objectives and principles of policy, concluding that although pay-as-you-go financing has not been replaced by funding, its overall logic has changed. The next section examines the influence of the EU on the Portuguese reform process. The supply side–oriented economic policy paradigm, dominant at the EU, helped create an economic environment since the early 1990s that has favored the introduction of pension reforms. However, the social policy agenda set at the EU aligned with that paradigm has also been an important element in the reform process. Finally, the last section emphasizes the critical relevance of economic performance on social security budgetary equilibrium, arguing that the budgetary difficulties identified in the present are mainly the result of restrictive macroeconomic policies unfavorable to employment and growth. A paradigmatic change in economic policy is a necessary condition to allow a different orientation for pension policy.

MAIN LEGISLATIVE CHANGES

In Portugal, social security is financed by a total contribution rate of 34.25 percent of earnings paid by the employee and employer. Out of this total, employees pay 11 percent and employers pay 23.25 percent. These contributions finance old-age benefits (20.21 percent, since 2010), survivors' benefits (2.44 percent), unemployment benefits (5.14 percent), and disability benefits (4.29 percent). The contributions also finance sickness, parenthood, and occupational disease. The legal age of retirement is 65, but benefits can be received at age 55 for workers with 30 years of contributions (with penalties for early retirement), though the award of early retirement benefits has been temporarily suspended from 2012 through 2014, except for the long-term unemployed.

The social security pension plan in Portugal was reformed in 2007.[1] This plan is mandatory for the employees and self-employed workers in the private sector. Civil servants are covered by a separate plan.[2] Other plans also exist but cover a limited percentage of the total active population.

This reform introduced three important changes in regard to retirement benefits. First, a "sustainability coefficient" was introduced in the formula for calculating pensions. This coefficient is a demographic adjustment factor, which reduces pensions by a certain percentage as life expectancy increases. It is equal to the ratio between life expectancy in 2006 and life expectancy in the year preceding retirement. The level of statutory pension is multiplied by the coefficient and is thus reduced as life expectancy increases. The decrease in pensions may be partially offset if workers decide to postpone retirement or if they increase their voluntary contributions to a new complementary public plan of individual accounts.

Second, the formula for calculating pensions was changed. After 2007, pension levels are calculated taking into consideration the earnings of the entire working life. Since 1994, pension levels were calculated on the basis of the average earnings of the 10 best years of the final 15.[3] A 2002 law stated that the earnings of the entire career would be taken into account for calculating the pension.[4] However, it also defined a transitional period, 2002–2016, during which the most favorable method of calculation—the former, the latter, or a weighted average of both—could be applied in order to guarantee beneficiaries the most favorable rule to determine the pension level. For that reason, the full impact of the measure was not felt. During the transitional period, only approximately 17.5 percent of pensions were calculated based on the earnings of the entire career, the method that could guarantee the most favorable pension amount (European Commission 2005, p. 2). The reform of 2007 accelerated the transition to the new method of calculation. The pension is determined by a weighted average of two terms: one is based on the best 10 years of earnings of the final 15, the other is based on the earnings of the whole career. The weight of each term depends on the moment of retirement and the length of the contributory career up to a specified moment of reference. For those who retire before 2016, the moment of reference is 2006; for those who retire after 2016, the moment of reference is 2001.

Third, new rules for indexing the benefits were approved, which came into effect in 2007.[5] The new method does not guarantee the maintenance of the real value of all benefits. Higher benefits will be indexed to prices only for higher rates of economic growth. In addition, the minimum wage is no longer used as reference for determining minimum pension levels. The process of gradual convergence of the minimum level of pension with the national minimum wage started almost 10 years before and was completed in 2005.[6] In 2006, pensioners with a career longer than 30 years were entitled to a pension equal to the minimum wage (net of employee contributions), and those with shorter careers were entitled to a certain percentage of the net minimum wage. However, immediately after, there was a reversal of this policy. A law published in the end of 2006 stated that thereafter the adjustment of the minimum levels of pensions should be dissociated from the minimum wage.[7] A new term of reference for calculating and adjusting the benefits is used, the *Indexante de Apoios Sociais* (IAS), which is defined every year by the government. As a consequence, the minimum pension level started to diverge from the net minimum wage, as Table 5.1 shows.

The reform also introduced new rules to encourage older workers to stay in the labor market such as higher penalties for early retirement and incentives to extend working life.

A CRITICAL ANALYSIS OF THE PORTUGUESE REFORM PROCESS

A Reform Focused on Cutting Spending

The reform was presented to the public as necessary to contain pressures on the social security budget and guarantee its fiscal sustainability (Ministry of Labour and Social Solidarity [MTSS] 2006a,b). The policy solution chosen was based exclusively on the reduction of benefit levels.

The option of cutting pensions is particularly adverse in the Portuguese case because, at the time the reform was introduced, the retired population had on average lower incomes and higher incidence of poverty than the rest of the population (Murteira 2008). This is explained by the late development of the Portuguese public pension system and by work histories characterized by low earnings and short contributory periods. Table 5.2 shows that more than 80 percent of old-age pensioners were entitled to an amount of pension lower than the national minimum wage. Thus, the strategy followed has placed the burden of the adjustment exclusively on pensioners, particularly on pensioners with the lowest incomes.

Table 5.1 Evolution of the Minimum Wage and the Minimum Pension Level

Years	Minimum wage (euros)	Net minimum wage (euros)	Minimum pension level (career > 30 years) (euros)	MPL/ Net MW (%)
2006	385.90	343.45	343.45	100.00
2007	403.00	358.67	354.10	98.70
2008	426.00	379.14	363.81	96.00
2009	450.00	400.50	374.36	93.50
2010	475.00	422.75	379.04	89.70
2011	485.00	431.65	379.04	78.20
2012	485.00	431.65	379.04	78.20

SOURCE: Author's calculations.

However, some analysts argue that the decrease in the benefit levels should not be a reason for concern because, up to 2007, the system could guarantee high replacement rates. Thus, the system could be considered "generous." This argument, although frequently mentioned, is not strong. It is important to understand why replacement rates were high while the majority of old-age pensioners received very low benefits. Analysis from previous research (Murteira 2008) helps to clarify this question. The average gross replacement rates were broken down by income quintile for several cohorts of men and women who retired

Table 5.2 Distribution of Old-Age Pensioners in 2005, by Pension Levels

Level of pension (euros)	Old-age pensioners	
	Number	%
<374.7	1,110,912	81.00
374.7–562.05	112,440	8.20
562.05–749.40	54,454	3.97
749.40–1124.1	53,094	3.87
1124.1–1873.5	29,553	2.15
1873.5–2997.6	8,521	0.62
frm 2997.6–3747.0	2,555	0.19
Total	1,371,529	100.00

SOURCE: Ministry of Labour and Social Solidarity (2006a).

before the rule change. The disaggregate data on replacement rates helps to explain the paradox. High replacement rates did not reflect the generosity of the social security pension system. The highest replacement rates were those of pensioners, especially women, with very low wage levels who were entitled to a minimum pension level. A high percentage of women had low incomes and short working careers. These women were entitled to a minimum pension level that was higher (in many cases much higher) than their previous wages. Thus, the fact that replacement rates were high does not mean that the system provided generous benefits. High replacement rates and low pension levels were two faces of the same coin.

Moreover, the reform may also be criticized from a methodological standpoint because it has focused on the means of policy (spending on pensions) and neglected its ends (the social objectives). The objectives to attain, in regard to income security, are not reported either in the text of the law or in the document that reveals the strategic lines of the reform (MTSS 2006b). The State Budget Report (Ministry of Finance and Public Administration [MFAP] 2006) presented the estimated effects of the new rules regarding the future reduction of public spending on pensions and the future decrease of real growth of average pension, as Figure 5.1 shows. This outcome was considered positive.

This conclusion results from a biased perspective that consists of assessing policy only by its budgetary consequences, ignoring the essential purpose of pension provision. The obsession with the means of pension policy has led to the neglect of the ends. An appropriate assessment of pension policy should focus on its ends, looking at the means in view of the ends. As the purpose of pension plans is to provide retirement income security, a consistent policy design requires a clear specification of this aim. Spending on pensions should be seen as the "constraint" to face, rather than the "objective," as Barr and Diamond (2008, p. 33) have observed.

The view that motivated the reform undertaken in the field of social security pensions in Portugal, based on cutting benefits in order to alleviate fiscal problems, represents a way of approaching the welfare state that has been deeply criticized by Atkinson. In particular, the author underlined the tendency to look exclusively at costs without considering the benefits of the welfare state: "The whole purpose of welfare state provision is missing from the theoretical model" (Atkinson 1999,

Figure 5.1 Expected Real Growth Rate of Average Pension

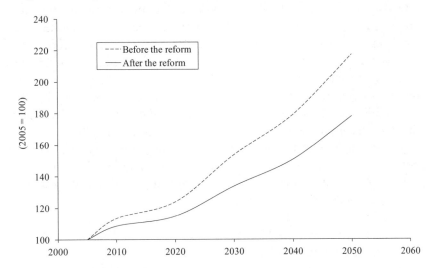

SOURCE: Ministry of Finance and Public Administration (2006).

p. 8). In the Portuguese debate the purpose of pensions was completely absent. As a consequence, the level of benefits has been taken as the adjustment variable in a policy aimed at containing spending.

The Structural Nature of the 2007 Reform

The reform was presented to the public as merely parametric, aimed at improving financial sustainability while preserving the overall logic of the system. However, there are sound reasons to argue that this reform had an important impact in the structure of the social security pension system. Thus, it might be better defined as structural.

The first reason is that it has produced a significant decline in the level of benefits, for both present and future pensioners but mainly for the latter. The three main measures introduced reduce the benefit levels because they affect both the replacement rate and the earnings path in the retirement period.

The replacement rate will decrease significantly over time because of the introduction of the "sustainability factor." According to the OECD (2007, p. 68), future benefits are expected to decrease around

20 percent as a result of the link to life expectancy. The replacement rate also decreases due to the new way of determining the benefits that are now based on the earnings of the entire career rather than the final earnings. Since working careers generally present rising earnings in later years, when pensions relate to the earnings of the entire career, the replacement rate is lower. Historical experience has shown that when pensions could be calculated according to the most favorable rule, between 2002 and 2004, only 17.5 percent of the new pensions were defined according to the new rule (European Commission 2005, p. 2). As a consequence, with the new formula, the large majority of pensions became more distant from the workers' final earnings and from the level of average earnings current in society at the time of retirement, meaning that replacement rates were reduced.

Moreover, pensioners' benefit levels over the retirement period will continue to diverge from the overall earnings path in society due to the unfavorable method of adjusting the benefits over time.

Thus far, the adverse effect of the reform on pensioners' economic well being has not been entirely felt: there is a transitional period for the application of the new calculation rule; the influence of the sustainability coefficient will be felt more acutely over time; and the negative effect of the new indexation rules is cumulative. The reduction of future pensions will be significant. OECD (2007) has estimated that future benefits will be more than 30 percent below the level pensioners would have been entitled to before the reforms. However, the reduction of future pensions might be higher than expected because of the effect of the new indexation rules, which is unpredictable.

The second reason for arguing that this reform was structural is that, although not explicitly, a new perspective regarding pension policy objectives has been adopted. The objective is no longer to enable people to maintain the previous living standards, but to provide a modest income protection.

A growing divergence between pension levels and wage levels was implicitly accepted. First, the new calculation rule expresses a different choice of objectives for pensions. When the objective is to safeguard the previous living standards, the benefits should be related to the final earnings. When pensions relate to the earnings of the entire career, they will diverge from workers' final earnings and from the average earnings current in society at the time of retirement. Second, the change in the way of adjusting pensions over time allows a growing divergence between pensioners' earnings path and the overall earnings path in the society. Both the reduction of the replacement rates for the majority of the retired population and the new rules of adjusting benefits over time show that the objective of enabling people to maintain the previous living standards in retirement has been abandoned. The new objective is to provide a modest income protection in retirement. A conception of social assistance, rather than what Myles has described as "contemporary notions of social security" (Myles 2002, p. 158), inspired this move.

The strategy of lowering pensions occurred at the same time the government declared the prevention of poverty among the elderly as a political priority. However, instead of reinforcing minimum income protection, the government has decided to dissociate the minimum pension levels from the minimum wage. At the same time, it has introduced a new means-tested benefit intended to alleviate old-age poverty (*complemento solidário para idosos*).[8] In the text of the law that introduced this benefit it is stated that the previous policy of general increase in the minimum levels of benefits was not sustainable and that it should be replaced by the strategy of concentrating the benefits of those in need.

Thus, the right to a minimum pension of the earnings-related plan has been questioned as a work-related right and started to be replaced by national solidarity mechanisms justified in case of need.

Furthermore, another profound change has occurred: the nature of pay-as-you-go (PAYG). The idea that it is possible to maintain in retirement the living standards achieved in the working period, which inspired the previous policy, was questioned.

The initial PAYG plans organized a mechanism of solidarity through work. Retirement pensions, like other social benefits, were guaranteed by the collectivization of a share of the total wages. In such a plan, the amount of contributions is immediately redistributed in the form of social benefits (pensions, unemployment benefits, sickness benefits, etc). In the original conception, a PAYG plan is contributory—benefits are defined on a commutative basis; since they are related to the employment status, their purpose is to replace earnings and require previous contributions—but it may involve a certain degree of redistribution in order to realize a set of social objectives. Therefore, benefits do not need to be strictly linked to contributions. A PAYG plan may include redistributive mechanisms such as the rules that establish minimum pension levels, the rules that guarantee higher replacement rates for the lowest incomes, or a calculation formula that takes into account the earnings of the final working years instead of the earnings of the whole career.

When the purpose is to safeguard in retirement the living standards achieved in the working period, pension levels should be close to the final wages. In this case, the pension may be seen as a "continued salary" (Castel 2009a,b; Friot 2010). This logic requires high replacement rates and indexation rules that guarantee a similar growth of pensions and wages over time.

Recently, PAYG plans in some countries have abandoned the previous logic, which based the right to resources on work and made pension levels dependent on the previous wage levels. In some cases, these plans have moved to a savings logic. Accordingly, each individual should be entitled to a sum of benefits closely related to what he has paid during his working period. Thus, the link between lifetime contributions and expected benefits should strengthen at the individual level. In this view, pensions are justified by the existence of "previous savings" (the contributions) and seen as an individual deferred income (Castel 2009a,b; Friot 2010).

In Portugal, the transition to a savings logic has already started. The logic of work-related rights is vanishing as the link between pensions and wages weakens. The reduction of the replacement rates, caused by the new pension formula and the introduction of the sustainability coefficient, increases the gap between the first pension and the final wages. These new rules contribute to strengthen the contributory nature of the plan and, thus, to the gradual transition to the model of pensions as individual deferred income. Also the new rules for indexing the benefits contribute to increase the gap between pensions and wages over the retirement period. Moreover, the link between pensions and wages also weakens due to the divergence of the minimum pension levels from the minimum wage. The plan is still PAYG but has a changing nature: the wage reference is disappearing, while the system moves from a work-based logic to a savings-based logic.

Thus, although the rule changes are parametric, the overall effect of the reform is structural: the level of future benefits will decrease significantly, social objectives have changed from safeguarding the preretirement living standards to the guarantee of a modest income protection, and a new logic is ruling PAYG.

THE STRATEGY OF SOCIAL RIGHTS
RETRENCHMENT IN PORTUGAL

The Portuguese social security pension system has been experiencing increasing political pressures. In recent years, we have identified a two-stage strategy for social rights retrenchment. Each stage presents a specific configuration.

In the first stage, marked by the 2007 reform conducted by a center-left government, the pressures were intended to contain spending. However, as observed ealier, this reform introduced significant changes in the structure of the social security pension system.

In the second stage, when a new right-wing government came into power in June 2011, the strategy for social rights retrenchment assumed a new configuration. The revenue side of social security budget has come under growing pressure. The new government has introduced several measures that reduce, directly or indirectly, the receipts from contributions. All the variables that influence the receipts from contributions came under pressure: the wage, the level of employment, and the contribution rate. In regard to the public sector, the government, in agreement with the *troika* (the European Commission, the European Central Bank, and the International Monetary Fund), has decided to reduce wages and employment. The private sector is recommended to follow the same route of wage reduction. In any case, wage reduction in the private sector is expected to occur as a consequence of massive unemployment. The third variable, the rate of contribution (*taxa social única*), has also been under downward pressure. The government has planned to reduce the employer contribution, arguing that it would reduce labor costs and thus improve the level of employment and external competitiveness of the economy. But, in regard to the reduction of the employer contribution, the government had to step back because of strong political opposition. These measures were planned when the social security budget was already extremely destabilized by the serious recession and massive unemployment that followed Portugal's bailout in May 2011. Massive unemployment has caused a significant decrease in receipts from contributions, an increase in spending on unemployment benefits, downward pressure on wages, and the growth of early retirement.

At the same time, a new political discourse has emerged. Invoking the excessive economic burden of social security, the government has introduced a new political speech on this subject intended to justify additional regressive reforms. The prime minister has announced that the reform of 2007 is not enough to guarantee the financial sustainability of the social security pension plan and that it is necessary to shift toward more funding and more private voluntary provision. Meanwhile, in April 2012, the government suspended the access to early retirement during the financial assistance period.[9] The financial assistance provided to Portugal after May 2011 by the European Central Bank, the European Commission, and the IMF was given on the basis of a policy program that required economic policy conditions. Following the demands of austerity established in the Memorandum of Understanding with the the *troika*, the new government has imposed deep cuts in expenditure, mainly in the wages of public servants and pensions, but also in a set of other social benefits, health care, and education. In 2013, after the periodical reviews of the *troika* for assessing the progression made with respect to the policy criteria specified in the memorandum, the government has accepted to impose additional cuts in expenditure. The focus will be on major budjet items, particularly the government wage bill and pension spending. A new reform of social security may be announced at any time.

The Influence of the EU on the Portuguese Reform Process

To understand the Portuguese reform process, we should not analyze it in isolation because it was significantly influenced by European prescriptions. The management of economic policy, imposing restrictive rules for the conduct of fiscal policy, and the social policy agenda set at the EU were important elements in that process.

The 2007 reform pensions, as well as the agenda of the current government, can only be understood by taking into consideration the social policy agenda set by the EU. The standpoint that has been adopted by both the previous and current government is in line with the social policy paradigm dominant in the EU. This one is aligned with the paradigm that has guided economic policy, especially since the Maastricht Treaty in 1992. In order to clarify this subject and understand how the EU has influenced pension reforms in the member states, it is worth mentioning the pressures imposed by restrictive macroeconomic policy and the influence of the European strategy for pensions.

The Economic Policy Paradigm Dominant in the EU

Especially since the Maastricht Treaty and the policy orientation adopted for the introduction of the single currency, the macroeconomic policy in the EU was defined in accordance to the prescriptions of the New Classical Economics (NCE). The same occurred with labor market and social protection policies.

The NCE defends monetary and fiscal policies based on rules rather than discretionary decisions of governments (Creel 2011). As the latter are considered to be moved by electoral purposes, rules are the only way to assign credibility to economic policies, a fundamental condition for guaranteeing its effectiveness. Therefore, economic policies should be ruled by restrictions imposed on the objectives or on the means.

Monetary policy should be conducted by an independent central bank and be committed to the objective of price stability. This commitment is fundamental in order to stabilize economic agents' anticipations and keep labor costs under control. In regard to fiscal policy, it should also be guided by strict rules. Two arguments justify it (Creel 2011). The first is the "Ricardian equivalence," stated by Barro (1974), according to which an expansionary fiscal policy has no effect on the level of economic activity. The argument may be summarized as follows: If a government tries to stimulate demand by increasing spending, the reduction of public savings will be offset by an increase of private savings. As people make perfect predictions of the effects of economic policy—assuming the rational expectations hypothesis—they will save more in the present in order to afford the future tax increases that will be necessary to pay off the increased debt. As a consequence, total spending will remain unchanged. Thus, demand-management intervention by governments is ineffective. The second argument states that the increase of the public debt may lead the central bank to increase money supply. According to the monetarist view, this will cause an increase in the price level. Both the inefficiency of fiscal policy and the importance of keeping price stability are arguments that justify the imposition of strict limits to budgetary policy.

Since Maastricht, EU countries have been submitted to a "culture of discipline" in the rules that guide macroeconomic policy (Fitoussi and Laurent 2009). According to the view that prevails in the EU, fiscal and monetary policy should have a limited role in stabilizing economies. The European Central Bank is responsible for guaranteeing the exclusive objective of monetary policy that is price stability. National fiscal policies have also been severely restricted by the Stability and Growth Pact and have been focused on the objective of balancing the budget. According to the dominant view, the role of the state in economic activity should be reduced to improve the performance of the economy. Therefore, it is essential to limit the growth of public expenditure. For this reason, a clause that prevents the governments from appealing to the European Central Bank to finance its deficits has been introduced. As a consequence, the governments have become dependent on deregulated and globalized financial markets.

Policies for the Labor Market and Social Protection

According to the paradigm that inspires European economic policy, growth and employment should not come through expansionary macroeconomic policies. These are replaced by the so-called structural reforms, such as the deregulation of the labor market or welfare retrenchment. Structural reforms in these two domains are recommended as a way to avoid distortions in the functioning of the labor market, promoting efficiency, and preventing high levels of public deficits and debts.

Policies for the labor market and social protection have been conceived in articulation with the supply-side orientation of economic policies. In regard to the functioning of the labor market, in this perspective unemployment is supposed to be caused by the malfunctioning of the labor market. It is considered largely voluntary, occurring when wages are above the level needed to clear the labor market. The source of massive unemployment is considered to be excessive regulation and high labor costs. Thus, the recommended solution is to make labor markets more flexible. Less regulation and the reduction of labor costs (wages and social contributions) are advocated in order to promote employment and the external competitiveness of economies.

Social spending, in turn, is considered unfavorable to economic growth. Social protection mechanisms are regarded as something that disturbs the market process. Welfare state programs, and social security pension plans in particular, are accused of contributing to the increase in the size of the government, causing inefficiency and originating huge public deficits and debts. It is assumed that the provision of welfare should not rely exclusively on public intervention. Instead, it should allow an increased role for the market, that is, private plans and voluntary provision. Additionally, pension plans should contribute to improve labor market efficiency by promoting employment and competitiveness. Thus, they should focus on containing labor costs and providing benefits that do not create disincentives.

Pressures Imposed by EU Macroeconomic Policy

The pressures for reforming social security pensions imposed by economic policies in the EU have been underestimated in most of the literature on the subject. In particular, the significant influence on pensions of the rules that guide fiscal and monetary policies in the EU should be underlined.

Since the Stability and Growth Pact, governments have been directly pressured to tighten fiscal policies (Fitoussi 2002, 2004). The imperative of balancing the budget has led the governments to cut public spending in general, and spending on pensions and other social transfer programs in particular. This fact has led to an attentive supervision of spending on pensions by the EU institutions charged with economic and financial affairs.

The imposition of the Maastricht "culture of discipline" in macroeconomic management materialized into restrictive fiscal and monetary policies (Fitoussi 2002, 2004). These policies have imposed indirect pressures on social security budgets. As restrictive macroeconomic policies have depressed growth and employment, they have undermined social security budgetary equilibrium. Under these circumstances, the pressure to impose reforms in social security pension systems increases.

The European Strategy for Social Security Pensions

At the same time, EU institutions have built a common political view about social security pensions, which is aligned with the mainstream in the international debate on pensions, inspired by the recommendations of the World Bank (1994) and the OECD (1996).

In the EU, social security pension system reform has been included in the political agenda after 1999. The effects of aging on pensions' spending have been under attentive supervision by the EU institutions charged with economic and financial affairs as a consequence of the budgetary discipline imposed by the Stability and Growth Pact. The member states were asked to adopt measures in order to guarantee the financial "sustainability" of PAYG plans by containing future spending and by encouraging the development of funded plans and voluntary provision. During the 1990s, and following these recommendations, many European countries have introduced reforms in social security pension plans with the implicit or explicit aim of containing spending.

Since 2001, the strategy designed for the field of pensions was pursued through the open method of coordination (OMC), which aimed to promote an increasing coordination of national reforms by building a consensual perspective regarding pension policy. It has contributed to define common principles and objectives, establish a common set of indicators to assess national pension arrangements, and offer periodic monitoring of progress made toward the common objectives. Although it has not imposed the same orientation to all member states, the OMC has been influential for decisions on national pension policy: it has contributed to build a shared view that has been translated into orientations for pension reforms. Palier (2006) has described the OMC as "a new form of intervention which is less aimed at institutional harmonisation or legislation than at harmonising ideas, knowledge and norms of action, in order to have common policy goals converging towards 'a common political vision' . . . The aim here is to achieve a Europeanization of social policy paradigm" (p. 8).

As mentioned earlier, the EU pension policy agenda is focused on reducing spending and organizing the plans in order to strengthen the "competitiveness" of national economies. First, it is assumed that the provision of welfare should not rely exclusively on public intervention; an increased role for the market should be allowed. Second, pension policy orientations are configured to meet the requirements of economic policies supply-side oriented. This view emphasizes that both contributions and benefits affect the functioning of labor markets. Pensions and other social benefits are analyzed in terms of their effects on labor costs and the incentives they embed. First, as the contributions required for financing pensions are a component of the labor costs, the contribution rate should be contained in order to avoid reducing labor demand. Therefore, cuts in social contributions are advocated to improve the performance of the labor market by favoring employment and the external competitiveness of economies. Second, generous pensions disincentivize the labor supply of older workers. Thus, in order to improve the functioning of the labor market to promote employment and competitiveness, pension policy should focus on containing the contribution rate to avoid the increase in labor costs, on providing benefits that do not create disincentives, and on "activating" older workers (European Commission 2006, p. 18).

This shared view inspired the reform programs developed in many member states, after 2003, like the one introduced in Portugal in 2007. The analysis of the progress in reforming pension systems in these countries, after the second round of the OMC (European Commission 2006), has identified common lines of reform. The conclusion was that, since 2003, when the first comprehensive analysis of national strategies in the area of pensions was reported (European Commission 2003), a general move has been observed in many member states regarding some features that may be summarized as follows. First, many countries have introduced rule changes such as incentives to extend working lives or disincentives to early retirement, the strengthening of the link between contributions and benefits, and the inclusion of life expectancy in pension formulas. Second, in many cases, the level of guaranteed minimum pensions has been increased to prevent the risk of poverty. Third, private provision has been promoted. It was recognized that, in general, the reforms caused the decrease in social security pensions, but it was admitted that it could be "compensated by longer working lives as well as by higher personal savings" (European Commission 2006, p. 3). Obviously, in Portugal these common lines of reform have been replicated in 2007.

ECONOMIC POLICY AND PENSION POLICY: PENSION POLICIES IN A CONTEXT OF INCREASING LONGEVITY

The increased pressures on public finances caused by an aging population has prompted many authors and policymakers who criticize state intervention in this sphere to recommend that the governments promote ambitious reforms of pension systems by means of rolling back spending. The "unsustainability/roll back argument" (Barr 2000b, p. 740) has been spread and consolidated as common sense.

Despite the recurrent use of this simple argument, it may be misleading because it neglects the decisive influence that economic performance has on the social security budget. The present difficulties in pension system financing are, to a great extent, the consequence of the economic dysfunctioning. Therefore, the analysis of pension policy should not be dissociated from the debate on macroeconomic policies.

Economic Growth, a Fundamental Issue

The economics of pensions has shown the relevance of promoting economic growth in order to face population aging.[10] Thompson (1998) has shown that, from an aggregate and real perspective, the economic cost of retirement equals the consumption of goods and services of the retired in relation to the total production of goods and services. The economic cost of retirement may be represented by the following expression:

$$\frac{C_R}{Y},$$

where C_R represents the consumption of retirees and Y represents total income. The analysis of this simple expression allows us to take two fundamental conclusions. First, retirement costs do not depend only on the consumption of retirees, but also on the level of total income. Thus, output is a central variable, as Barr (2001, 2004) and Barr and Diamond (2008) have emphasized. Second, pensions represent a claim on the output (Barr 2004).

Thus, the problem with pensions is essentially a distributive issue: it is the question of defining the rule that specifies pensioners' share in total income. Pensioners' income share depends on the distribution of income between capital and labor and on the division of the labor income between workers and pensioners. Thus, the social bargaining that leads to income distribution and so defines capital and labor shares and the political decision regarding the way the latter is divided between workers and pensioners are critical issues.

To sum up, in society's perspective, pensions represent a claim on the output. If life expectancy increases, other things equal, pensioners' share in spending will grow. At a given level of output, the adjustment may be realized by increasing contributions (of the employer or the employee), by reducing the benefits, or by increasing the legal age of retirement in line with rising life expectancy to avert the growth of the dependency ratio. However, in order to face rising life expectancy there is also a fourth solution: to increase the supply of goods and services. So, policies that promote economic growth are central. If the output grows, the distributive problem will become easier. There are two basic strategies for rising output: to increase labor productivity or to increase the number of workers (by reducing unemployment, by increasing women's participation in the labor market, by rising the legal age of retirement, or by immigration).

The public debate on the future of pensions has focused on two of the possible options: reducing pensions or increasing the age of retirement. In both cases, the burden of the adjustment is placed on the elderly. The relevance of policies that promote economic growth and full employment as a means to deal with future problems posed by demographic aging has been underestimated. However, a serious debate on pension policy cannot be dissociated from the debate on the model of macroeconomic regulation, income distribution in society, and the way labor income is divided between workers and pensioners.

The problem posed by the change in the age structure of the population—an increasing share in spending—has to be faced independently of the method of financing pensions. A shift toward funding would not avoid it. As Barr (2004) has shown, PAYG and funded plans represent two sorts of claims on future production, that is, two different ways of claiming the share of pensioners in national output. In the first case, the question is decided in the political process. In the second case, the question is decided in the market sphere. If the role of private plans and of voluntary provision increases, the pressures on public finances will reduce—because the retirement costs will not burden the public budget—but the economic cost of retirement will rest unchanged, unless it could be proved that a shift toward funding would lead to a higher increase in output. It is often argued that funding increases savings and hence will lead to higher productive investment and economic growth. Although there is a vast economic literature on this subject, there is a great controversy regarding both the causal link between funding and saving and the effect of saving on productive investment.[11]

Economic Policy and Pension Reforms in Portugal

The EU has declared concern for the future of pensions. However, European macroeconomic policies followed in the last two decades, inspired by the prescriptions of the New Classical Economics, have not been conceived in order to promote growth and full employment. Instead, the restrictive rules that have guided macroeconomic policies, focused on restrictive fiscal policy, price stability, and a strong euro, have depressed growth and employment, especially in peripheral countries like Portugal. Economic policies have contributed to deepen the social security budgetary problems and thus helped to present the reforms as unavoidable. Moreover, in Portugal, as in many developed countries, labor income share has decreased significantly in the last decades.

In Portugal, population aging has provided the argument to the former center-left government to restructure the system by reducing spending on pensions. In the years preceding the 2007 reform, social security has been characterized by a significant financial destabilization. The budgetary difficulties identified were, to a great extent, the outcome of economic policies—restrictive fiscal policy, monetary policy focused on price stability, and a strong euro in a context of external trade liberalization—that have depressed growth and employment. Since the introduction of the single currency, Portugal has experienced a decade of low growth and increasing unemployment, as Table 5.3 shows.

A low rate of economic growth and unemployment are big threats to the financial balance of social security. The official diagnosis mentions it: "As a consequence of a set of negative factors, like the slowdown of economic growth, a parallel increase in unemployment, the maturation of the system and the consolidation of schemes of anticipation/flexible age of reform, we have assisted, in the last five years, to an increased deterioration of the financial balance of the social security system . . . " (MTSS 2006a, p. 14).

Unemployment leads to the decrease in contributions and to a downward pressure on wages, which translates into lower contributions. Moreover, it causes an increase in spending on unemployment benefits and favors early retirement. In this context, retirement may

Table 5.3 Real Growth Rate of GDP and Unemployment Rate

	2000	2001	2002	2003	2004	2005	2006	2007	2008	2009	2010	2011
GDP real growth rate (%)	3.40	1.70	0.80	−0.80	1.30	0.50	1.40	2.40	0.00	−2.90	1.40	−1.60
Unemployment rate (%)	3.90	4.00	5.00	6.30	6.70	7.60	7.70	8.00	7.60	9.50	10.80	12.70

SOURCE: Banco de Portugal.

be the appropriate alternative for older workers facing the risk of un-employment. Early retirement becomes more frequent and creates additional financial pressures on pension systems. The budgetary problems identified were also conditioned by the increased maturity of the system, mentioned in the same report. Furthermore, these difficulties were aggravated by several measures of reduction or exoneration of contributions, expanded after 1999 with the purpose of stimulating employment, based on the idea that high labor costs are the main cause of unemployment. Population aging has also imposed financial pressures, but at a slow and gradual rate.

Thus, economic policies have contributed to deepen the budgetary problem and, as a result, to present the reform as unavoidable. At the same time, the social security plan came under growing political pressure. In particular, the recommendations from the EU level, regarding benefit retrenchment and the design of the plans, have been influential for decisions on national pension policy.

THE PRESENT CRISIS

The present crisis has revealed the adverse effects of economic policies oriented by the New Classical Economics in stabilizing economies with regard to growth, employment, and the external equilibrium of several member states, particularly the peripheral nations. After the global recession in 2008, some EU countries had to face problems of public debt financing. However, in order to manage the crisis, the leaders of the EU have imposed budget austerity to these countries, thereby contributing to deepen the recession and worsen the public finance crisis. The governments were asked to cut their deficits even when they had to face serious recession.

According to the understanding of European leaders, the present crisis is the consequence of the lack of rigor and effectiveness in the governance of the euro zone. Thus, discretionary decisions of national governments and parliaments with regard to fiscal policy should be subject to additional constraints in order to enforce budget consolidation. The commitment to this view has been embodied in the fiscal pact signed in March 2012 by European leaders. Expansionary fiscal policy is considered ineffective with regard to growth and responsible for increasing deficits and debts. The proposed solution to promote growth is to deepen structural reforms, which should improve competitiveness at the national level. Inspired by this view, European leaders have called for additional regressive reforms of the labor market and welfare systems. Thus, a "race to the bottom" for wages and social benefits is emerging.

As a consequence, welfare systems have been under growing pressure. Restrictive rules on monetary and fiscal policies result in a growth path that puts social protection systems under increasing stress in times of recession, since the receipts from contributions decrease while social expenditures are increasing. However, structural reforms promoting labor market flexibility and welfare state downsizing have not reduced massive unemployment in European countries, as predicted by the New Classical Economics. Instead of acting in favor of growth and employment, the decline in wages and social benefits has caused a decrease in effective aggregate demand and thus contributed to deepen the recession.

CONCLUSION

The 2007 reform of the social security pension system in Portugal was presented to the public as fundamental to contain pressures on the social security budget and guarantee its financial sustainability. The reform has been described as merely parametric, aimed at reducing the level of benefits for improving financial sustainability while preserving the overall logic of the system. However, it did not have a limited impact in the structure of the social security pension system. It might be better described as structural.

This chapter has argued that the Portuguese process of pension reform was deeply influenced by European guidelines and policies. The economic policy paradigm dominant in the EU helped to create an economic environment since the early 1990s that has favored the introduction of pension reforms. Since Maastricht, the imposition of restrictive rules in macroeconomic management has contributed to impose pressures for reforming pensions. As the governments were recommended to cut spending on pensions and other social transfer programs, there were direct pressures to lower public deficits and debts. There were also indirect pressures, since restrictive rules on fiscal policy have caused the slowdown of growth and the increase of unemployment, destabilizing social security budgetary equilibrium. However, a European strategy for the field of pensions, compatible with economic policies supply-side oriented, was designed in parallel. An open method of coordination was followed, which has been an important factor in the process of reforming pensions in many member states. It has contributed to build a common view on this subject and to define guidelines for policy that have been translated into common trends in reforms. The Portuguese reform in 2007 and the new political discourse that calls for an additional reform have been aligned with the EU orientation for pensions.

The chapter has also emphasized that the present difficulties in pension system financing are, to a great extent, the consequence of economic dysfunctioning. This fact, however, has been underestimated in the public debate, which has been dominated by the argument that spending on pensions will be unsustainably high because of population aging. The use of this simple argument may be misleading as it underestimates the decisive influence that economic performance has on pension systems budgetary equilibrium.

Economic growth is crucial, as the problem posed by the change in the age structure of the population is one of an increasing share in spending. If output grows, the distributive problem becomes easier. However, economic policies inspired by the New Classical Economics have had extremely adverse effects in stabilizing economies with regard to growth, employment, and the external equilibrium of several Member States, particularly the peripheral nations. A paradigmatic change in economic policy is fundamental to allow the appropriate policies for growth.

Furthermore, the discussion on the future of social security pensions should not be dissociated from the debate on income distribution in society. In a system financed on a PAYG basis, pensioners' income share depends on the distribution of income between capital and labor and on the division of the labor share between workers and pensioners. Ultimately, pension policy is about political choices.

Notes

1. Law n.° 4/2007, January 16, and Decree-Law n.° 187/2007, May 9.
2. Significant measures intended to harmonize the public scheme with the scheme that covers civil servants were introduced. See Law n.° 60/2005, December 29. Notice that Decree-Law n.° 187/2007 also applies to the calculation of pensions for civil servants whose working career started after September 1, 1993, in accordance with Decree-Law n.° 286/93.
3. Decree-Law n.° 329/93, September 25.
4. Decree-Law n.° 35/2002, February 19. See also DecreeLaw n.° 17/2000, August 8, art.° 57°3.
5. Law n.° 53-B/2006, December 29.
6. Ordinance n.° 1316/2005, December 22.
7. Ordinance n.° 1357/2006, November 30.
8. Decree-Law n.° 232/2005, December 29.
9. The official speech of the present government includes two policy orientations: increasing the labor market participation of older workers and promoting complementary private retirement savings. These orientations seem to have been inspired by the proposals of the EU social policy agenda defined in the Green Paper (European Commission 2010) and the White Paper (European Commission 2012).
10. See, for example, Barr (2001, 2004); Barr and Diamond (2008); and Thompson (1998).
11. First, funding might not increase savings, since an increase in mandatory savings can be offset by a reduction in voluntary savings. Second, increasing savings might not increase productive investment. Savings do not convert automatically into productive investment. However, if there is a low rate of economic growth, increasing savings may have a depressive effect on the level of economic activity, and thus reduce productive investment. Third, an increase in productive investment might not have a significant effect on growth. This is the reason why Barr (2004, p. 207) argues that funding, as a mechanism intended to promote economic growth, is both indirect and debatable. On the effects of pensions on saving and investment, see Barr (2004), Barr and Diamond (2008), and Thompson (1998). The "myths" on the advantages of funding have been examined by Barr (2000a, 2001, 2004); Barr and Diamond (2008); Orszag and Stiglitz (2001); and Thompson (1998).

References

Atkinson, A. B. 1999. *The Economic Consequences of Rolling Back the Welfare State*. Cambridge MA: MIT Press.

Barr, Nicholas. 2000a. "Reforming Pensions: Myths, Truths, and Policy Choices." IMF Working Paper No. 00/139. Washington DC: International Monetary Fund.

————. 2000b. Review of *The Economic Consequences of Rolling Back the Welfare State*, by Anthony B. Atkinson. *Economic Journal* 110(467): 739–823.

————. 2001. *The Welfare State as Piggy Bank: Information, Risk, Uncertainty and the Role of the State*. Oxford: Oxford University Press.

————. 2004. *Economics of the Welfare State*. 4th ed. Oxford: Oxford University Press.

Barr, Nicholas, and Peter Diamond. 2008. *Reforming Pensions: Principles and Policy Choices*. Oxford: Oxford University Press.

Barro, Robert. 1974. "Are Government Bonds Net Wealth?" *Journal of Political Economy* 82(6): 1095–1117.

Castel, Nicolas. 2009a. *La Retraite des syndicats: Revenu différé contre salaire continué*. Paris: La Dispute/SNÉDIT.

————. 2009b. "Poursuite du salaire ou contributivité? Les retraites au péril des comptes individuels." Les notes de l'IES n°.1. Institut Européen du Salariat.

Creel, Jérôme. 2011. "Les politiques macroéconomiques: des mutations fortes." In *La pensée économique contemporaine*, Cahiers français n°. 363. Paris: La documentation française, pp. 57–61.

European Commission. 2003. *Joint Report from the European Commission and the Council on Adequate and Sustainable Pensions*. Brussels: European Commission.

————. 2005. *National Strategy Report: Adequate and Sustainable Pension Systems—Portugal—Summary*. Report submitted to the European Commission. Brussels: European Commission.

————. 2006. *Adequate and Sustainable Pensions: Synthesis Report*. Luxembourg: Office for Official Publications of the European Communities.

————. 2010. *Towards Adequate, Sustainable and Safe European Pension Systems*. COM (2010) 365 final, July 7. Brussels: European Commission.

————. 2012. *An Agenda for Adequate, Safe and Sustainable Pensions*. COM (2012) 55 final, February 16. Brussels: European Commission.

Fitoussi, Jean-Paul. 2002. *The Stability (and Growth) Pact and Monetary Policy*. Brussels: European Parliament—Committee for Economic and Monetary Affairs.

————. 2004. *Reform of the Stability and Growth Pact*. European Parliament—Committee for Economic and Monetary Affairs.

Fitoussi, Jean-Paul, and Éloi Laurent. 2009. "Macroeconomic and Social Policies in the EU 15: The Last Two Decades." Documents de travail de l'OFCE 2009-20. Paris: OFCE.

Friot, Bernard. 2010. *L'enjeu des Retraites*. Paris: La Dispute/SNÉDIT.

Ministry of Finance and Public Administration (MFAP). 2006. *Orçamento de Estado para 2007: Relatório*. Lisboa: MFAP.

Ministry of Labour and Social Solidarity (MTSS). 2006a. *Relatório Técnico sobre a Sustentabilidade da Segurança Social*. Lisboa: MTSS.

———. 2006b. *Linhas Estratégicas da Reforma da Segurança Social*. Lisboa: MTSS.

Murteira, Maria Clara. 2008. "Pension Policies and Income Security in Retirement: A Critical Assessment of Recent Reforms in Portugal." Papeles de Trabajo del Instituto de Estudios Fiscales 12/08. Madrid: Instituto de Estudios Fiscales.

Myles, John. 2002. "A New Social Contract for the Elderly?" In *Why We Need a New Welfare State*, Gøsta EspingAndersen with Duncan Gallie, Anton Hemerijck, and John Myles, eds. Oxford: Oxford University Press, pp. 130–172.

Organisation for Economic Co-operation and Development (OECD). 1996. *Ageing Populations: Pension Systems and Government Budget*. Paris: OECD.

———. 2007. *Pensions at a Glance: Public Policies across OECD Countries*. Paris: OECD.

Orszag, Peter R., and Joseph E. Stiglitz. 2001. "Rethinking Pension Reform: Ten Myths about Social Security Systems." In *New Ideas about Old Age Security*, Robert Holzmann and Joseph E. Stiglitz, eds. Washington, DC: World Bank, pp. 17–56.

Palier, Bruno. 2006. "The Europeanisation of Welfare Reforms." Cambridge, MA: Inequality Summer Institute, Kennedy School of Government, Harvard University.

Thompson, Lawrence H. 1998. *Older and Wiser: The Economics of Public Pensions*. Washington, DC: Urban Institute Press.

World Bank. 1994. *Averting the Old Age Crisis: Policies to Protect the Old and Promote Growth*. New York: Oxford University Press.

6

The Norwegian Government Pension Fund as an Investor in Global Markets

Magdalena Mosionek-Schweda
University of Gdańsk

Because of population aging, many countries have established reserve funds to mitigate the effects of future deficits in their social security programs (Jarrett 2011). According to the OECD, in 2009, 17 of 34 member states had social security reserve funds. They have accumulated a total of $4.554 trillion, of which about $2.540 trillion belonged to the U.S. Social Security Trust Fund (OECD 2011).

The purpose of this chapter is to describe a special reserve fund, the Norwegian Government Pension Fund. Its uniqueness is reflected in both its organizational structure and its principles of accumulation and investment of resources. This fund consists of two parts: Pension Fund-Global and Pension Fund–Norway. In view of a clearly defined commitment to the social security program of the latter, and a general commitment of the former, only the latter is recognized as a reserve fund in the OECD statistics. This chapter, however, mainly focuses on the Global Fund, which is one of the largest investors in the global financial market.

This chapter addresses issues related to the development and the operation of the Norwegian Government Pension Fund Global (GPFG), which the Norwegian government uses to invest funds derived from the extraction of oil. After 15 years of regular fuel revenue receipts and through active investment policy, GPFG became the second-largest pension fund in the world (after Japan) and the first in Europe, with assets of NOK 3.496 trillion ($626 billion, based on $1.00 = 5.58 kroner),

This chapter first provides an overview of Social Security programs in Norway. It then discusses the Norwegian Government Pension Fund, focusing on the Norwegian Pension Fund Global.

ORGANIZATION OF THE SOCIAL SECURITY PROGRAM IN NORWAY

The involvement of the Norwegian government in the organization of social protection of the population began in the late nineteenth century with the establishment of accident insurance for factory workers in 1885. The start of the development of the social security program took place in 1957, and 10 years later an additional mandatory retirement plan depending on the amount of remuneration of labor was implemented. In 1967, social benefits introduced for different groups prior to the Second World War were integrated in a single National Security program (Ambasada Norwegii w Polsce 2010). The current social security program consists of three components (Lovdata 1966, 1998, 2002; Norwegian Labour and Welfare Organisation [NAV] 2012):

1) The National Insurance Scheme, under an act of February 28, 1997;

2) The Family Allowance Scheme, regulated by an act of March 8, 2002;

3) The Scheme for Cash Benefits for Families with Small Children, established by an act of June 26, 1998.

In 2006, the social security reform process began. One of the most important changes was the establishment of a new institution, NAV. This office started its operations on July 1, 2006, and replaced the two previous institutions, Norwegian National Insurance (*Trygdeetaten*) and the Norwegian Labour and Welfare Service (Aetat). NAV's primary objective is to create opportunities for employment, while at the same time protecting the rights to social security benefits (NAV 2007–2009). The organizational structure includes 457 local NAV offices. The first offices were established in the autumn of 2006, while the target number was reached in March 2011.

The social security program is financed by contributions from employees, the self-employed, and employers, and also from government subsidies. The amount of the contribution is determined annually by the Parliament (NAV 2012). In 2012, four rates applied:

1) 7.8 percent of income from employment, paid by workers;

2) 11.0 percent of the income from the self-employed;

3) 14.1 percent of the gross payroll for employers (with no ceiling on earnings);

4) 3.0 percent of other income (e.g. pensions).

The benefits of social security include old-age, survivor's and disability pensions, temporary assistance grants for the chronically ill and those recovering from accidents, care allowances for persons with disabilities, rehabilitation benefits, compensation for accidents at work, benefits for single parents, unemployment, sickness and maternity benefits, medical sickness and maternity allowances, and funeral benefits (NAV 2012).

The right to individual benefits usually depends on the length of membership in the social security program. Most of the benefits, however, are calculated on the base rate, the G value (from *grunnbeløp*), determined annually by the Parliament in May. Since May 1, 2011, this rate amounts to NOK 79,216 (NAV 2011c) ($14,196).

THE PRINCIPLES OF FUNCTIONING AND THE REFORMS OF THE NORWEGIAN SOCIAL SECURITY PROGRAM

Norwegian authorities reformed the social security program, taking effect starting January 1, 2011. The program is currently undergoing a period of transition in which old and new rules operate simultaneously. The most important aspects of the current system and the changes are indicated below.

The Norwegian retirement system consists of three components referred to as pillars. The first pillar is the basic pension received from the social security program (*Folketrygden*). The amount of the benefit depends on the amount of income, the duration of membership in the program and the contribution period, marital status, and whether the spouse receives benefits from Folketrygden. The retirement pension from this part of the system consists of the basic pension (*grunnpensjon*), the supplementary pension (*tillegspensjon*) and/or the extra allowance (*særtillegg*) and the care allowance for pensioners with dependent children and/or a spouse (NAV 2012).

The basic pension is granted to persons with at least three years of membership in the program between the ages of 16 and 66. The amount of the basic pension benefit is determined by the length of the insurance period and is independent of both the amount of income earned during the activity period and the contributions paid into the system during the activity period. A full basic pension is received by members of *Folketrygden* after a minimum of 40 years. If the membership period is shorter, the amount of benefits is reduced accordingly (NAV 2011a). A full basic old-age pension is 100 percent of the base G rate (NOK 79,216 since May 1, 2011) (NAV 2011c).

The supplementary pension (*tilleggspensjon*) was introduced in 1967 with the purpose of maintaining a standard of living after retirement close to the level of the work period (NAV 2012). The amount of the benefit is strictly dependent on income, measured by the average number of pension points, and the qualifying years of contributions. In order to obtain supplementary pension rights, the insured needs to exceed the G rate of the pensionable salary for a period of at least three years, with the G rate being the income threshold above which the pension points are counted. The part of income that exceeds the G rate is divided by this rate. Thus, workers earning twice the G rate receive one pension point. This rule applies to pension points calculated on the basis of pensionable salary not exceeding 6G. For income between 6G and 12G, only one-third is taken into account to calculate the number of pension points. Income exceeding 12G is not taken into account. The average final pension points for determining the supplementary pension is calculated as the average of the 20 best years in terms of pension points (NAV 2012).

The extra allowance (*særtillegg*) is granted to pensioners not entitled to a supplementary pension or if the supplementary pension is less than the *særtillegg*. The right to the basic pension is necessary to obtain the extra allowance. The amount of the allowance is decided by Parliament as a percentage of the basic G in two rates, normal, amounting to 94 percent of G and reduced, which is 74 percent of G (NAV 2010).

The age for receipt of social security benefits in Norway is 67 for both men and women. Workers are allowed to continue work after benefit receipt until age 68 with full pension entitlement. At age 68, however, until age 70, if the annual income of the retired person exceeds twice the rate of G, the pension amount above this level is reduced by 40 percent (NAV 2011a).

The pension reform implemented on January 1, 2011, introduces changes in the retirement age, the principles of calculation and payment of benefits and the possibility of combining an old-age pension with further work. The new, flexible, retirement program is primarily aimed at providing the insured with the following (NAV 2012):

- The ability to receive a retirement pension after age 62, if the insured has acquired adequate pension rights. Everyone is still entitled to receive benefits at age 67.

- The selection of the "retirement standard"—the insured worker decides whether to receive the full old age benefit from their pension account, or a partial benefit: 20 percent, 40 percent, 50 percent, 60 percent, or 80 percent.

- The right to change the "level of retirement" once a year.

- The possibility of combining the entitlements and labor income without reducing the received pension benefit.

In addition, those born after 1962 acquire pension rights according to the following new rules (NAV 2012):

- The amount of the old-age pension depends on all the years in which the income accounting for pension points was obtained, until age 75. Based on the new rules, the contributions of the insured create a pension fund, and the amount of the benefit depends on the accumulated capital value. According to the existing rules, the amount of pension was calculated on the basis of the 20 best years of work and allowed full pension after 40 years of participation in the program.

- The funds accumulated in the pension fund (a notional account, rather than an invested account) are indexed annually by the wages growth indicator for those before retirement, and by that indicator decreased by 0.75 percent for persons receiving a benefit;

- The pension fund grows by 18.1 percent of the insured income in excess of the equivalent of 7.1 G.

Persons born between 1943 and 1953 acquire pension rights and receive benefits in accordance with the existing terms and conditions. Persons born between 1954 and 1962 acquire the rights based in part on new and old rules.

The changes introduced in the Norwegian social security program guarantee a greater freedom as to when, and to what extent, the insured person starts drawing a pension. The changes also allow a person to work and receive an unreduced pension, which helps to increase future benefits by raising retirement savings. Despite the right to receive a pension at age 62, the new rules for calculating entitlements encourage prolonged years of work. The flexibility of pension savings withdrawal also applies to persons born between 1943 and 1953, to whom the regulations from before the reform apply.

The effects of the implemented reforms were evident right when the new regulations were enforced. In January 2011, 13,600 persons under age 67 took the advantage of the possible pension savings withdrawal. In total, in the first quarter of 2011, 17,834 people aged 62–66 opted to receive benefits, of whom 83.5 percent were male (NAV 2011b). About 60 percent of this group remained in the labor market using the possibility of joining work with drawing pension benefits (NAV 2011e). In the first quarter of 2011, NAV paid pensions to 685,226 people, an increase of about 32,000 compared to the first quarter of 2010. In total, the participation of pensioners in the Norwegian community at that time was 13.88 percent (NAV 2011d).

In addition to the social security program, the second pillar, consisting of employee pension plans (*Obligatorisk Tjenestepensjon* [OTP]), was introduced in 2006 as a part of the retirement system reform. The Norwegian OTP is mandatory for both employees and employers. The third pillar covers all additional, optional forms of benefits offered by private pension funds and other financial institutions. The scope of its organizational system, however, is not specified by the legislature.

THE ORIGINS AND DEVELOPMENT OF THE NORWEGIAN GOVERNMENT PENSION FUND

The Norwegian Government Pension Fund has been operating in its present form since January 1, 2006. Its origins, however, date back to the 1960s. It consists of two separate funds: the Government Pension Fund Global (GPFG), which is the successor of the Government Petroleum Fund, and the Government Pension Fund Norway (GPFN), derived from the Social Insurance Fund. The Norwegian Government Pension Fund is owned by the Norwegian Government and the Ministry of Finance.

The current administration of GPFG and GPFN has been entrusted to two institutions, a special unit operating in the National Bank of Norway called Norges Bank Investment Management (NBIM) and Folketrygdfondet (Norwegian Ministry of Finance 2012). Each of these funds was created at a different time and, although together forming the Norwegian Pension Fund, are independent of each other, governed by separate legislation and adopting different strategies.

The GPFN was established in 1967 under the Social Security Act as the Social Insurance Fund (Lovdata 1966). As mentioned above, in 2006 it was converted into GPFN, managed by *Folketrygdfondet*, an independent entity, under an act of June 29, 2007, fully owned by the state (Lovdata 2007). The aim of GPFN is to accumulate and grow savings in the social security program for the purpose of payment of future pension benefits. The initial capital of the GPFN derived from the surplus generated in the social security program since its establishment in 1967 until the late 1970s. Currently, the proceeds to the fund are profits from its investment activities. The total net gains (net of management costs) increase the GPFN assets and no transfers to the state budget or payments of current benefits occur (Norwegian Ministry of Finance 2012). The value of assets held in the fund at the end of 2011 stood at NOK 129.4 billion ($23.19 billion), of which NOK 78.3 billion ($14.0 billion) is in equity securities, and NOK 51.1 billion ($9.2 billion) is in financial assets with fixed income (SSB 2012b). The investment portfolio of the fund shares included 48 Norwegian companies (with a total value of NOK 60.4 billion) and 90 companies in other Nordic countries (with a value of NOK 17.9 billion). Among the debt securities, almost

70 percent were corporate bonds of Norwegian companies (worth NOK 35.5 billion); the fund also held government bonds worth NOK 6 billion and foreign debt securities worth NOK 9.6 billion (SSB 2012c). In contrast to the GPFG, the GPFN investment activity is limited to the Norwegian market and the regulated markets of Nordic countries (Finland, Denmark, and Sweden, with the exception of Iceland). GPFG, founded more than 30 years later than the GPFN, is the focus of the remainder of the chapter.

The basis for its establishment was an act in June 1990 that created the Government Petroleum Fund (the Oil Fund) (Lovdata 1990). Through this fund, the Norwegian government accumulated and invested the excess funds from the extraction of crude oil discovered at the end of 1969. Until the establishment of the Oil Fund, the revenues from extractive industries were used for about 20 years for current public expenditure and national debt redemption. In the 1970s, however, it was evident that the revenues from the petroleum sector are indefinite as they relate to nonrenewable resources. To avoid overheating the Norwegian economy and in view of the long-term use of oil wealth, the Norwegian authorities decided to direct one-third of the net income of the state generated by the oil production to a special fund. The first transfer of funds, however, took place only in 1996; the fund received approximately NOK 2 billion in 1996 (Norwegian Ministry of Finance 2012).

After 15 years of regular fuel revenue receipts and through an active investment policy, GPFG became the second-largest pension fund in the world (after Japan) and the largest in Europe. The fund is also the largest shareholder in the European capital market with about 1.8 percent of shares listed on stock exchanges in Europe and one of the largest investors in the world, with approximately 1 percent share in the global capital market (Towers Watson 2011). The value of assets held in GPFG at the end of the first quarter of 2012 amounted to NOK 3,496 trillion ($627 billion). Figure 6.1 shows the market value of the fund on a quarterly basis from 1998 to 2012.

As mentioned above, the predecessor of today's GPFG was the Oil Fund, transformed into GPFG in 2006. From that time, its purpose is not only to support the government in the long-term, sustainable use of revenues from the petroleum sector, but also to multiply these means in order to finance future pension payments in the public social security

**Figure 6.1   Government Pension Fund Global Market Value, 2002–2012
(quarterly data in NOK billions)**

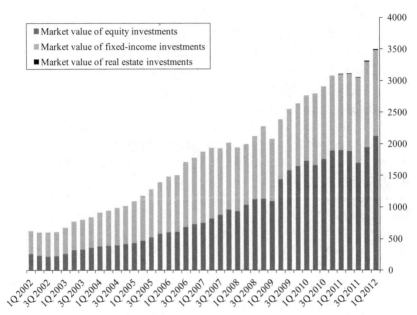

SOURCE: NBIM, Government Pension Fund Global first quarter 2012, Oslo
(2012b, p. 2).

system (OECD 2011). The fund, however, is an instrument for general
saving with undefined future liabilities to the social security program or
any other social or economic area. It is not an instrument of Norwegian
foreign policy, and is not used for the purpose of achieving political or
strategic objectives. The functioning of the GPFG (*Statens pensjonsfond – Utland*) is based on three basic principles (Ambasada Norwegii
w Polsce 2012):

1) Annual revenues of the fund are derived from the Norwegian
    state oil production, financial operations associated with the ex-
    traction and profits generated by the fund.

2) The transfer of funds to the budget may not exceed an amount
    equal to the expected rate of return on investment, set at 4 per-
    cent per year. With this principle, the government can only

withdraw the profits earned by GPFG without diminishing its capital. In addition, short-term fluctuations in oil and gas prices do not impact the fiscal policy.

3) The fund's assets are invested exclusively outside Norway. This is to ensure the diversification of investments and the reduction of the adverse impact of fluctuations in oil prices on the domestic economy.

Due to the lack of clearly defined social security pension liabilities of the pension fund, as well as the lack of the connections between the fund and the social security program (GPFG revenues are independent of the contributions of the insured), it is not a typical social security reserve fund established in some countries, such as the United States, with the aim of securing future pension payments. As emphasized by the Norwegian authorities, the idea of the GPFG is a long-term, rational management of resources from the oil deposits to benefit both today's and future generations of the residents of Norway (Norwegian Ministry of Finance 2012). According to the forecasts of the Ministry of Finance, in 2020 the market value of the fund will amount to NOK 6.285 trillion ($1.126 trillion) (Norwegian Ministry of Finance 2011). Assuming that at that time Norway will be inhabited by about 5.5 million people (SSB 2012a), the amount per person will exceed NOK 1.1 million ($197,000). At the end of 2011, the fund's value per capita amounted to about NOK 670,000 ($120,000).

THE INVESTMENT STRATEGY OF THE GOVERNMENT PENSION FUND GLOBAL

GPFG is a unique investor considering not only its large asset value, but also its lack of necessity of achieving short-term investment objectives. Its investment policies are designed to take into account the specific characteristics of the fund and the specificity of the markets in which the assets are invested. For this reason, the Ministry of Finance and the National Bank of Norway carry out a continuous review of the fund's investment strategy to develop it in the best direction to increase funds accumulated in the fund and to achieve the desired rate of return at a moderate level of risk. It is the basic principle to be respected by NBIM, the entity responsible for managing the assets of GPFG (Norwegian Ministry of Finance 2010). The real average annual rate of return of the fund for the period 1997–2011 was 2.7 percent and therefore below the 4 percent estimated by the Ministry of Finance. The annual performance of the GPFG is characterized by extremes, from a loss of −23.3 percent to profits of 25.6 percent (Norwegian Ministry of Finance 2012). The Norwegian Government points out, however, that GPFG is based on a long-term investment objective, and the loss-making assets in the investment portfolio have a great potential for growth in the future.

GPFG investment policy has evolved with the growth of its assets (Table 6.1). The first transfers from the state budget to the fund (then *Statens petroleumsfond*) were invested exclusively in government bonds, in accordance with the investment policy of the Norwegian Central Bank. In 1998, NBIM was established—the body responsible for the management of the investment policy of the fund in accordance with the guidelines of the Ministry of Finance. In that year, it was decided to include stocks in the investment portfolio on the condition that they not exceed 40 percent of the fund (Norwegian Ministry of Finance 2012). Nine years later, this limit was raised to 60 percent, and in the subsequent year the Ministry decided to permit real estate investments limited to 5 percent of the portfolio (Norwegian Ministry of Finance 2010).

The diversification of the GPFG portfolio pertains to different categories of investments, as well as geographical dispersion. For the purpose of the investment policy of the fund, the following three regions were determined: Europe, America/Africa, and Asia/Oceania, with the investment limits within each of these regions defined separately for investments in equity and debt securities. So far, they were established, respectively, as 50 percent, 35 percent, and 15 percent for equities, and 60 percent, 35 percent, and 5 percent for investments in fixed income securities (NBIM 2012a). This indicates that more than half of the GPFG assets were located in securities and real estate in Europe. The current financial crisis not only shook the capital markets, but also revealed a number of anomalies and problems in the public finances of certain European countries. The changes observed in global finance in 2008–2010 contributed to the GPFG management decision to change

Table 6.1 Stages of Development of the Government Pension Fund Global Investment Policy

Year	Events
1969	The discovery of oil in the North Sea—extraction since 1971.
1990	The decision of the Norwegian Parliament to set up the Government Petroleum Fund for long-term management of revenues from oil sales.
1996	The first transfer of funds to the Fund in the amount of approximately NOK 2 billion.
1997	The decision of the Ministry of Finance to start investing in equity funds—the fund previously invested only in government bonds.
1998	January 1—the NBIM commencement—NBIM manages the fund on behalf of the Ministry of Finance. The change in the structure of the investment portfolio of the fund—40 percent of the portfolio conversed from debt to equity instruments.
2000	Five emerging markets added to benchmark index.
2002	Corporate bonds included in debt instruments benchmark index.
2004	The establishment of ethical guidelines for the fund's investment plan.
2006	Name changed to: Government Pension Fund Global.
2007	The decision of the Ministry of Finance to increase the limit of investment in equities from 40 percent to 60 percent and the inclusion of small and medium-sized enterprises to the portfolio.
2008	The decision to start investing in real estate to a maximum of 5 percent of the fund's assets. The inclusion of all emerging markets in benchmark index.
2009	Evaluation of ethical guidelines. The share of stocks in the portfolio of the fund has reached the limit of 60 percent in June. The fund reached a record rate of return, 25.6 percent.
2010	Rules for investing in real estate adopted.
2011	The first investments in real estate (located in London and Paris).
2012	A new benchmark for investments in debt instruments. New rules of geographic diversification of investments in equity.

SOURCE: Author's study based on Norwegian Ministry of Finance (2012, pp. 13–39).

the geographical spread of the fund investments by reducing the share of European investment in the fund and increasing its commitment to emerging markets. The category of emerging markets includes 23 countries, among others: Argentina, Chile, Brazil, Mexico, Poland, the Czech Republic, Russia, and Hungary (NBIM 2012a). The new rules of geographical diversification were introduced progressively since 2012, and this process is expected to take about six years.

In addition to the investment guidelines of the Ministry of Finance, the fund management is obliged to comply with the rules developed by the Council of Ethics. The council, operating since 2004, is preparing recommendations for the Ministry of Finance on exclusion from GPFG portfolio of companies operating in the production of weapons, destroying the environment, disrespecting ethical standards, and violating human rights. By the end of 2011, based on council recommendations, a total of 55 companies were excluded, among others: British American Tobacco Plc., Philip Morris International Inc., and Japan Tobacco Inc. (the tobacco industry); Wal-Mart Stores, Inc. (human rights violations); Alliant Techsystems Inc., General Dynamics Corp., and Hanwha Corp. (cluster weapons); and Singapore Technologies Engineering Ltd. (landmines) (Council on Ethics 2012).

THE INVESTMENT PORTFOLIO OF THE GOVERNMENT PENSION FUND GLOBAL IN 2011

In 2011, GPFG assets increased by approximately NOK 234 billion, and at the end of this period, their value amounted to NOK 3.312 trillion. As a result of persisting high oil prices on the world markets, the government receipts transferred to the fund were the highest since 2008 and amounted to NOK 271 billion (SSB 2012b). Table 6.2 presents the basic information on the investment portfolio and the financial performance of GPFG between 2006 and 2011 (since the transformation of the Oil Fund into the Pension Fund).

In 2011, the value of the fund's assets was almost two times higher than in 2006. This value is dependent on transfers from the state budget, rates of return on investments, and changes due to fluctuations in the Norwegian krone (all GPFG investments are made outside Nor-

Table 6.2 Government Pension Fund Global Market Value, Annual Results, and Cash Flows from the State Budget, 2006–2011 (NOK billion)

	2011	2010	2009	2008	2007	2006
Equity instruments	1,945	1,891	1,644	1,129	958	726
Fixed-income instruments	1,356	1,186	996	1,146	1,061	1,058
Real estate investments	11	0	0	0	0	0
Transfer of funds from the budget	271	182	169	384	314	288
Generated profit/loss	−86	264	613	−633	504	124
Change due to fluctuations in krone	49	−8	−418	506	−154	−28
Total net change	234	437	365	257	235	384
Total GPFG value	3,312	3,077	2,640	2,275	2,019	1,784

SOURCE: Author's study based on NBIM, *Government Pension Fund Global Annual Report 2006, 2007, 2008, 2009, 2010, 2011.*

way). In the analysed period, the worst result from investing activities was achieved in 2008—the rate of return was −23.3 percent (in international currency) and it was the weakest result since the establishment of the fund.[1] The loss of NOK 633 billion, however, was compensated by record transfers from the state budget (NOK 384 billion) and the weakening of the Norwegian krone against the currencies in which the fund invests (NBIM 2009). At the end of 2011 the loss amounted to NOK 86 billion. With funds from the state budget and the depreciation of NOK the assets increased eventually by NOK 234 billion, but this was the lowest figure since 2005.[2] A negative rate of return in 2011 (−2.5 percent in international currency) was the consequence of negative results from investments in equity; the declines in stock markets in Asia, the United States and Europe generated the loss of −8.8 percent. The rising prices of debt instruments, however, resulted in a 7 percent return on investment in this type of GPFG securities. Comparing these figures with their reference indexes (the FTSE Global for shares, the index prepared by Barclays Capital for bonds) shows that the rate of return on investment in shares is 0.48 percentage points lower than its benchmark, while in the case of bonds, the result is 0.52 percentage points higher (NBIM 2012a).

Based on these figures, the changes to the investment policy of GPFG can be observed in the structure of the investment portfolio, i.e., a gradual increase in the share of stocks. As a result, starting from 2009, the shares occupy a dominant position in the structure of the investment. At the end of 2011, GPFG held shares of a market value of about NOK 1.945 trillion (an increase of NOK 54 billion compared to 2010), which accounted for 58.7 percent of total assets, slightly below the permissible limit of 60 percent of the investment in such instruments (see Figure 6.2). At the same time, 41 percent of the GPFG assets were invested in the fixed income securities, significantly exceeding the 35 percent limit adopted for the strategic investment portfolio. The market value of debt instruments has increased over 2011 by NOK 170 billion to the level of NOK 1.356 billion (NBIM 2012a).

In 2011, the GPFG investment portfolio included the first real estate investment. In April 2011, the management of the fund finalized

Figure 6.2 Strategic and Actual Structure of the Government Pension Fund Global Investment Portfolio, 2011 (%)

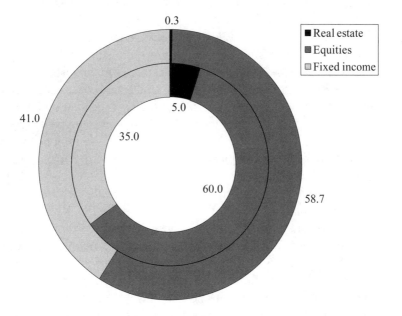

SOURCE: Author's study based on NBIM (2012a, p, 14).

the purchase of a 25 percent stake in the Crown Estate's Regent Street in London, with a value of NOK 4.2 billion (approximately GBP 452 million). Three months later, the fund acquired a 50 percent interest in 7 properties located in Paris and the surrounding area with a total value of NOK 5.5 billion (EUR 702.5 million). By the end of the year, the involvement in real estate had increased by another 2 buildings located in London at the Regent Street and three in Paris. In total, GPFG held shares in 13 buildings (114 premises), primarily office and retail space. The total market value of these investments at the end of 2011 was approximately NOK 11 billion, which accounted for only 0.3 percent of the value of the investment portfolio with an acceptable level of 5 percent. Due to the transaction costs, the return on investment in real estate in 2011 was negative and amounted to −0.79 percent (−4.37 percent in international currencies) (NBIM 2012a).

The Ministry of Finance plans to gradually increase the fund's involvement in the real estate market to reach the 5 percent threshold in 2020. Given the projections on the value of the fund's assets (Norwegian Ministry of Finance 2011), about NOK 250–300 billion of GPFG assets is expected to be invested in the European real estate market in the target year.

At the end of 2011, GPFG held stocks, bonds, and real estate shares registered in 68 countries (Norwegian Ministry of Finance 2011). Table 6.3 shows the capital structure of the GPFG investment portfolio in terms of geographic diversification in 2011. About 50 percent of its shares were listed on the European markets, 35 percent on the markets in the Americas, Africa, and the Middle East, and 15 percent in Asia and Oceania. The rates of return on investments in these regions (measured in international currency) were, respectively, −12.1 percent, −2.4 percent, and 15.5 percent.

Analysing the fund's commitment to national stock markets of individual countries (Table 6.3), the largest share (30.3 percent) of the GPFG investment portfolio was placed in the securities listed on the markets in the United States (2,041 investments with a total value of more than NOK 588.4 billion), followed by the British market (16.3 percent of the GPFG portfolio, 397 investments worth NOK 317.7 billion), France (6.9 percent), Switzerland (6.3 percent), Germany (5.8 percent), and Japan (5.6 percent). The investments in securities of Japanese companies accounted for 40 percent of the total value of shares purchased in the Asia-Pacific (NBIM 2012c). As a result of the earthquake and tsunami that hit Japan in March 2011, their value has decreased by 18.7 percent. More negative returns were received on investments made in the four countries considered to be the largest emerging markets, i.e., India (−34.4 percent), China (−21.8 percent), Russia (−19.5 percent), and Brazil (−10,1 percent) (NBIM 2012a).

At the end of 2011, the fund held securities issued by 8,005 companies, while in the previous year this number was equal to 8,496. According to the investment policy of the Ministry of Finance, the fund is not allowed to exceed 10 percent of the shareholding of one company. In the analysed period, the highest share was recorded in the Irish company Smurfit Kappa Group, in which the fund held 9.6 percent of shares worth NOK 773 million. In total, the participation of the fund exceeded 5 percent in 53 companies (17 companies in 2010). The 10 largest investments in equity securities included companies from Switzerland, the UK and the United States (see Table 6.4) with an oil sector company, Royal Dutch Shell Plc, on the top of the ranking, as GPFG acquired 2.2 percent of its shares worth nearly NOK 31 billion (NBIM 2012a).

The fund's investments in fixed income securities include bonds, inflation-indexed bonds, corporate bonds, securitized debt instruments and bonds issued by public entities such as regional authorities or state-owned enterprises. The GPFG debt investment portfolio in 2011 was dominated by government bonds (46 percent), followed by securitized debt instruments (18 percent) and corporate bonds (14 percent). The fund had a total of 5,215 series of debt securities issued by 1,404 entities, while in the previous year it was a series of 8,659 issued by 1,686 entities. Ninety-four percent of these investments were denominated in Euros, U.S. dollars, British pounds, and Japanese yen (NBIM 2012a).

CONCLUSION

GPFG is one of the largest investors in the global capital market. A characteristic feature of its investment activity is a long-term approach to investment. The main idea of the fund's management is growing the GPFG assets for future generations. Such an investment objective en-

Table 6.3 GPFG Investments in Equity in the Global Capital Market, 2011

Region/country	Investment value (NOK million)	Number	Region/country	Investment value (NOK million)	Number
Europe	966,343	1,567	Africa	9,564	89
Austria	6,119	28	Egypt	750	31
Belgium	16,505	44	Morocco	33	1
Cyprus	111.6	3	South Africa	8,781	57
Czech Republic	903	4	Asia	244,624	3,481
Denmark	18,300	36	China	27,235	1,016
Faeroe Islands	8.9	1	Hong Kong	26,030	327
Finland	15,688	44	India	10,365	120
France	136,215	162	Indonesia	4,427	15
Georgia	56,646	1	Japan	109,633	1,267
Germany	112,797	140	Kazakhstan	174	3
Greece	2,066	29	Malaysia	5,993	79
Guernsey	280	5	Philippines	1,619	26
Hungary	1,407	6	Singapore	7,243	102
Ireland	4,509	25	South Korea	28,856	92
Italy	34,941	118	Taiwan	19,554	401
Jersey	34.9	1	Thailand	3,495	33
Lithuania	1.6	1	Latin America	41,881	174
Luxembourg	431	3	Brazil	33,308	98
The Netherlands	37,745	56	Cayman Islands	10.5	1
Poland	5,844	48	Chile	3,141	33

Portugal	6,681	23	Colombia	367.7	8
Russia	25,246	69	Mexico	4,754	30
Spain	45,077	75	Panama	10	1
Sweden	48,714	85	Peru	290.1	3
Switzerland	121,811	103	Middle East	4,005	73
Turkey	6,936	57	Bahrain	454	1
Ukraine	152.8	3	Israel	3,342	65
Great Britain	317,758	397	United Arab Emirates	209.1	7
North America	641,671	2,333	Oceania	32,646	288
Bermuda Islands	56	2	Australia	31,830	269
Canada	53,151	290	New Zealand	815.4	19
USA	588,464	2041			

SOURCE: Author's own study based on NBIM (2012c, pp. 1–46).

Table 6.4   The Largest GPFG Investments in Equity Securities, 20011

Issuing entity	Country	Value of shares held (NOK billion)
Royal Dutch Shell Plc	Great Britain	30.983
Nestlé SA	Switzerland	25.346
HSBC Holdings Plc	Great Britain	19.583
Novartis AG	Switzerland	19.281
Vodafone Group Plc	Great Britain	18.858
BP Plc	Great Britain	17.277
Exxon Mobil Corp	United States	16.901
Roche Holding AG	Switzerland	16.279
Apple Inc	United States	16.027
GlaxoSmithKline Plc	Great Britain	15.775

SOURCE: Author's own study based on NBIM (2012a, p. 43).

ables the fund management to focus on prospective investments with above-average returns in the future instead of achieving short-term results. The current financial crisis and the collapse of the capital markets resulted in impairment of investments for many investors. At the same time, GPFG consistently implemented its investment objective by acquiring low-priced shares with a potential for growth in a long-term perspective. For instance, in the second half of 2011, GPFG allocated NOK 150 billion to the purchase of shares in the European market.

Establishing the Government Petroleum Fund and then converting it into a Pension Fund is a testimony to the rational management of Norwegian wealth. Although GPFG has no clearly defined obligations to the social security program, it is stressed in any document governing the operation that it was founded for the benefit of future generations. It is undoubtedly a financial, as well as social, success.

Notes

1. The GPFG investments in international securities are not converted into kroner in connection with financial reporting and are not hedged against moves in the krone. Changes in the krone exchange rate do not affect the fund's international purchasing power. Consequently, the return is generally measured in international currency, a weighted combination of the currencies in the fund's benchmark indices for equities and bonds. This is known as the fund's currency basket and consisted of 35 currencies at the end of the first quarter of 2012 (NBIM 2012b).
2. In 2011, the Norwegian krone weakened by 1.9 percent against the British pound, 2.7 percent against the U.S. dollar, 8.2 percent against the Japanese yen, and strengthened by 0.7 percent against the euro. The fund held 83 percent of the investments in these currencies.

References

Ambasada Norwegii w Polsce. 2010. *System ubezpieczeń społecznych* [Social Insurance System]. Warszawa: Ambasada Norwegii w Polsce. http://www .amb-norwegia.pl/About_Norway/policy/Opieka-socjalna/insurance   (accessed June 12, 2012).

———. 2012. *Inwestowanie zysków z ropy naftowej na rzecz przyszłych pokoleń* [Investing oil profits for the benefit of future generations]. Warszawa: Ambasada Norwegii w Polsce. http://www.amb-norwegia.pl/About_ Norway (accessed June 12, 2012).

Council on Ethics for the Government Pension Fund Global. 2012. *Annual Report 2011*. Oslo. http://www.regjeringen.no/pages/1957930/Annual_ Report_2011.pdf (accessed June 12, 2012).

Jarrett, P. 2011. "Reformy emerytalne w Polsce i na świecie widziane z Paryża." Zeszyty BRE Bank-CASE, nr 113-/2011, Centrum Analiza Społeczno-Ekonomicznych, Warszawa.

Lovdata. 1966. *Lov av 17. juni 1966 nr. 12 om folketrygd (folketrygdloven)*. Oslo. http://www.lovdata.no (accessed June 10, 2012).

———. 1990. *Lov av 22. juni 1990 nr. 36 om Statens petroleumsfond opphe-ves*. Oslo: Lovdata. http://www.lovdata.no (accessed June 10, 2012).

———. 1998. *Lov av 26. juni 1998 om kontantstøtte til småbarnsforeldre (kontantstøtteloven)*. Oslo: Lovdata. http://www.lovdata.no (accessed June 10, 2012).

———. 2002. *Lov av 8. mars 2002 nr. 4 om barnetrygd (barnetrygdloven)*. Oslo: Lovdata. http://www.lovdata.no (accessed June 10, 2012).

————. 2007. *Lov av 29. juni 2007 nr. 44 om Folketrygdfondet*. Oslo: Lovdata. http://www.lovdata.no (accessed June 10, 2012).

Norges Bank Investment Management (NBIM). 2009. *Government Pension Fund Global Annual Report 2008*. Oslo: NBIM. http://www.nbim.no/ Global/Reports/2008 (accessed June 12, 2012).

————. 2012a. *Government Pension Fund Global Annual Report 2011*. Oslo: NBIM. http://www.nbim.no/en/press-and-publications/Reports/810/1062 (accessed June 12, 2012).

————. 2012b. *Government Pension Fund Global first quarter 2012*. Oslo: NBIM. http://www.nbim.no/Global/Reports/2012/Q1/1Q_2012%20report .pdf (accessed June 12, 2012).

————. 2012c. *Government Pension Fund Global, Holdings of bonds at 31 December 2011*. Oslo: NBIM. http://www.nbim.no/en/Investments/holdings-/ (accessed June 12, 2012).

Norwegian Labour and Welfare Organisation (NAV). 2007–2009. Guides issued by the Norwegian Labour and Social Affairs Department received in NAV local office in Stavanger. Oslo: NAV.

————. 2010. *Særtillegg*. Oslo: NAV. http://www.nav.no/Pensjon/Pensjon (accessed June 12, 2012).

————. 2011a. *Alderspensjon*. Oslo: NAV. http://www.nav.no/Pensjon/ Alderspensjon (accessed June 12, 2012).

————. 2011b. *Alderspensjonister. Kjønn og alder. 31. mars 2002-2011. Antall og prosent (2011)*. Oslo: NAV. http://www.nav.no/Om+NAV/ Tall+og+analyse/Pensjon/Alderspensjon (accessed June 12, 2012).

————. 2011c. *Grunnbeløpet (G) i folketrygden*. Oslo: NAV. http://www.nav .no/Om+NAV/Satser+og+datoer/Grunnbeløpet (accessed June 12, 2012).

————. 2011d. *Over 30,000 nye alderspensjonister*. Oslo: NAV. http://www .nav.no/Om+NAV/Tall+og+analyse/Pensjon/Alderspensjon/Alderspensjon (accessed June 14, 2012).

————. 2011e. *Seks av ti nye alderspensjonister under 67 år jobber*. Oslo: NAV. http://www.nav.no/Pensjon/Seks+av+ti+nye+alderspensjonister+und er+67+%C3%A5r+jobber.280227.cms (accessed June 14, 2012).

————. 2012. *Ny alderspensjon fra folketrygden, 2. opplag januar 2011*. Documents issued by the Norwegian Labour and Social Affairs Department received in NAV local office in Stavanger. Oslo: NAV.

Norwegian Ministry of Finance. 2010. *Management Mandate for the Government Pension Fund Global Laid down by the Ministry of Finance 8 November 2010 pursuant to Act no. 123 of 21 December 2005 on the Government Pension Fund*. Oslo: Norwegian Ministry of Finance.

————. 2011. *The Revised National Budget 2012*. Oslo: Norwegian Ministry of Finance. http://www.statsbudsjettet.no/Revidert-budsjett-2012 (accessed June 12, 2012).

———. 2012. *The Management of the Government Pension Fund in 2011, Meld. St. 17 (2011-2012) Report to the Storting.* Oslo: Norwegian Ministry of Finance. http://www.regjeringen.no/pages/37868600/PDFS/ STM201120120017000EN_PDFS.pdf (accessed June 12, 2012).

Organisation for Economic Co-operation and Development (OECD). 2011. *Pensions at a Glance 2011: Retirement-Income Systems in OECD and G20 Countries, Part II, Assets in Pension Funds and Public Pension Reserve Funds in OECD Countries, 2009.* Paris: OECD. http://www.oecd-ilibrary .org/statistics (accessed June 12, 2012).

Statistisk sentralbyrå (SSB). 2012a. *Folkemengden 1. Januar. Registrert 2011. Framskrevet 2012–2100.* Oslo: SSB. http://www.ssb.no/emner/02/03/ folkfram (accessed June 12, 2012).

———. 2012b. *Statens pensjonsfond Norge, balanse, 2. halvår 2011.* Oslo: SSB. http://www.ssb.no/emner/12/01/10/folketrygdfond (accessed June 12, 2012).

———. 2012c. *Statens pensjonsfond Norge. Obligasjoner, aksjer, andeler og grunnfondsbevis, etter debitorsektor.* Oslo: SSB. http://www.ssb.no/emner (accessed June 12, 2012).

Towers Watson. 2011. *Top 300 Pension Funds, Analysis as at 2010 Year End.* Brussels: Towers Watson. http://www.towerswatson.com (accessed June 12, 2012).

7
Pension Reforms in Central and Eastern European Countries, 1998–2012

Maciej Żukowski
Poznań University of Economics

Since the end of the 1990s, a number of countries in Central and Eastern Europe carried out structural pension reforms, including the introduction of a privately managed pension system, the so-called second-pillar pension system. The reforms were clearly influenced by the book *Averting the Old Age Crisis*, published in 1994 by the World Bank. The Central and Eastern European (CEE) countries that implemented this type of pension system include Hungary (1998), Poland (1999), Latvia (2001), Bulgaria (2002), Croatia (2002), Estonia (2002), the Former Yugoslav Republic (FYR) of Macedonia (2003), Slovakia (2005), and Romania (2008).

This chapter covers a wide topic: social security pension reform in Central and Eastern Europe. The chapter surveys the main tendencies and discusses the reforms in the region in general terms, with a more detailed discussion about Poland, which was one of the forerunners of both the structural reforms in the late 1990s and the reforms at the time of crisis. The chapter concentrates on structures and types of mandatory general pension systems without going into details of the systems' design.

The chapter starts with a brief description of the heritage of communism in pension systems and the early transition. The next section deals with the structural pension reforms in the late 1990s and early 2000s. The following section presents basic differences between countries, concerning solutions within pension systems and their situation. The next section is devoted to the impact of crisis on pension systems and the resulting "second wave of reforms." Conclusions follow.

HERITAGE OF COMMUNISM AND EARLY TRANSITION

When the CEE countries started their transition from communism to democracy and from a centrally planned economy to a market economy, the heritage of communism was largely negative. However, in the pension area, contrary to many others, the countries inherited existing and functioning institutions.

The pension systems in the CEE countries had many similar characteristics in the early 1990s (Barr and Rutkowski 2005; Hirose 2011):

- Social security pension systems, financed on a PAYG basis, were the only source of income in old age, as occupational or individual pension plans did not exist.

- The systems were fragmented, with privileges for some groups, such as lower retirement age or more generous benefit formulas.

- Access to pensions was easy: the normal retirement age was low, there were many early retirement possibilities, and disability pensions were granted relatively easily.

- Even if pensions were financed by contributions (the "Bismarck" approach), the entire contribution was paid by the employer and pensions were only partly related to contributions, due to many redistributive aspects in the benefit formulas.

- There were no records of contributions at an individual level and no clear lines of demarcation between the state budget and the budgets of the social security systems.

At the same time, there were also differences between CEE countries concerning solutions in the pension system or generosity of pensions. CEE countries entered the transition to the market economy with inherited pension systems that had been adjusted to the circumstances of a centrally planned economy. In the early transition, some changes were introduced that made the pension systems compatible with a market economy (Barr and Rutkowski 2005), including

- indexing pensions to cope with high inflation;

- improving incentives, such as through increasing the number of years used to calculate a pension; and

- strengthening administration.

Poland, like most other CEE countries, has a long tradition of social insurance that was still present under communism, although with some important elements of a state redistribution system. The Polish pension system was in a sense between the traditions of "Bismarck" and "Beveridge" (Żukowski 1994).

The transformation process influenced the Polish pension system: the number of contributors fell and the number of pensioners rose, partly as a result of special early retirement plans connected with unemployment. This, together with an increase in pension levels, led to a financial crisis. These were costs of a successful policy protecting incomes of retirees in the difficult time of an economic and social transformation.

Several reform plans met with political resistance, and changes introduced affected only some parameters of the system, without a structural reform (Żukowski 1996). Unlike many other areas of the economy, the pension system was reformed only in the "second wave" of the reforms.

There are several reasons why the pension reform was made only 10 years after the beginning of transformation. First, Poland had inherited from the communist era an old-age security system that was able to function under the changed circumstances, unlike many other areas that had to be built from the beginning, such as taxes, banks, capital market or—in the social policy area—labor market policy. Second, for exactly the above reasons, at the beginning of the transformation some important preconditions for functioning of pension funds, which were an element of almost every reform concept, were absent (capital market, banks, insurance). Third, a political consensus necessary for such a deep reform was absent in Poland for a longer period. Still, however, with time, the understanding of the problem, especially of the systematic burden of the system, has been growing.

STRUCTURAL PENSION REFORMS

Many CEE countries introduced structural social security pension reforms in a second wave of reforms. These reforms created "multitier pension systems" (Żukowski 1997), with a mandatory second tier (or pillar) of privately managed pension funds. As these new second pillars replaced a part of the previous social security PAYG systems, the structural reforms were also described as (partial) privatization of old-age security. These pension reforms in CEE countries were influenced by the World Bank report (1994) and followed the examples of some countries in Latin America (Müller 2003).

The first two CEE countries to introduce such a reform were Hungary (1998) and Poland (1999). Several other countries followed: Latvia (2001), Bulgaria (2002), Croatia (2002), Estonia (2002), the FYR of Macedonia (2003), Slovakia (2005), and Romania (2008).

As a result of these structural pension reforms, the new EU member states are a majority of countries within the EU with a mandatory second tier (Table 7.1). The exceptions were the Czech Republic, Slovenia, and Lithuania, which preserved their "Bismarckian" PAYG systems with no mandatory pension funds.

Apart from the common feature of replacing a portion of the PAYG plan with a fully funded plan, the exact reform patterns in these countries differed in many respects. In the PAYG social security systems (now called the first-pillar pension systems), some countries (such as Poland and Latvia) introduced notional defined contribution accounts, while the others kept the defined benefit formula, but often reformed through, for example, the extension of the qualifying period in terms of years of work needed to receive a benefit. Also, the second-pillar pension systems differed in terms of contribution rate, administration, and coverage.

There are various explanations of the structural pension reforms in CEE countries. The role of international organizations, especially the World Bank, was stressed, especially in relation to the high foreign debt of the countries involved (Müller 1999, 2003). It was shown that the reforms were fostered by a transnational advocacy campaign (Orenstein 2008).

Economic objectives, such as accumulation of capital and economic growth, played a crucial role. The pension reforms were treated as a vehicle of modernization to accelerate the development of market economies. The reforms were introduced in specific circumstances of transition: "extraordinary" conditions of a transformation of almost all economic, social, and political institutions. In this situation, the political will to enact deep reforms was stronger than the political resistance to change.

Table 7.1 Types of Old-Age Security Systems in the EU-27

General state pension system (first tier)		Supplementary pension plans (second and third tiers)		
Pensions	Based on:	Voluntary		Obligatory
Earnings-related	Insurance/earnings (defined benefit)	Austria Luxembourg Greece Spain Lithuania Czech Rep. Finland	Germany Belgium Portugal Slovenia Cyprus Malta	France (o) Hungary (i) Estonia (i) Slovakia (i) Bulgaria (i) Romania (i)
	Insurance/contributions (notional defined contribution)	Italy		Latvia (i) Poland (i) Sweden (i)
Flat-rate	Insurance (paying contributions)	Ireland		UK (s, o, or i)
	Residence			Denmark (o) Netherlands (o)

NOTE: s = state; o = occupational; i = individual.

In Poland, after several years of discussions on pension reform, the reform concept "Security through Diversity" (Office of the Government Plenipotentiary for Social Security Reform 1997) was to a large extent implemented. The new system took effect on January 1, 1999. Three factors enabled such a structural change in the old-age security system: 1) the critique of the old system, 2) the reform concept, and 3) an appropriate organization of the work on the reform, including political consensus.

The main objectives of the reform were both microeconomic and macroeconomic. The first microeconomic concern was to create a tighter link between contributions and pensions, thus strengthening the incentive to work and the disincentive to evade making contributions. The other microeconomic objective was to lower—in the longer term—social insurance contributions paid by the employer in order to reduce labor costs and to increase employment. The key macroeconomic aim was to lower the level of public expenditures on pensions, as a proportion of gross domestic product, to relieve public finance for other aims toward growth. The other aim was to induce people to save more voluntarily.

The new old-age pension system covered younger insured workers (under age 30) in full. Those aged 30–50 were given the option until the end of 1999 to participate (and split pension contributions accordingly) in both new pillars (PAYG and funded) or to stay in the new PAYG one with the entire contribution. The insured who were older than age 50 were not covered by the reform—they will retire according to the old rules.

The pension reform in Poland replaced a one-pillar system with a multipillar one. The new system consists of two obligatory parts: the first is pay as you go, which is administered by Social Insurance Institution (ZUS), and the second one is fully funded and privately managed. Between 1999 and 2011, these plans had contribution rates of 12.22 percent and 7.30 percent, respectively. Additional sources of income security, among them occupational pension plans, constitute the third, voluntary pillar.

Pensions from the first pillar will be based on the principle of notional defined contributions, whereas the old pensions have been defined benefit pensions. The new pension formula includes only two components: the sum of indexed contributions paid, divided by average life expectancy at retirement age in the calendar year of retirement. For persons born after December 31, 1948, who had been insured in social insurance before January 1, 1999, a "starting capital" according to the old pension rules will be assessed and recorded on the individual account in ZUS.

The same defined contribution formula (with real capital) will also be used in the second pillar. The newly created open-ended pension funds are administered by private pension fund societies, organized as joint stock companies. The insured may choose a fund and change the choice. The funds are supervised by a state agency, and there are strict regulations concerning functioning of the funds. A multistep procedure is foreseen in case of fund insolvency until another pension fund society overtakes a fund management. Every fund has to achieve a minimum rate of return, relative to the results of all funds.

IMPACT OF FINANCIAL CRISIS ON PENSION SYSTEMS—
SECOND WAVE OF REFORMS

When the global financial crisis disrupted financial markets in 2008, the rate of return on investments from pension funds dropped dramatically. Moreover, the difficult state of public finances started to make further financing of the reform's transitional period increasingly difficult. This led to a discussion on "reforming the reform" in many countries. Extreme measures were taken in Hungary where the second pillar was renationalized in 2010. Poland, which pioneered the structural reforms with Hungary in the late 1990s, reacted also, but differently, reducing the contribution rate to the second pillar (Fultz 2012). A similar strategy to scale back the privatized pension systems, rather than to eliminate them, was developed in Slovakia, Romania, Bulgaria, Estonia, and Latvia (Hirose 2011; Orenstein 2011).

The crisis has also facilitated some pension system reforms to address both the current financial problems and future challenges, especially related to demographic developments. For example, later retirement has been legislated in several countries, including Poland (Hirose 2011).

In Poland, the pension system remained relatively stable in the 2000s. The reform debates concerned the "completing" of the reform started in 1999, and some issues have remained open until now (Golinowska and Żukowski 2011). In 2008, the issue of early retirement finally was solved, giving some restricted categories of workers who have worked under special (difficult) conditions bridging pensions starting in 2009.

The financial markets crisis revealed the weaknesses of the pension reform, which started in 1999. It was the reform itself that led to worsening of the financial situation of the Social Insurance Fund, and especially of its part related to old-age pensions. The reform created a large funded tier out of a part of a previously entirely PAYG system, which created a big deficit for the expenditure on current pensions. The financial markets crisis, which started in 2008, led to a further deterioration of old-age insurance finances: increasing subsidies to the social security system contributed to a growing deficit of the government budget. This provoked debates on introducing changes to the pension system, including the withdrawal of crucial structural elements of the new system.

A debate started in 2010 on a reduction of the contribution rate to the funded second pillar, with the money going to the notional defined contribution part, in order to lower the budget subsidies to the social security pension system and thus to lower the public debt. The discussions continued in 2011 with clear polarization of positions. Most economists criticized the proposal, claiming it was rescuing the present public finances at the cost of future generations (or at least governments) and dismantling the pension system and pension reform that had started in 1999. The government was successful in passing the law in Parliament. Beginning May 1, 2011, the contribution rate to the second pillar was reduced from 7.3 percent to 2.3 percent.

Another structural change that had not been tackled for political reasons was increasing the retirement age. Again, the financial markets crisis facilitated the reform. After the Parliamentary elections in October 2011, the new government, backed by the same Parliamentary coalition and led by the same prime minister, announced plans to increase the statutory retirement age. Starting in 2013, the statutory retirement age was raised by three months every year, reaching age 67 for both genders, in 2020 for men and in 2040 for women. After a short but intensive debate, the change was legislated in May 2012 and implemented in January 2013.

CONCLUSION

Most CEE countries introduced structural pension reforms as part of the transformation of their socioeconomic systems following the end of communism in Central and Eastern Europe. Modernization may thus be seen as the main objective in the first wave of pension reforms.

The second wave of pension reforms was closely related to the financial crisis that revealed problems of the pension systems and facilitated changes. However, contrary to some comments, no "death of pension privatization" occurred (Orenstein 2011). The second wave of pension reforms in CEE countries may be seen as an adjustment of pension systems to the circumstances.

There have been differences between the countries in terms of solutions and pension systems. In the first wave, most CEE countries opted for the introduction of the second pillar of privately managed pension funds. However, both the solutions in the main public PAYG systems differed, and the patterns of the second pillars were different. In the second wave, the countries again reacted differently.

References

Barr, Nicholas, and Michał Rutkowski. 2005. "Pensions." In *Labor Markets and Social Policy in Central and Eastern Europe. The Accession and Beyond*, Nicholas Barr, ed. Washington, DC: World Bank, pp. 135–170.

Fultz, Elaine. 2012. "The Retrenchment of Second-Tier Pensions in Hungary and Poland: A Precautionary Tale." *International Social Security Review* 65(3): 1–25.

Golinowska, Stanisława, and Maciej Żukowski. 2011. "The Impact of the Economic and Financial Crisis on the Polish Pension System." *Journal of Social Policy Research* 57(3): 267–285.

Hirose, Kenichi. 2011. "Trends and Key Issues of the Pension Reform in Central and Eastern Europe—A Comparative Overview." In *Pension Reform in Central and Eastern Europe in times of Crisis, Austerity and Beyond*, Kenichi Hirose, ed. Budapest: International Labour Organization, Decent Work Technical Support Team for Central and Eastern Europe, pp. 3–71.

Müller, Katharina. 1999. *The Political Economy of Pension Reform in Central-Eastern Europe*. Cheltenham, UK, and Northhampton, MA: Edward Elgar.

———. 2003. *Privatising Old-Age Security. Latin America and Eastern Europe Compared*. Cheltenham, Northampton: Edward Elgar.

Office of the Government Plenipotentiary for Social Security Reform. 1997. *Security through Diversity: Reform of the Pension System in Poland*. Warsaw: Office of the Government Plenipotentiary for Social Security Reform.

Orenstein, Mitchell, A. 2008. *Privatizing Pensions: The Transnational Campaign for Social Security Reform*. Princeton, NJ: Princeton University Press.

———. 2011. "Pension Privatization in Crisis." *International Social Security Review* 64(3): 65–80.

World Bank. 1994. *Averting the Old Age Crisis: Policies to Protect the Old and Promote Growth*. Washington, DC: World Bank.

Żukowski, Maciej. 1994. "Pensions Policy in Poland after 1945: Between 'Bismarck' and 'Beveridge' Traditions." In *Beveridge and Social Security:*

An International Retrospective, John Hills, John Ditch, and Howard Glennerster, eds. Oxford: Oxford University Press, pp. 154–170.

———. 1996. "Das Alterssicherungssystem in Polen–Geschichte, gegenwärtige Lage, Umgestaltung. *Zeitschrift für ausländisches und internationales Arbeits- und Sozialrecht* 10(2): 97–141.

———. 1997. *Wielostopniowe systemy zabezpieczenia emerytalnego w Unii Europejskiej i w Polsce. Między państwem a rynkiem [Multitier old age security systems in the European Union and Poland. Between state and market]* Poznań: Poznań University of Economics.

8

Pension Reform and the Measurement of Risk in Occupational Pension Plans in Poland

Marek Szczepański
Poznań University of Technology

Tomasz Brzęczek
Poznań University of Technology

Poland belongs to a relatively small group of European countries that, in the late 1990s and early 2000s, introduced comprehensive, structural reforms, changing the whole structure of their pension systems. Earlier structural pension reforms had been introduced in Sweden (1998) and Hungary (1998). In Poland, this took place in 1999, and it was followed by Bulgaria (2000), Latvia (2001), Croatia (2002), and Estonia (2002). Recommendations contained in a World Bank report (1994) have had a significant impact on the shape of structural pension reforms. A representative of the World Bank in Poland was even directly involved in introducing the pension reform. The basic element of structural pension reform was the introduction of a capital-financed segment into social security systems (privately managed individual accounts), which in effect meant the partial privatization of the pension system (Żukowski 2006).

Despite the similarities between these structural reforms, there were also significant differences. One of them was the underdevelopment of the third-pillar, employer-provided supplementary pension systems in all the reformed pension systems of the postsocialist countries. In this respect they differ, for example, from the Swedish model. In Sweden, occupational pension plans play an important role in securing the finances of future retirees, covering the majority of employees due to widespread collective bargaining agreements.

In 2011, Poland made a partial reversal from the original reform that involved the diversification of risk between the PAYG and the fully funded segments. Funded second-pillar pension plans are mandatory in Poland, following the original reform, and cover nearly the entire labor force. Since June 2011, the mandatory second-pillar pension funds—the individual account pension funds, managed by private financial institutions—have been funded with contributions of only 2.3 percent of wages. Previously, the fully funded segment had received contributions of 7.3 percent. In 2013, the 2.3 percent was raised to 2.8 percent. The total mandatory pension contributions is 19.55 percent of pension of wages, which was not changed. The difference between 2.3 or 2.8 percent and 7.3 percent is transferred to the Polish Social Security fund (ZUS), which provides social security benefits through a notional defined contribution plan.

While the reform of the public pension system in Poland since 1999 has been the subject of many studies in Poland and abroad (see Góra [2009] and Góra and Palmer [2004]), the operation of supplementary pension systems, and especially the still underdeveloped voluntary employer-provided occupational pension system, has not received such interest, with a few exceptions (see Szczepański [2011]). Only a few researchers have tried to explain why the potential hidden within the occupational pension plans has not been utilized in Poland.

With these plans, benefits cannot be taken before retirement age. Contributions are made on an after-tax basis. The plan must be offered to more than 50 percent of the employees of the company. The employer is required to contribute to the plan, with a maximum employer contribution of 7 percent of the employee's wages. Employees can voluntarily contribute. Voluntary employer-provided pensions cover only a small percentage of the labor force. This chapter attempts to explain why. It focuses on the conceptual and empirical identification of different types of risk involved in employer-provided individual account (defined contribution) pension plans. It examines the state of risk awareness on behalf of the employer-sponsors related to the investment of funds accumulated in occupational pension plans. It compares the investment performance of Employees' Pension Funds investment with the results of other types of investment funds operating on the Polish financial market, and uses risk as an explanation for why most of Polish employers have not adopted pension plans for their employees.

RISK CLASSIFICATION OF OCCUPATIONAL PENSION PLANS

The economic literature defines risk, for which there are many types, as an event with the possibility of different results achieved with a certain probability. Risk is most broadly classified depending on the outcome of an event (Fabozzi and Modigliani 2009, pp. 23–31; Monkiewicz and Gąsiorkiewicz 2010, p. 35): pure risk refers to situations in which a random event occurs and results in loss or no loss, and speculative risk exists when the result of an event is a loss or gain in relation to initially assumed expected outcome.

Operation of occupational pension plans is subject to risk of bankruptcy, break of contract, or an event insured within Employees' Pension-Insurance Fund (such as occupational disease or accident). Such funds operate in many countries (such as the United States and Germany), but not in Poland. More speculative risk factors of occupational pension plans include, for example, the risk of political and legal regulations, investment risk, and financial or business risk.

The classification of risk factors into systematic and specific ones remains important from the point of view of risk management (Fabozzi and Drake 2009, pp. 555–574; Monkiewicz and Gąsiorkiewicz 2010, p. 36). Systematic risk concerns events a company cannot alter because they result from the macro environment. In the case of an occupational pension plan, these factors include

- demographic risk, especially the longevity of employees in a company pension plan;
- political risk due to legal regulations and their frequent changes to which pension institutions have to adapt;
- interest rate risk affects investment performance;
- currency risk, which affects the results of foreign investments and revenues of an enterprise importing or exporting goods;

- risk of market valuation of asset class and the associated economic risks;

- risk of purchasing power due to the uncertain future rate of inflation;

- risk related to market liquidity of assets; and

- risk related to market conditions for reinvestment (market reinvestment risk).

Table 8.1 summarizes the systematic (macroeconomic) and specific (microeconomic) business risks of occupational pension plans according to their operational and financial-investment activity.

Specific risk concerns a single occupational pension plan and is thus called micro risk here. The following factors of this risk have been distinguished:

- Business risk, including market-demand risk of business activity of an enterprise with a pension system and an entity that manages it.

- Management risk, which is conditioned by an improper management of an enterprise and its pension system and capital. This risk can be limited by public supervision of pension institutions.

- Breach of contract risk—the source of its origin is the failure to meet conditions agreed between the parties to the transaction and written in the contract.

- Risk of insurance event regarding participants in the occupational pension plan in the form of life insurance.

- Liquidity of assets risk results from the investment strategy, just as other factors.

- Risk of the investment preferences of participants regards an approved return rate and its term structure tailored to the age of the insured.

- Risk of a financial instrument valuation is a problem with risky investment efficiency in terms of the ratio of expected return and its volatility measured with, for example, standard deviation.

Table 8.1 Risk Classification of Occupational Pension Plans

Business risk	Systematic risk (macroeconomic)	Specific risk (microeconomic)
Operating risk	Demographic (especially longevity)	Business
	Political	Management
		Breach of contract
		Insured event
Risk of financial and investment activities	Interest rate	Liquidity of assets
	Currency	Investment preferences of beneficiaries
	Market conditions on asset class	
	Inflation and purchasing power	Valuation of financial instruments (investment efficiency)
	Market liquidity of assets	
	Conditions for reinvestment	Financial (financial status)
		Bankruptcy
		Reinvestment strategy

SOURCE: Authors' study based on Fabozzi and Drake (2009, pp. 555–574)

- Market reinvestment risk due to assets durability and time horizon of portfolio of given fund.

- Financial risk associated with interest and repayment of borrowed foreign capital and its liabilities, which in the case of occupational pension plans relates to pension disbursement.

- Risk of bankruptcy. It may result in a company's bankruptcy caused by two previously described types of risk, the risk of contract breach and the financial risk.

A SURVEY ASSESSING OCCUPATIONAL PENSION PLAN RISK IN POLAND

The risk of occupational pension plans is a complex concept, which consists of all the previously mentioned factors. Occupational pension plans in Poland have operated since 1999, which is a relatively short time period (the tradition of employer sponsored plans, which is longer than that of social security, reaches the era of industrial revolution). Most of the employers do not have enough experience with investments of pension funds and do not understand all aspects of risk connected with pension savings. Lack of experience and knowledge about risk management of pension plans has a significant impact on whether employers introduce such a plan. Of course, there are also other important reasons why there are very few occupational pension plans in Poland (for example, complicated registration procedures, not enough tax incentives for pension plans' sponsors, and situation on labor market).

The Financial Supervision Commission is obligatorily provided by occupational pension plans with information on such risk factors, such as the rate of return. Others, such as currency risk, depend on the investment strategy of the fund. Yet other factors, such as business risk or the risk of the investment preferences of participants, can be judged best by business enterprises providing occupational pension plans to their employees.

For this reason, an indirect risk assessment has been chosen in the form of a survey of company representatives providing occupational pension plans. In February 2011, 1,099 companies were running occupational pension plans. The survey included 100 companies that were selected using stratified random sampling. There were three strata of pension plans concerning different legal forms (capital fund, capital-insurance fund, employees financial program). The strata fraction in the sample was proportionate to the fraction in the population. The survey was done by telephone, with an answer rate of about 90 percent.

Responses were measured using the following scales:

- Binomial scale—yes/no in order to assess the most important risk factors and recommendations for regulators.

- Ordinal scale to assess the level of risk (rating scale: low, medium, high, and hard to tell).

- Ordinal scale to assess communication, risk reduction tools, and system design (rating scale: definitely yes, probably yes, it's hard to say, probably not, definitely not).

- Nominal scale to assess appropriate strategies for investors with different preferences toward risk (rating scale: the level of risk and income corresponding to the majority of participants, etc.).

The most important risk factors are listed in Table 8.1. Figure 8.1 shows the proportion of respondents that recognized the individual risk factors as the most important. This is a multiple-choice question in which one can indicate any number of factors as the most important: it can be one, several, or all of the risk factors. Only 17 percent of respondents indicated one most important factor, which indicates high importance of several factors. Among other respondents, the most numerous group was the one that indicated two most important factors (31 percent), while 17 percent marked three factors. Four and five factors were selected by 13 percent of respondents; more factors were selected by the remaining 9 percent of respondents.

Investment risk was recognized as the most important factor for most (63 percent of respondents). It is understood as an uncertainty of the rate of return. Sixty-two percent of respondents indicated the macroeconomic risk of the situation on the financial markets and the economy as a whole, while 41 percent of respondents indicated a microeconomic risk of an enterprise's activity.

Fig. 8.1 Respondents' Percentage Indicating Importance of Chosen Factors of Risk

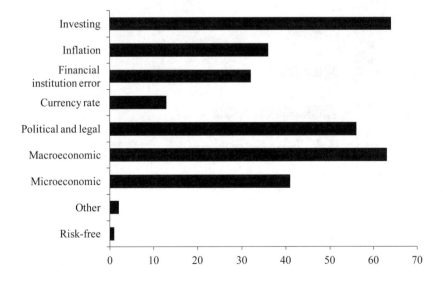

SOURCE: Authors' calculations.

A significant proportion of the companies surveyed (as many as 56 percent) pointed to the importance of legal-political risk. About one-third of all companies considered inflation and financial institutions settling accounts of occupational pension plans as important risk factors. Thus, they referred to external risk management. Only 12 percent of the surveyed companies confirmed that foreign exchange risk poses a threat to pension plans, and only 2 percent indicated other important risk factors and mentioned manipulation and the lack of knowledge.

Because the representatives of companies identified investment risk as the greatest source of risk, another question regarded the assessment of its level in the financial market and in pension plans. Figure 8.2 shows that the risk of financial markets is rated as average for more than half of the respondents and high for the remaining 40 percent. Twenty-four percent of respondents indicated a high level of risk in financial markets, noting that it has been higher after the crisis, while 16 percent of respondents said that although this risk is high, it has not increased as a result of the crisis. However, the perceived level of risk of occu-

Figure 8.2 Assessment of Investment Risk Level of the Occupational Plans and Whole Capital Market (% of Positive Answers)

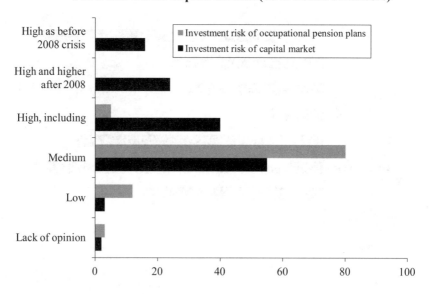

SOURCE: Authors' calculations.

pational pension plans is lower than the risk of the financial market. Eighty percent of respondents believe that it is of an average level, and 12 percent believe that it is actually low.

The risk of the investment preferences of pension participants covers a mismatch between the level of risk aversion of the pension plan and its participants due to a single investment pool. In Poland, participants of occupational pension plans can choose one of the investment funds offered by the financial institution that manages their pension plan (for example, fund investing in securities or treasury bonds). They have the right to move their assets from one fund to another.

With the exception of one form of pension plan (the occupational pension fund, which does not have to be managed by an external financial institution), workers do not have any influence on investment strategy of a given pension fund. Therefore, we asked representatives of employers offering pension plans about how they select plan risk preferences (see Figure 8.3). Most respondents chose strategies accepted by a company's management in consultation with representatives (34 percent) or strategies that were the most popular among participants. Both of those choices are irrational because they lack finance and investment education and experience—some people's preferences even appeared to resemble gambling, which was observed during the stock market boom (Griffin, Harris, and Topaloglu 2003). That means that plans should take into account the risk of mismatch and irrational pref-

Figure 8.3 Risk-Return Preferences in Occupational Pension Plans

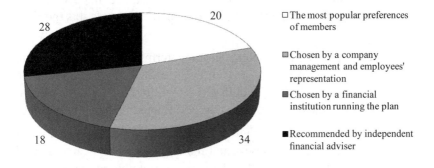

SOURCE: Authors' calculations.

erences. The most rational preference strategy is that recommended by an independent consultant (chosen by 28 percent of enterprises). The least frequently chosen option was the risk-return strategy recommended by the financial institution managing the occupational pension plan (18 percent). Once again, results suggest a lack of confidence by employers in financial institutions as agents of the occupational pension plan (principal-agent conflict). Risk preferences should be matched to the diverse age structure of participants and its dynamics in time.

We now evaluate the management of occupational pension plans regarding the information provided to participants about the risks and protection against them, as well as the principles of the design of occupational pension plans. Figure 8.4 shows consecutive percentage stakes regarding the distribution of responses by the representatives of employers to the following six questions:

1) Do you believe that employees/participants of the program and their employers are aware of all the risks associated with a given pension plan? Most of the companies and their insured employees are informed about the risks, according to the representatives of the employers. Only 20 percent believe that communication from occupational pension plans or their managing institutions remains insufficient.

2) Does the current pension plan structure provide their participants with adequate protection against the risk of investment and other risks associated with the financial market? Most companies indicate very little protection against such risks.

3) Occupational pension plans in Poland are defined contribution plans. All the risks rest on the participants. Is this the right solution?

4) Defined benefit pension plans predetermine pension amounts in proportion to wages. If such occupational pension plans were available in Poland, would you be willing to offer them to your employees, being aware of the additional financial obligations?

5) In mixed (hybrid) programs, part of the investment risk is assumed by the employer, and the employee also bears some of it (i.e., a program with a defined contribution but a guaranteed minimum benefit). If such occupational pension plans were

available in Poland, would you be willing to offer them to your employees, being aware of the additional financial obligations?

6) Do we need to introduce a pension guarantee fund?

Replies for questions 3–6 are shown in Figure 8.4 and indicate that the majority of companies involved in occupational pension plans in Poland consider the plans with a defined contribution as imperfect, but they are not willing to accept plans where the risk is carried onto them. They do call for the introduction of a pension guarantee fund, which would take over the obligations of an occupational pension plan if the company went bankrupt. In another question, respondents indicated that the guarantee fund should be financed jointly by employers and the state (38 percent), employers and employees (36 percent), employers only (13 percent), the Treasury (9 percent), or only by the workers (4 percent).

For questions about changes in regulation of occupational pension plans, the majority of business representatives surveyed did not support any changes, including an increase in the Financial Supervision Commission's control over occupational pension plans, an implementation

Figure 8.4 Respondents' Opinions on Risk Management and Plan Construction (%)

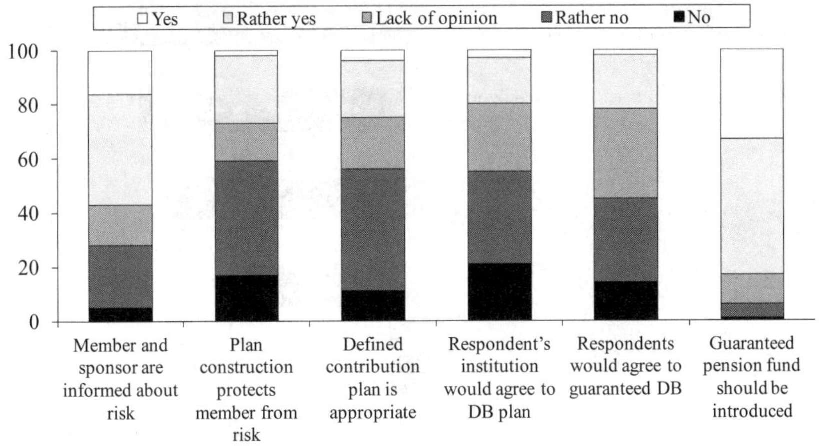

SOURCE: Authors' calculations.

of pension plan design choice, or an increase in the role of employers and employees in the investment strategy (see Figure 8.5). Almost 50 percent of business representatives noted the need for regulation by obliging an agent managing an occupational pension plan to provide information more frequently.

INVESTMENT EFFECTIVENESS OF OCCUPATIONAL PENSION PLANS IN POLAND

Efficiency refers to the results-to-effort ratio. Converted into percentage it becomes the rate of return. In the case of an investment activity, the rate of return itself is not an appropriate indicator of performance because it does not include effort in the form of volatility risk valuation of a financial instrument or its stock market price. Valuation risk of a financial instrument is related to operational and financial risk of an issuer (and, in the case of the stock exchange instruments, of li-

Figure 8.5   Respondents' Recommendations for System and Regulation of Pension Occupational Plans (%)

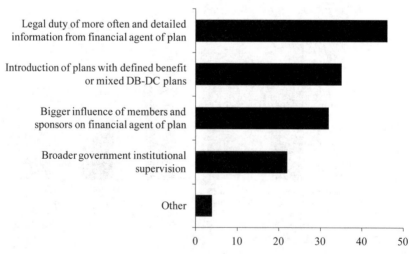

SOURCE: Authors' calculations.

quidity risk and the situation on the capital market). Therefore, the rate of return of a fund is calculated per unit of measure of risk and compared to this ratio value calculated for the Polish financial market. The risk of actively managed portfolios is measured in one way (the classic measure is the standard deviation of the rate of return), and in another for passively managed portfolios, which eliminates the specific risk. There are also a few methods to conduct a comparison with market effectiveness.

A number of performance measures of capital investment have been developed, and we will briefly describe the three most versatile and widely used ones. Each ratio has its own interpretation, as well as pros and cons. These ratios assume the calculation of efficiency under conditions of multiple market valuation of financial instruments or other investment assets, which is usually satisfied in the case of instruments listed on a stock exchange or other regulated markets.[1]

1) The Sharpe ratio is the average rate of return attributable to one percentage point of the variation of the rate of return, measured by standard deviation (see Fabozzi and Modigliani [2009, pp. 162, 191]; Ostrowska [2007, p. 252]). An investment that obtains the highest value of this ratio is considered the most efficient strategy. The construction of this index assumes that the portfolio rate of return exceeds the risk-free rate of return. Otherwise, the index loses its ability to assess the efficiency of the portfolio (see Brzęczek [2004, p. 7]; Węgrzyn [2006 p. 11]).

2) The Treynor ratio determines the rate of return for taking the average market risk (see Fabozzi and Modigliani [2009, pp. 157, 191]; Ostrowska [2007, p. 249]). Portfolio bonus for the risk taken (excess portfolio return over the risk-free rate) is divided by its market risk measure/coefficient β (see Fabozzi and Modigliani [2009, p. 195]). The Treynor ratio calculated for the evaluated portfolio is compared to the surplus market rate of return. As in the previous case, the higher the ratio, the more efficient the portfolio. This ratio takes into account only the market risk of the portfolio, so it is useful for the assessment of well-diversified portfolios. Like the Sharpe ratio, it can be used if the bonus for portfolio risk remains positive.

3) Jensen's Index, or Jensen's alpha, refers to the rate of portfolio return relative to the market risk taken, as well as to the market return rate (see Fabozzi and Modigliani [2009, p. 203]; Ostrowska [2007, p. 249]). The efficiency of investment is evaluated by comparing the index to zero. Positive values indicate that the fund is performing better than the market, and negative values indicate a weaker result than the market average. Generally, the higher the ratio, the better the portfolio's management.

The Sharpe, Treynor, and Jensen ratios cannot be compared because the first two convert surplus return per unit of risk of different type, and the third compares it to the market rate of return.

Table 8.2 lists two groups of institutions. Occupational pension plans in the form of Employees' Pension Funds are separate funds managed by enterprises; financial institutions are only agents for them. The second group, mutual open pension funds, is only financed by enterprises, but is fully managed by investment fund corporations, including insurance management companies. Therefore, the evaluation of the efficiency of investments was made separately in both groups. An average monthly rate of return from employee and mutual pension funds was calculated along with its standard deviation for the years 2009–2011. The risk-free monthly rate of return was calculated on the basis of the interest rates on three-year retail Treasury bonds during the analyzed period per month (6.35 percent / 12 = 0.53 percent). On this basis, the Sharpe, Treynor, and Jensen ratios were determined. The results are presented in Table 8.3.

The monthly rate of return for employee pension plans is 0.55 percent and is only slightly higher than the interest rate of Treasury bonds. The rate of return from the WIG index (the index of broad market of basic shares of the Warsaw Stock Exchange in Poland) was much higher, and the highest rate of return was achieved by investment fund corporations. However, the analyzed period begins after the slump of 2008, which significantly improves the performance of risky assets funds. The second difference is the level of risk for strategies listed in Table 8.3. Total risk measured with standard deviation from the rate of return is far smaller for occupational pension plans than for mutual pension funds and WIG index. Similar proportions are maintained between the

Table 8.2 Authorities Managing the Occupational Pension Plans Grouped by Form of a Plan

Management entity	Number of occupational pension plans managed
Inter-Company Employee Pension Institution PZU SA	1
Employee Pension Institution NESTLE SA POLAND	6
Employee Pension Institution "New World" SA	19
Employee Pension Institution of Polish Telecom	3
Employee Pension Institution UNILEVER POLAND SA	7
Investment Fund Institution BPH	16
BZ WBK AIB SA Investment Fund Corporation	2
Aviva Investors SA Investment Fund Corporations	10
Investors SA Investment Fund Corporation	8
ING SA Investment Fund Corporation	62
KBC SA Investment Fund Corporation	3
Legg Mason SA Investment Fund Corporation	40
Pioneer Pekao SA Investment Fund Corporation	7
PKO SA Investment Fund Corporation	7
TREASURY SA Investment Fund Corporation	3
Allianz Polska SA Investment Fund Corporation	4
PZU SA Investment Fund Corporation	104
Spółdzielcze Kasy Oszczędnościowo-Kredytowe S.A. Investment Fund Corporation	24
Union Investment SA Investment Fund Corporations	1
Aviva SA Life Insurance Company	133
Generali Życie SA Insurance Company	36
Nordea Poland SA Life Insurance Company	3
Pierwsze Amerykańsko-Polskie Towarzystwo Ubezpieczeń na Życie i Reasekuracji Amplico Life S.A.	41
PZU SA Life Insurance Company	472
Sopot Life Insurance Company Ergo Hestia SA	1
Allianz SA Life Insurance Company	99
Warta SA Life Insurance Company	4
Total	1,116

SOURCE: Financial Supervisory Commission reports, accessed November 20, 2012.

Table 8.3 Investment Efficiency of Employee Pension Plans, 2009–2011 (per month)

Measure	Occupational pension funds[a]	Asset management company associated within IZFiA[b]	Capital Market Benchmark WIG index
Average rate of return (%)[c]	0.55	1.35	1.13
Standard deviation of return (%)	2.15	2.95	6.96
Sharpe Ratio	0.01	0.28	0.09
Coefficient ß	0.30	0.37	1.00
Treynor ratio (%)	0.07	2.25	0.60
Jensen index (%)	−0.16	0.01	0.00

[a] The monthly rate of return and performance indicators were calculated on the basis of valuation of shares of all five employee pension funds (source: Financial Supervision Authority and the Warsaw Stock Exchange Bulletins 2012, 2011, 2010).

[b] The calculations for investment funds are based on their net assets and managed capital flows (source: Statistics of IZFiA–Chamber of Fund and Asset Management).

[c] Average rate of return of the analyzed group of entities, in the case of employee pension funds is not a weighted value of the assets of entities (the results would seek one pension fund with by far the largest assets), while in the case of investment funds, the weighted value of assets.

SOURCE: Authors' calculations.

amounts of market risk measured by the beta coefficient. Calculating the rate of return on its percentage point variation (Sharpe ratio), employee pension funds turn out to be less efficient than the Polish capital market represented by the WIG index. Mutual pension funds appear to be much more efficient than the market.

In conclusion, employee pension funds are characterized by low risk but do not offer a higher rate of return than Treasury bonds. This suggests that the continued operation of this form makes sense only in the form of bond funds. An alternative is to transfer these funds to mutual funds, which are much better prepared for global investing.

CONCLUSION

Four general conclusions can be drawn from the replies of employers offering employee pension plans in Poland:

1) Respondents point to investment performance and economic conditions as the most important risk factors for occupational pension plans. They note, however, other important political and business risk factors for the sponsors of employee pension funds.

2) The perceived risk of financial markets is high, while the investment risk of employee pension plans regarding their investments remains on an average level. Replies suggest the existence of the agent-principal problem (the so-called theory of agency costs). Only 20 percent of enterprises with occupational pension plans chose an investment strategy recommended by financial agents of the program. The respondents note a significant risk of error of an agent.

3) The current design of occupational pension plans is not considered optimal by the majority of respondents. In their opinion, the only major change needed is the introduction of a guarantee fund. The vast majority of respondents are in favor of a guarantee fund for the payment of benefits under occupational pension plans, as is the case in Germany (the fund protects against the risk of insolvency of the employer-sponsor of the program). In Germany both defined benefit and defined contribution plan types are found, as well as hybrid types, although even defined contribution plans are legally required to have some sort of guarantee to workers, such as return of contributions. Such a solution could be implemented in Poland, where all occupational pension plans are defined contribution plans. From the other side, the same guarantees, if they were implemented, could be treated as another obligation for employers and stop at least some of them from creating pension plans in their companies. It is always easier to declare some safety measures than finance them. And such a guarantee fund most likely would be financed by employers and not the state. There is also a need to better inform both employers—the sponsors—and employees (participants of pension plans) on the level of risk associated with the investment strategies used by financial institutions managing a program (i.e., selected to support the investment fund companies, life insurance companies, or em-

ployee pension funds). This confirms the previously indicated agent-principal problems.

4) Employee pension funds are characterized by low risk but do not offer a higher rate of return than Treasury bonds. This suggests that the continued operation of this form makes sense only in the form of bond funds. An alternative is to transfer these funds to investment funds, which are more prepared for global investment and as a sector have been more effective than the Polish capital market. This shows that there are benefits to large-scale investments, which are not available for employee pension funds.

These findings may constitute a starting point for discussion on the institutional framework to reduce the risk for employee pension plan participants, but also for the companies that offer such programs to their employees.

Note

1. The selected set of performance indexes was considered sufficient. For specific purposes other indexes are used: information, Sortino, M2, etc. (see Węgrzyn [2006, pp. 53–62]).

References

Brzęczek, T. 2004. "Procedura wyboru portfela akcji zapewniającego kontrolę ryzyka niesystematycznego." [Procedure for the selection of equity portfolio ensuring control over non-systematic risk.] *Badania Operacyjne i Decyzje* [Operations Research and Decisions] no. 3-4.

Fabozzi, Frank J., and Pamela Peterson Drake. 2009. *Finance: Capital Markets, Financial Management, and Investment Management.* Hoboken, NJ: Wiley & Sons.

Fabozzi, Frank J., and Franco Modigliani. 2009. *Capital Markets: Institutions and Instruments.* Saddle River, NJ: Prentice Hall.

Góra, M. 2009. *Integralny charakter systemu emerytalnego w Polsce* [Integral nature of the pension system in Poland], *Jeszcze raz o "Bezpieczeństwie dzieki różnorodności* [Once again about the "Security through Diversity"], Forum Obywatelskiego Rozwoju, "Zeszyty FOR," May.

Góra, M., and E. Palmer. 2004. "Shifting Perspectives in Pensions." IZA Discussion Paper No. 1369. Bonn: IZA.

Griffin, J. M., J. H. Harris, and S. Topaloglu. 2003. "The Dynamics of Institutional and Individual Trading." *Journal of Finance* 58(6): 2285–2320.

Monkiewicz, J., and L. Gąsiorkiewicz, eds. 2010. *Zarządzanie ryzykiem działalności organizacji* [Institution Operation Risk Management]. Warszawa: C. H. Beck.

Ostrowska, E. 2007. *Rynek kapitałowy. Funkcjonowanie i metody oceny* [The capital market. Operation and evaluation methods]. Warszawa: Polskie Wydawnictwo Ekonomiczne.

Szczepański, Marek. 2011. "The Role of Occupational Pension Plans in an Optimal Polish Pension System." In *Imagining the Ideal Pension System: International Perspectives*, D. M. Muir and J. A. Turner, eds. Kalamazoo, MI: W. E. Upjohn Institute for Employment Research, pp. 249–264.

Węgrzyn, T. 2006. *Charakterystyka wybranych wskaźników oceny efektywności zarządzania portfelem w Metody matematyczne, ekonometryczne i informatyczne w finansach i ubezpieczeniach, część 2, Prace Naukowe AE w Katowicach* [Characteristics of selected indexes to assess the effectiveness of equity portfolio management at mathematical, econometric and computing methods in finance and insurance, Part 2, Scientific Papers of the University of Economics in Katowice].

World Bank. 1994. *Averting the Old Age Crisis. Polices to Protect the Old and Promote Growth: A Summary*. New York: Oxford University Press.

Żukowski, M. 2006. *Reformy Emerytalne w Europie* [Pension Reforms in Europe]. Poznań, Poland: Publishing House of Poznań Academy of Economics.

Part 3

Reforms in Australia, Asia, Africa, and the Americas

9

Australian Pensions

An Equitable Solution in a Postcrisis World?

Ross Clare
Association of Superannuation Funds of Australia

PROVIDING SUPPORT FOR RETIREMENT IN AUSTRALIA

Australia has a classic three-pillar retirement system:

1) A mandatory contribution, generally to an individual account defined contribution plan, (made by employers) which is currently 9 percent of wages, increasing to 9.25 percent from July 2013 and then currently legislated to gradually increase to 12 percent by July 2019.

2) Voluntary contributions to pensions, primarily to defined contribution plans, many of which attract tax concessions.

3) A government means-tested pension, called the Age Pension, commencing at age 65 for males and (currently) 64 for females but increasing to age 67 over the next decade. Veterans (pensioners who have been in the armed services) receive identical benefits but receive them five years earlier than civilians. The Age Pension is not earnings related, It is paid at a higher rate to low-income persons due to the operation of a means test but is received by most retirees.

All elements have been subject to changes for fiscal and other reasons.

The voluntary contributions are from a number of sources:

• Employers (usually large companies and governments) that pay a higher rate than the law requires for mandatory pensions.

- Members paying pretax contributions from their salary package. The limit of tax-preferenced contributions has fallen significantly in recent years.

- Members paying after-tax contributions, which are subject to a contribution cap of $A150,000 a year or $A450,000 in a three-year period. (In early 2013, U.S.$1.00 = A $0.96. Currency conversion rates vary over time.)

- The government cocontribution, which matches after-tax contributions up to an amount which is currently A$500.00 a year for low-income earners.

The taxation structure for pensions is relatively complicated, but in broad terms most members of defined contribution funds are taxed concessionally (at a reduced and flat rate) in regard to contributions and investment earnings. Benefits, both lump sum and in income stream form, are tax free when received at age 60 and over. Thus, with T representing taxed, t representing concessionally taxed, and E representing exempt from tax, this system can be characterized as ttE. By comparison, the U.S. tax arrangement for most types of pensions is EET.

Despite the regular changes that governments have made for fiscal or equity reasons, the broad structure is robust and is supported by voters, politicians, and industry.

A critical element of Australia's retirement system, including the government mandated private pensions, is that members generally carry all the investment risks themselves because their pensions generally are defined contribution plans. While around 10 percent of employees are in defined benefit plans, most of these are closed to new members. In the long term, almost all members will have defined contribution pensions. However, there will be at least some defined benefit pensioners in the system for many decades to come.

Also important for the living standards of retirees are

- a high level of home ownership among retirees, and

- government funding on a means-tested basis of residential aged care and some other aged care.

The focus of this chapter is on mandatory and voluntary pensions and the means-tested Age Pension.

A BRIEF HISTORY OF SUPERANNUATION (PENSIONS) IN AUSTRALIA

Occupational superannuation in Australia first emerged in midnineteenth century. The term *superannuation* was in common usage in the early nineteenth century to refer to the pension received after retirement from the former employer. In most other countries, the term "private pensions" tends to be used to describe what is known as superannuation in Australia. While it is not entirely clear why the term superannuation is used in Australia, it does provide a clear distinction for private arrangements from the government-provided Age Pension. It also is more consistent with the availability of lump sum benefits from pensions in Australia, which are taken by a substantial number of retirees.

From its earliest days in Australia (with the establishment of a pension fund for its staff by the Bank of Australasia in October 1842) up to the 1940s, pensions were only available to a select, mostly male, group of salaried employees in the public sector and some large companies. Employer-supported pensions for wage staff tended to be less generous, with smaller benefits and smaller employer contributions in plans that were noncompulsory.

By 1974, 32.2 percent of wage and salary earners were covered by pensions, made up of 40.8 percent of male wage and salary earners but only 16.5 percent of females. Most pension assets were in defined benefit plans.

In 1983, the newly elected Labor Government expressed support for the principles of employee pensions and initiated discussions with the Australian Council of Trade Unions (ACTU) on the possibility of broadening access to pensions as part of the Government's Prices and Incomes Accord with the trade unions.

The process of making employee pensions a more or less universal entitlement began in September 1985 when, with the support of the government, the ACTU sought a 3 percent pensions contribution to be paid by employers to industry funds specified in relevant industrial labor agreements, which set the minimum wages and conditions for many but not all employees in Australia.

This submission was supported by arguments addressed to

- the implications arising from the trend towards an aging of the population including the workforce;
- the effects of the trend for earlier retirement;
- the existing dependency on Age Pensions and the projected significant increase in the dependency of the aged on the working population with an explosion of Age Pension costs; and
- the fact that a large percentage of the workforce was not covered by existing pension plans and that wide disparities existed in coverage according to sex, industry, occupation and income levels. In particular, it was submitted that women, manual workers and those in the lower income level were less adequately covered than others.

As new labor agreements were progressively negotiated according to the guidelines in the national wage case decision, pension coverage increased rapidly. In the four years after the introduction of employer contributions linked to labor agreements, employee coverage grew from around 40 percent to 79 percent. In the private sector, coverage grew from 32 percent in 1987 to 68 percent in 1991.

This was a major achievement for collectively bargained pensions, but more was needed in terms of coverage and rate of contributions. Accordingly, the government at the time announced in the 1991–1992 budget that it would introduce a mandatory pension system through the implementation of the Superannuation Guarantee. The Superannuation Guarantee pension system is based on using the taxation power of the Australian government to provide a very powerful incentive for employers to make pension contributions of the required amount. The guarantee part of the superannuation guarantee is about a requirement for contributions being made rather than a guarantee of investment earnings or eventual retirement income.

The Superannuation Guarantee system—the mandatory pension system—came into effect on July 1, 1992, starting at a minimum contribution level of 3 percent. A schedule of future increases in the rate of the Superannuation Guarantee contributions was also set, with a contribution rate for all employees of 9 percent of earnings. Employers already making contributions that met the requirements of the Superannuation Guarantee were not required to make additional contributions. Employees now generally are able to choose the fund to which they want to contribute, but many employees have contributions made to the fund that their employers have selected as the default fund or that is specified as a default fund in an industrial award. There are hundreds of corporate, retail, industry, and public sector funds and nearly 500,000 small Self-Managed Superannuation Funds.

While there has been growth in the number of self-managed super-annuation funds, the numbers of the other types of funds have decreased over time. Self-managed superannuation funds are funds where each member is also a trustee of the fund. There is a general prohibition on membership of such funds by someone who is an employee of another member of the fund. The result is that a small business owner cannot include his or her employees in the self-managed superannuation fund of which the business owner is a member. They have less than five members each, and they differ from the various individually managed accounts in other countries in that they are a private trust arrangement that does not require a financial institution to be involved as a provider.

The coverage of the system was very broad, using wide definitions for employer and employee. However, there were some exceptions, chiefly those earning less than A$450 per calendar month, part-time employees aged under 18, and those over 65. As well, the Super-annuation Guarantee does not apply to the self-employed (other than to owner-managers who receive wages and technically are employees of a company they control). Around 30 percent of the self-employed make voluntary contributions, partly driven by the tax concessions available for this. Some self-employed persons will have a private pension because of previous periods when they have been an employee. Some contractors who might be regarded as self-employed by other legal pro-visions are also covered in the compulsory system through an extended definition of employee.

In May 2010, the Australian Treasurer announced that compulsory employer pension contributions were to increase to 12 percent by July 2019. The increase in mandatory Superannuation Guarantee contribu-tions is a gradual process, starting with 0.25 percent in the 2013–2014 financial year, and then a 0.25 percent increase in 2014–2015. For the following five years after the 2015 financial year, the Superannuation Guarantee rate will increase by 0.5 percent until it reaches 12 percent by July 2019. A new government was elected in September 2013 and as part of its election policies indicated an intention to legislate a two year pause in the phased increase in the rate of contributions.

THE AGE PENSION NOW AND INTO THE FUTURE

The Age Pension—the means-tested pension—is funded out of general tax revenue by the Australian government. It does not require either a history of social security contributions by the person or a history of work; rather, receipt is determined by reaching the eligibility age, being a resident in Australia for 20 years, and qualifying under the applicable asset and income tests. The maximum benefit provided by the Age Pension as of September 1, 2012, is A\$20,142 for a single person and A\$30,368 for a couple. The Age Pension is taxable, but due to a variety of rebates, those receiving the maximum benefit generally do not pay any income tax. People with higher income and assets in retirement receive a reduced Age Pension. Many people receive a partial Age Pension, but persons at the top of the income distribution do not receive any benefit from the Age Pension.

Table 9.1 shows budget standards for a modest and comfortable lifestyle as indicated by the Association of Superannuation Funds of Australia (ASFA) retirement standard. These budget standards are based on a typical retiree at age 65 and are widely used in Australia as an indicator of adequacy of retirement income. They are updated regularly on the ASFA Web site (www.superannuation.asn.au). ASFA is a private-sector, not-for-profit organization whose members are pension funds and service providers to pension funds.

While these values do not reflect the situation of every retiree, they allow us to gauge the average needs for different lifestyle expectations given cost of living in Australia as of December 2012. These are compared with the maximum annual benefit of the Age Pension as of September 2012.

It is clear that the Age Pension is close to meeting the modest lifestyle needs of retirees. As the benefit is linked to national average wages and the modest lifestyle is linked to prices, the Age Pension will gradually close in on the modest lifestyle for at least a period of some years.

Table 9.1 The Age Pension Compared to the ASFA Retirement Standards

	Modest lifestyle single	Modest lifestyle couple	Comfortable lifestyle single	Comfortable lifestyle couple
Yearly total ($)	22,585	32,555	41,186	56,339
Age Pension ($)	20,142	30,368	20,142	30,368
Difference from Age Pension ($)	2,443	2,187	21,044	25,971

NOTE: All values in Australian dollars.
SOURCE: ASFA (2013).

The ASFA retirement standard is adjusted for changes in prices every quarter, but every four or five years it is adjusted more substantively for changes in the pattern of expenditure by retirees and for increases in the general living standard of the community. For a comfortable lifestyle, retirees need to build their own pension savings, as the Age Pension by itself will be inadequate.

THE FISCAL SUSTAINABILITY OF THE AGE PENSION

Australia is unusual in that the future financial impact of programs such as the Age Pension is required to be assessed on a regular basis in what is known as the Intergenerational Report (IGR) which is prepared by the Australian Treasury. The IGR came to life as a key requirement of the 1998 Charter of Budget Honesty Act. The charter requires an intergenerational report to assess the long-term sustainability of policies over the 40 years following the release of the report, including the impacts of demographic change. The IGR has played a major role in raising community awareness of long-term fiscal challenges and, in so doing, placed greater focus on government decisions with long-term consequences.

For instance, in the fiscal year 2009–2010 budget, the government announced increases to Age Pension benefits, particularly for single persons, following an inquiry process that indicated the desirability of increasing such payments. These increases were introduced along with a suite of budget-saving measures designed to offset their long-term costs. The budget-saving measures included a gradual rise in the qualifying age for the Age Pension (to be phased in from 2017 to 2023), means testing of the private health insurance rebate, as well as reforms to family payments and pensions. The package of changes was projected to be budget neutral by 2021–2022 and through to 2049–2050 as a result of the effect of the expenditure saving measures offsetting the increase in the costs of he Age Pension.

Australia was relatively unusual in the international community in that it weathered the global financial crisis without significant impacts on economic activity, unemployment, or fiscal outcomes. While the current budgetary situation is not without challenges, with the then government recently formally announcing that a target of a budget surplus in 2012–2013 would not be met, the budgetary situation has been sufficiently robust to support both the increase in the Age Pension benefits and the increased tax expenditures associated with higher compulsory contributions to pensions. In regard to the latter, there was an explicit linking of the introduction of a new resources rent tax associated with certain mining activities with the legislation increasing the Superannuation Guarantee contribution rate. The legislation increasing the Superannuation Guarantee contribution reduced income tax receipts due to the reduction in net wages, which is only partially offset by the tax on contributions, while the resources rent tax provided an offsetting increase in taxes. As noted earlier, the government elected in September 2013 proposes a two-year pause to the increase in the rate of compulsory contributions.

However, over a longer time period, aging of the population will still contribute to pressure on government spending and fiscal sustainability. The Intergenerational Report (IGR) prepared by the Australian Treasury projects total spending to increase to 27.1 percent of GDP in 2049–2050, around 4.75 percentage points higher than its projected low point in 2015–2016. In today's terms, that is the equivalent of adding around $A60 billion a year to government spending.

Around two-thirds of the projected increase in spending over the next 40 years is related to health, reflecting pressures from aging, increased community expectations, and the funding of new technologies. Growth in spending on age-related pensions and aged care is also significant, both as a proportion of GDP and in real spending per person. Currently, about a quarter of Australian government spending is on health, age-related pensions, and aged care. The Intergenerational Report projects that Australian government spending on these functions will increase significantly over the next 40 years, pushing their share of spending to almost one-half.

As a proportion of GDP, spending on health is projected to rise from 4.0 percent to 7.1 percent. Age-related pensions and aged care are projected to rise from 2.7 percent and 0.8 percent of GDP to 3.9 percent and 1.8 percent, respectively, in 2049–2050. Figure 9.1 provides further details by each major expenditure category.

Excluding public debt interest, the Intergenerational Report projects a fiscal gap of 2.75 percent of GDP (or around $A30 billion in today's dollars) by 2049–2050.

Much of the increase in government expenditure on Age Pensions is due to population aging. Unlike some countries, such as Japan, the Australian population will continue to grow, as annual rates of population

Figure 9.1 Projected Expenditure by Major Category

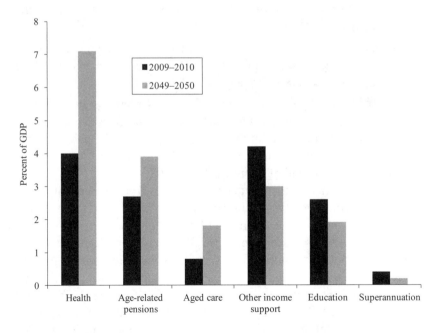

SOURCE: Australian Treasury (2010).

growth are projected to slow gradually, from 2.1 percent in 2008–2009 to 0.9 percent in 2049–2050. Australia's population is projected to grow from around 22 million people to 35.9 million people in 2050.

As well, average Australian mortality rates have fallen significantly, with life expectancies rising for both men and women. These changes have added to population growth and the proportion of older people in the Australian population. As a result, the number of Australians aged 65 and over is projected to grow from around 3 million in 2010 to 8.1 million by 2050, from 2.1 percent of the population to 5.1 percent. As a result, the number of people of eligible age for the Age Pension is projected to increase by around 150 percent by 2049–2050.

There are other factors that affect the projections of age-related pension spending:

- A decline in the proportion of pensioners receiving a full Age Pension, because of the increased value of individuals' mandatory pension and other private assets and income.

- The proportion of people with a partial Age Pension is projected to increase significantly while the proportion of the eligible age group not receiving any Age Pension is projected to rise slightly.

- As noted earlier, the increase in the level of the Age Pension benefits has been largely offset by other policy measures, such as raising the eligibility age.

When the next Intergenerational Report is prepared in or before 2015, it can be expected to take into account the phased increase in compulsory pension contributions from 9 percent to 12 percent. This will further moderate the increase in age-related pension spending, particularly toward the end of the projection period.

Of course, there are consequences flowing from compulsory pension contributions for the public sector's contribution to private (and therefore national) saving as a result of the compulsory pension system. This public sector contribution arises from the tax-preferred status of compulsory pension contributions and the assumption by the Australian Treasury that other expenditures are cut back to allow for this tax expenditure. The public sector's contribution is estimated to be about 0.4 percent of GDP currently, rising gradually to nearly 0.7 percent of GDP by the end of the decade, and then staying around that level to the middle of the century.

The estimated net fiscal cost to the government budget is smaller than the public sector's contribution to private saving, because budget savings arising from the compulsory pension system reduce the net fiscal cost of compulsory pensions. This is because growth in net wages is less than it would otherwise be because of the increase in pension contributions, leading to increases in expenditure on Age Pension and other government payments indexed to movements in average net wages being less than they would otherwise be.

Equity clearly is a key issue in the debate about pension and retirement income reform. There is strong government and community concern that the assistance provided to retirement income should be spread fairly according to need. There also is a strong tradition in Australia of support for what we colloquially call a "fair go." In the context of pensions, this means that no groups should face barriers to participation in the retirement income system.

One statistic that gained some currency in public debate in Australia was that 5 percent of individuals account for 37 percent of tax-preferred pension contributions. However, that is no longer the case and is now something of an urban myth—that figure, calculated by the Treasury, related to 2005–2006, when pension policy settings were significantly different than they are now. For instance, in 2005–2006, a maximum deductible contribution limit of $A100,587 applied for each employee aged 50 and over and for the self-employed aged 50 and over. For those aged 35–49 the figure was $A40,560 a year.

By fiscal year 2009–2010, a new set of tax-preferred contribution caps was in force (after a number of variants along the way). These caps permitted annual contributions of no more than $A25,000 a year for those under age 50 and $A50,000 a year for those aged 50 and over. However, the $A50,000 a year cap was a transitional one and expired on June 30, 2012. The government has announced its intention to replace these caps with a general cap of $A25,000 a year except for those aged 50 and over with less than $A500,000 in pension savings, where a $A50,000 a year cap would apply. However, the introduction of this higher cap for those aged 50 and over has been delayed due to budgetary reasons.

Tax-preferred contributions include employer contributions (including contributions made under a salary sacrifice arrangement where wages are traded for extra contributions), and personal contributions claimed as a tax deduction by a self-employed person.

Tax Assistance for Pensions after the New Tax-Preferenced Contribution Caps

Clear empirical evidence indicates that the contribution caps have reduced the tax-preferenced pension contributions made by upper-income earners. This is reflected in Table 9.2, which sets out estimates of the proportion of tax-preferenced pension contributions made on behalf of wage earners in the various marginal income tax bands applying in 2009–2010. These estimates are based on data especially extracted for ASFA from a large scale survey of Australian households, namely the Household, Income and Labour Dynamics in Australia (HILDA) Survey.

These estimates of employer contributions are consistent in broad terms and produce overall results consistent with aggregate pension contributions as reported by the Australian Prudential Regulatory Authority (APRA), which is one of the government regulators of the financial services industry (including pensions), and Australian Taxation Office statistical publications.

As is clear from the table, pension contributions are not spread entirely evenly across all taxpayers or income ranges. This is because one of the basic characteristics of pensions is that contributions are linked to employment, particularly full-time employment. Those taxpayers on very low incomes are not receiving pension contributions made by their employers or are receiving the benefit of only relatively small contribution amounts.

Individuals on a low income in any given year will not necessarily be on a low taxable income for all of their lives. Many individuals who have low taxable incomes from employment are undertaking part-time employment when they are studying or when they also have family responsibilities that prevent them from undertaking full-time work. However, over their lifetime they will have many years, usually decades, of full-time work. As well, wages often increase in real terms over the course of a career. The distribution of taxable incomes and tax concessions for pension contributions in any given year is not a good indicator of assistance delivered over a lifetime.

Table 9.2 Employer Contributions by Income Range, 2009–2010

Taxable income range ($A)	Marginal income tax rate (%)	% of wage earners	Value of employer contributions[a] $A million	% of employer contributions[a]
0–6,000	0	5.4	54	0.1
6,001–37,000	15	31.5	4,255	7.9
37,001–80,000	30	42.7	23,120	43.0
80,001–180,000	38	18.0	20,280	37.7
180,001+	47	2.4	6,050	11.3

[a] Based on data extracted for ASFA from Wave 10 of the HILDA survey.
SOURCE: Clare (2012a).

However, even in regard to a single year, as indicated by Table 9.2, around 90 percent of employer contributions relate to individuals on less than the top marginal tax rate, with over 50 percent of contributions relating to individuals on a marginal income tax rate of 30 percent or less.

The top 5 percent of employees (in terms of income) accounted for less than 20 percent of the total pension contributions in 2009–2010.

While upper-income earners typically have more pension contributions than lower-income earners, the amount related to upper income earners is now much lower than it was previously. While a higher figure may have applied back in 2005–2006, the impact of the contribution caps has been considerable. The various changes that have been made to the pension tax rules also may have affected confidence in contributing to pensions also leading to lower discretionary contributions.

Table 9.3 provides estimates of the amount of tax concession by personal income tax rate. It also factors in the receipt of the cocontribution (government matching contribution), which is only available to low-income earners making personal contributions.

Table 9.3 indicates that in recent times less than 15 percent of the government assistance for pension contributions flows to those on the top marginal rate. This compares to the around 30 percent of aggregate personal income tax collections that is paid by that group of taxpayers. While upper-income earners do receive assistance for their pension contributions, the overall personal tax system imposes a substantially higher tax burden on upper-income earners compared to those earning

Table 9.3 Employee Tax Concessions by Income Range, 2009–2010

Taxable income range ($A)	Marginal income tax rate (%)	Value of tax concession[a] $A, millions	% of total tax concession for employer contributions	Value of tax concession and cocontribution $A, millions	% of total tax concession and cocontribution[b]
0–6,000	0	−8	−0.1	192	1.5
6,001–37,000	15	68	0.6	1,068	8.3
37,001–80,000	30	4,462	39.2	4,662	36.4
80,001–180,000	38	4,968	43.6	4,968	38.8
180,001+	47	1,906	16.7	1,905	14.9
All employees		11,396	100.0	12,795	100.0

[a] Takes into account the Medicare levy, the phasing out of the Low Income Tax Offset, and the phasing in of the Medicare liability.
[b] Column does not sum to 100 because of rounding.
SOURCE: Clare (2012a).

lower incomes. It could be argued that the general tax and transfer system in Australia should and does do most of the "heavy lifting" in terms of improving vertical equity.

Table 9.3 also indicates that the bulk of government assistance for pensions flows to those on either the 30 percent or 38 percent tax rates. Such taxpayers make up a very large part of the full-time workforce in Australia. Providing the bulk of tax assistance to this group makes sense from a public policy point of view. In contrast to very low-income earners and those who never have significant wage incomes during their lives, they have the potential to finance through savings significant income in retirement.

For those on the top marginal tax rate, achievement of significant savings in the form of pension savings has the potential to make them totally self-funded in retirement, with no reliance on the government-provided Age Pension.

The Australian government has also legislated to provide a new matching contribution of up to $A500 annually for eligible low-income earners from the 2012–2013 income year. The payment will be 15 percent of the eligible tax-preferred contributions (including employer contributions) made by or for individuals with adjusted taxable incomes of up to $A37,000. Individuals will also need to meet a test where at least 10 percent of their incomes must be from employment or business sources and they are a resident of Australia or New Zealand. Individuals also can benefit from the cocontribution in regard to personal contributions that are not tax-preferred.

By its very nature, new matching contributions will only provide assistance to low-income earners on either the 0 or 15 percent tax rate. However, the government elected in September 2013 has indicated its intention to abolish this government contribution for low income earners.

As well, the phased increase in the rate of compulsory contributions to 12 percent will have its greatest impact on low- and middle-income earners, given that those earning higher incomes commonly already receive the benefit of contributions in excess of 9 percent of wages and/or will adjust voluntary salary sacrifice contributions if there is an increase in compulsory contributions.

Table 9.4 compares the distribution of government tax relief and contribution assistance for pensions in 2009–2010 for employees on

Table 9.4 Current and Proposed Government Assistance for Pension Contributions by Income Range

Taxable income range ($A)	Marginal income tax rate (%)	Current value of tax concession and cocontribution[a] ($A, millions)	% of current total tax concession and cocontribution[b]	Value of proposed total tax concession and government contributions[a] ($A, millions)	% of proposed total tax concession and government contributions
0—6,000	0	192	1.5	210	1.4
6,001–37,000	15	1,068	8.3	1,640	11.0
37,001–80,000	30	4,662	36.4	5,732	38.3
80,001–180,000	38	4,968	38.8	5,465	36.6
180,001+	47	1,905	14.9	1,905	12.7
All employees		12,795	100.0	14,952	100.0

[a]Takes into account the Medicare levy, the phasing out of the Low Income Tax Offset, and the phasing in of the Medicare liability. Based on 2009–2010 tax rates.
[b]Column does not sum to 100 because of rounding.
SOURCE: Clare (2012b).

the basis of current policy settings and what it would have been if a 12 percent mandatory contribution rate, the low income matching contribution payment and the current rate of cocontribution had all applied in that year. While it will be some years before all the measures are fully in place this approach illustrates what the eventual impact on the distribution of government assistance by income level will be.

The combined effect of the government proposed measures would have, if they had applied in 2009–2010, increased the total assistance for retirement saving for employees earning less than $A80,000 a year from $A5,920 million to around $A7,580 million. Expressed as a percentage of total government assistance, the share of those earning less than $A80,000 a year would have increased from 46.2 percent to 50.2 percent. Clearly, the measures strongly favor those on lower incomes.

GOVERNMENT ASSISTANCE FOR BOTH MANDATORY PENSIONS AND THE AGE PENSION

There is also a direct link between the level of retirement savings and the subsequent reduction in the government Age Pension. In considering the equity of government assistance for retirement income, it also is necessary to take into account the amount of the Age Pension that will eventually be provided on average to persons on various levels of earnings and pension contributions during their working life.

This was done in research conducted in 2009 by George Rothman of the Australian Treasury Retirement & Intergenerational Modelling & Analysis Unit. This research places emphasis on a "whole of life" or life cycle perspective where Age Pension benefits in the retirement phase are included. The cost to government of its retirement income policies as a whole is modelled using the Treasury's comprehensive RIMGROUP model.

The base case for this analysis is the retirement income framework following the 2009 government budget. Significant changes in that budget included

- a significant increase in Age Pension payments of $A32.49 a week for single pensioners and $A10.14 a week combined for couple pensioners, together with changes to the income test,

whereby the pension taper rate for new pensioners, which reduces the Age Pension for persons receiving higher levels of income, is 50 percent rather than 40 percent;

- a gradual increase in the age for eligibility for an Age Pension
beginning in 2017 so that this age reaches 67 in 2023; and

- a reduction in the annual cap on tax-preferenced pension contributions from $A50,000 to $A25,000 for those younger than 50
and the transitional cap for those in their 50s from $A100,000 to
$A50,000. This limit applies to the combined compulsory and
salary sacrifice contributions. Individuals generally will not exceed this limit as the result of compulsory contributions alone
given there is a cap on compulsory contributions per job that is
below the tax-preferenced cap.

The analysis in the Treasury paper indicates that these measures
have added considerably to the equity of Australia's retirement income
system, both by gender and income. The tax-preferenced contribution
caps budget measure also was found to add even more vertical equity
to the system with the saving to government revenue impacting mostly
on the top two deciles of the income distribution for both men and
women.

**Table 9.5 Net Present Value of Cost to Government of Retirement
Income System by Income Level ($A, millions)**

Decile	NPV1-women	NPV1-men	NPV1-both
1	1,750	1,600	3,350
2	1,700	1,600	3,350
3	1,650	1,600	3,300
4	1,650	1,600	3,300
5	1,650	1,600	3,200
6	1,650	1,750	3,400
7	1,900	1,800	3,700
8	1,850	1,950	3,800
9	1,850	2,050	3,950
10	1,800	2,450	4,250
All	17,500	18,050	35,550

NOTE: Columns do not precisely add up to the totals because of rounding.
SOURCE: Clare (2012b).

The research also indicates that the total amount of government support does not vary much across the income deciles or by gender. Table 9.5 sets out the Treasury forecasts of government assistance for those born in 1960 and retiring in 2027. The proportion of assistance provided in the form of tax expenditures on pensions increases with higher income with a more or less equivalent decrease in the value of Age Pension expenditures.

Overall government support for the Age Pension was found to account for 82 percent of the government assistance to women for their retirement and 68 percent of the assistance provided to men.

One group that receives above average assistance is men in the top income decile. For the other income deciles, the withdrawal of the Age Pension largely matches the assistance given to higher pension contributions. However, this became irrelevant for those who are not entitled to even a partial Age Pension. Limiting the tax-preferred contribution cap to $A25,000 a year for those aged 50 and over with more than $A500,000 in pension is a policy response to this distributional finding.

THE REAL EQUITY CHALLENGE

The real issue in regard to equity is that too many Australians have too little in retirement savings rather than too much. While much public debate has focused on the top 1 percent or 5 percent of income earners, there has been little or no debate on how to advance outcomes for the other 99 percent or 95 percent.

If excessive government assistance is a problem, it is restricted to a very small number of individuals. This is particularly the case since the introduction of progressively tighter caps on both tax-preferred and non-tax-preferred contributions. When properly measured, the total government assistance for retirement income in the form of both the Age Pension and tax concessions for pensions is broadly even across the entire income distribution.

After the recent contribution cap and rebate changes to private pensions, 87.3 percent of the tax concessions for pensions will flow to individuals on less than the top marginal tax rate, up from the around 85 percent, which applied before the changes. The share of total concessions flowing to individuals on the top marginal tax rate was around 50 percent in 2007–2008, with the reduction in the share since then due to the introduction of contribution caps and higher rates of tax on the contributions of certain upper-income earners, together with the top marginal rate applying to a smaller proportion of taxpayers.

ASSISTING THOSE WHO REALLY NEED ASSISTANCE

Evidence from surveys of pension account balances held by individuals indicates that compulsory pensions have been very effective in lifting coverage rates and average pension account balances (Table 9.6).

The increase in the mandatory Superannuation Guarantee contribution rate to 12 percent will further improve pension balances at retirement, but it will be 40 or 50 years before the system is fully mature, meaning that all workers will be under that regime for their full careers.

However, voluntary contributions have remained flat in recent years in response to both tax changes and investment return developments. In particular, contribution caps and other changes to pensions are limiting the amount of voluntary salary sacrifice contributions, including by individuals seeking to catch up on contributions late in their careers. Salary sacrifice contributions are made when an individual trades part of his salary for additional employer contributions.

Longitudinal data indicate that a significant proportion of the population have higher incomes (with associated capacity to make higher contributions) for a relatively limited portion of their working careers. A higher contribution cap generally, or at least for those aged 50 and over, would assist those who need to catch up and have a capacity to do so.

While the pension cocontribution (matching contribution) made by the government has been effective in lifting personal contributions of low-income individuals, the design parameters of the cocontribution and recent cutbacks to them have made the cocontribution less effective than it could be. There is a case for both a higher maximum cocontribution and a lower matching rate in order to encourage greater additional contributions.

Table 9.6 Pension Coverage and Pension Holdings of Men And Women Who Were Not Yet Retired, by Annual Salary Income, 2006 and 2010

Annual wage and salary income ($)	2006			2010		
	% with pension	Pension balance of those with super ($)		% with pension	Pension balance of those with super ($)	
		Mean	Median		Mean	Median
Men						
<28,000	75.1	37,312	5,700	79.9	43,553	5,000
28,000 – < 58,000	96.7	70,698	30,000	96.8	62,853	25,000
58,000 – < 80,000	98.1	134,981	65,000	98.7	108,092	50,000
80,000+	97.8	207,801	110,000	98.6	212,025	110,000
Total	91.4	99,506	35,000	93.9	109,609	40,000
Women						
<28,000	80.7	32,807	9,000	80.9	37,622	8,500
28,000 – < 58,000	96.8	56,253	25,000	96.6	52,885	29,000
58,000 – < 80,000	98.6	102,844	55,000	98.2	98,071	50,000
80,000+	97.7	158,652	88,000	98.9	142,855	75,000
Total	89.4	55,433	21,000	90.9	63,412	26,000

NOTE: Population weighted results.
SOURCE: HILDA data.

The $A450 a Month Threshold for the Superannuation Guarantee Mandatory Contributions

While there may have been a rationale for the income threshold below which contributions are not required when the mandatory Superannuation Guarantee pension system was first introduced, it would make sense to remove it now given that nearly all employees have a pension account, and processes for making contributions are now more efficient. Around 250,000 individuals, the majority of whom are women, would benefit from removal of the threshold through higher eventual retirement savings. The cost to both employers and to the Australian budget from removing the threshold would be very modest.

The Self-Employed

Nearly 10 percent of the labor force are self-employed. While tax concessions have led to some self-employed persons saving for retirement through pensions, average balances and coverage have remained relatively low. Around 29 percent of the self-employed have no pension savings (this is more common for males than females). There is a strong case to extend compulsory pensions to include the self-employed.

Individuals on Paid Parental Leave

Paid parental leave is considered by the government to be equivalent to wages in terms of income tax and other treatment of individuals. Consistent with this, it would be appropriate for the Superannuation Guarantee mandatory pension contributions to apply to such payments, which it does not currently do.

One of the reasons that the average pension balance of women is lower than that of men is time out of the paid workforce for parental reasons. Paying Superannuation Guarantee mandatory contributions on parental leave payments would help reduce this difference in entitlements. The effects of compound interest also would be very favorable in regard to pension contributions made on behalf of women who take parental leave, mostly in their 20s and 30s. The cost to the Australian government budget would be just over $A20 million a year.

Indigenous Australians

Indigenous Australians have lower coverage and lower balances on average than the general population, again largely related to differences in paid labor force experience. Pension coverage for indigenous Australians is about 70 percent for men and 60 percent for women, compared to rates of 85 percent for men and 80 percent for women for the population more generally. Average (mean) balances are also lower than for the equivalent Australian population as a whole (Table 9.7).

Increases in the pension coverage and average pension balances of indigenous Australians will clearly be associated with improvements in involvement in paid work and in wages. Labor market measures rather than pension policies drive labor market outcomes.

However, current pension arrangements and administrative requirements do not always mesh well with the circumstances and needs of indigenous Australians, particularly those in remote areas who may have difficulty communicating with their pension fund administrators and in claiming benefits or identifying lost accounts.

There is scope for the pension industry and the regulators to work toward a regulatory framework and administrative arrangements that can better cope with the special needs of indigenous Australians. Such arrangements also would be likely to benefit many other Australians.

Table 9.7 Pension Coverage And Pension Holdings of Aboriginal and Torres Strait Islander Men and Women Who Were Not Yet Retired, 2006 and 2010

	2006			2010		
	% with pension	Pension balance of those with super ($A)		% with pension	Pension balance of those with super ($A)	
		Mean	Median		Mean	Median
Men	68.3	49,589	9,000	70.7	55,743	14,000
Women	52.1	42,109	10,000	60.6	39,909	15,000
Persons	59.5	46,069	10,000	65.3	47,863	15,000

NOTE: Population weighted results. Not enough cases to break down by age.
SOURCE: Clare (2012b).

Recently Divorced Men and Women

Survey data indicate that the distribution of pensions is now much more even for those who have recently divorced compared to when amendments were made in 2002 to the Family Law Act to allow the splitting of pension account balances. The extent of disparities in particular decreased between 2006 and 2010. While a number of factors would have contributed to this, the growing maturity of the compulsory pension system leading to higher average account balances for both men and women would have played a role, along with more women having pensions in their own right. The figures also are consistent with the parties in a marriage making more use of the splitting arrangements.

Exposure to Investment Risk

Currently in Australia, around 90 percent of individuals in the preretirement phase who have a pension, and around 75 percent of those recently retired with a pension, are exposed to investment risk. The proportion is higher in the preretirement phase given that the newer and younger fund members have been predominantly enrolled in defined contribution arrangements.

As shown in Table 9.8, investment returns in Australia, as in many other countries, have not been favorable in recent years. The global financial crisis had a significant impact, particularly given the 65–70 percent exposure on average of most funds to equities.

Investment returns in 2012–2013 were relatively high, with preliminary estimates indicating an average rate of return for default members of funds of over 15 percent.

The rationale for relatively high levels of exposure to equities in defined contribution plans (accumulation funds) is that this will generally lead to higher retirement benefits for members. Most individuals will be a member of a pension fund for a period of 40 years or more. Subject of course to individual decisions regarding exposure to investment risk and volatility, there is an argument that such exposure should be sustained throughout a member's career.

However, market volatility means that at least some members will wish to shift assets into cash over the five years before retirement. This will allow them to cater for any required lump sum benefit and their

Table 9.8 Average Annual Fund Investment Returns to June 30, 2012

Year	Real returns (%)
1	0.3
5	−0.7
10	5.2
15	5.5
20	7.0
25	7.2
30	10.0
35	10.8
40	9.9
50	9.9

SOURCE: Annual survey published by ASFA.

initial pension drawdowns. Life cycle investment options can provide such an investment strategy. However, while they are suitable for some individuals, they may not be suitable for others.

Historical analysis also indicates that a typical life cycle fund would have delivered poorer outcomes for most members over most periods in Australia, such as 1900–1970, 1970–1999, and 1900–1999. Now is also not a good time to switch allocations from equities to bonds as returns to bonds are at historical lows and recent returns from equities, especially Australian equities, have been relatively strong, with double-digit returns in calendar 2012, particularly the second half of 2012.

While consumer satisfaction with pensions tends to follow with a lag in developments in investment returns, there has been little pressure in Australia for the government to cover any investment losses faced by fund members due to general developments in investment markets. The only policy response to the global financial crisis was to reduce the minimum drawdown factor for individuals who have an individual account–based (defined contribution) income stream in retirement. There are compensation arrangements that can be called upon in the case of members suffering loss due to fraud or theft in a regulated fund, but fortunately fraud or theft are relatively rare in the regulated pension funds. Compensation in these cases is effectively funded by members of other regulated pension funds through special levies struck by the government in such cases.

INCOME STREAMS IN RETIREMENT

In an ideal world, the objective of pensions should be focused on the provision of income during the whole of retirement. However, there are a number of reasons why it is difficult to structure the Australian system around regular reliable pension payments. These include the following:

- When pension contributions began to be included in labor agreements in 1986 as deferred pay (in lieu of a possible productivity wage rise), it was promoted to members as an addition to the Age Pension. The Superannuation Guarantee pension has increased the value of contributions, but the message has not changed— members consider that the private pension account balance is their own money and they expect flexibility of payments.

- The government allows all members above age 60 to retire and draw a tax-free lump sum or pension. Most older Australians also are subject to low or nil rates of personal income tax given low average incomes and various tax rebates. As a result, there is only a limited incentive for individuals to leave money in the system during retirement.

- There are no longer maximum withdrawal factors on account-based defined contribution pensions, so nobody is forced to draw their benefits over time.

- Members can buy lifetime annuities from the private sector (albeit from a small number of suppliers), but current sales are well under 100 a year in total. Consumer research indicates that most Australians are unrealistic about the pricing of an indexed lifetime annuity and expect much more than fair value. Without compulsion or incentives, most members will not buy these products.

- Many members retire with small benefits, and they appear comfortable with leaving the money in an interest-bearing bank account rather than in a pension. This may be influenced by their perception of safety in the bank or by a short time horizon where they do not value higher (but uncertain) returns. They may also value instant access to their funds.

- Many people today retire with some debt (including mortgages) or the need to carry out home repairs or consumer durable purchases, and it is a rational decision to take a pension lump sum to clear all such expenses or debts before retiring.

- Around a third of total pension savings and around half of post-retirement pension balances are held in Self-Managed Superannuation Funds, which have less than five members and where each member is also a trustee of the fund. Such fund members generally value control highly and are wary of purchasing an income stream from a third party such as a life insurance company or managed fund.

The above situation has made the provision of income streams, particularly those that protect members from their longevity risk, difficult. In addition, transitional arrangements, especially if compulsion is involved, can be problematic due to the plans made by those approaching retirement.

That said, the evidence available indicates that many Australians do take an income stream from their pension in retirement, albeit one that is account based, where the individual can access the entire account balance should they choose to do so. This is particularly the case when larger amounts are involved.

As shown in Table 9.9, around 70 percent of males aged 60–64 who have recently retired have a pension with an average balance of around $A380,000. This is a drop in coverage of around 20 percentage points compared to those who are in the same age group who have not retired. The average balance is also higher than for those not retired, which suggests that those with lower balances are more likely to cash out and invest (or spend) elsewhere.

For women, the drop in coverage is greater, at around 30 percentage points. Again, the average balances for those retaining retirement savings in a pension, at around $A255,000, is higher than for those in the same age group who have not retired.

These figures strongly suggest that the great bulk of recent retirees keep their retirement savings primarily in a pension account and draw down an income stream. Those retirees who take their retirement savings out of the pension system are a minority. However, even for this minority there is no evidence that the pension savings are used pri-

Table 9.9 Pension Coverage and Pension Holdings of Men and Women Who Were Recently Retired, 2006 and 2010

Age group	% with pension	Pension balance of those with super ($A) Mean	Pension balance of those with super ($A) Median	% with pension	Pension balance of those with super ($A) Mean	Pension balance of those with super ($A) Median
		2006			2010	
Men						
<60	70.2	283,430	200,000	89.8	528,105	386,000
60–64	76.7	573,228	500,000	68.8	381,703	250,000
65–69	48.1	421,618	200,000	65.7	299,161	164,000
70+	41.6	283,938[a]	162,000[a]	32.3	273,218[a]	90,000[a]
Total	60.7	419,841	280,000	60.8	367,336	245,000
Women						
<60	62.1	322,945	100,000	63.7	135,501	53,000
60–64	53.1	273,135	195,000	58.6	255,485	120,000
65–69	46.4	129,491	90,000	41.7	205,855	70,000
70+	41.6[a]	48,358[a]	15,000[a]	7.1[a]	184,000[a]	184,000[a]
Total	54.5	254,647	100,000	53.0	191,474	102,000

[a]Estimate not reliable.
NOTE: Population weighted results. "Recently retired" if "currently retired and observed not retired (i.e., employed) at some stage in the last three years."
SOURCE: HILDA data.

marily for immediate consumption purposes, such as an overseas trip. While some commentators claim that that frequently happens, such assertions are more in the line of urban myths than being supported by any objective research. However, in the past it is likely that the rate of taking lump sums was higher, in part due to account balances of those in defined contribution pension schemes being relatively low. For lower account balances, the tax benefits of remaining within the private pension system are not large. Elderly Australians, particularly elderly women, commonly have low or no private pension account balance because they either never had pension contributions in the first place or they have exhausted their pension account balances.

However, clearly there is scope for more retirement benefits to be taken in income stream form.

Designing better postretirement arrangements

The primary purpose of pensions is to provide financial security in retirement. This purpose is not currently being achieved as much as it could be in Australia, as there are many potential leakages that are at a cost to the system's integrity and the taxation concessions provided.

These potential leakages include

- using pension benefits too fast, which manifests in several ways, such as having insufficient longevity protection and excessively running down retirement savings to either fund excessive consumption and/or debts that were built up in the lead up to retirement in the knowledge that a lump sum would be available; and

- using pension benefits too slowly (i.e., poor lifestyle in retirement) and leaving these benefits for others in the estate.

While the evidence available indicates that most retirees make sensible decisions regarding the investment of their retirement savings, there is scope to strengthen arrangements in advice, defaults, and compulsion.

The ASFA currently has a major project under way with the aim of facilitating or requiring the better provision of retirement income streams. This work is well under way but is not yet complete.

The following 11 guiding principles have influenced ASFA's thinking:

1) The main focus of pensions should be on income streams in retirement, as opposed to lump sums or estate planning. Pensions in the postretirement phase should be designed to ensure that pension income streams, in conjunction with full or partial Age Pension payments, provide income and dignity in retirement until death.

2) The retirement income system (including both tax concessions and Age Pension payments) must be perceived to be fair, when assessed across all components of the system and across the lifetime of individuals, including both the pre- and postretirement phases.

3) Changes should not undermine confidence in the system; that is, in terms of both the changes made and the need for long lead times.

4) The system must be comprehensive, covering people in different types of employment structures, such as employees, contractors, and the self-employed.

5) The retirement income system needs to be flexible, recognizing the need to take into account the varying patterns of work and lifetime income that exist. Phased retirement should also be encouraged as a means of helping people stay in the workforce longer, not as a tax evasion mechanism.

6) The retirement income system should be robust and able to withstand a range of reasonable economic conditions without significantly reducing the expectations of the individuals involved.

7) The means test for the Age Pension has an important role to play in determining the amount of government assistance that retirees receive. In particular, those individuals or family units who earn below average wages, or who spend time out of the workforce (e.g., to raise a family or because they cannot get a job) should receive substantial support from the government to achieve a basic income in retirement. On the other hand, individuals and couples who continue in paid employment past customary retirement age and/or who have substantial pension and other assets that support a lifestyle in retirement more substantial than that described in the ASFA Retirement Standard at the comfortable level should receive little or no Age Pension.

8) The mandatory pension system needs to have a relatively high degree of guidance and constraints (including good default systems) in order to protect people from unwise or excessively short-term actions. For example, it needs to

    • require long-term savings with restricted access prior to retirement,

    • provide income in retirement, and

    • reduce risks during both the accumulation and retirement phases.

9) There needs to be access to deferred annuities, the purchase of which could start in either the accumulation or drawdown

stage. This will necessitate the removal of prudential supervision and tax regulatory roadblocks in order to allow the offering of deferred annuities in either the accumulation or drawdown phase.

10) Incentives and default settings should be the initial approach to obtaining the desired outcomes. However, if such arrangements are not effective in producing desired outcomes, then consideration may need to be given to introducing a degree of compulsion with respect to the taking of income streams in retirement. For instance, this could be achieved through the application of tax penalties with respect to taking benefits in any one of the following:

- as a lump sum,

- in the form of a noncomplying income stream, or

- if there is noncompliance with either the minimum or maximum drawdown factor of a complying account based income stream.

11) The requirements should apply to all pension structures, including self-managed superannuation funds, which are small plans, where provisions are relevant.

CONCLUSION

The Australian pensions system is not without its shortcomings. Among other things it is too complex, particularly in regard to the taxation of contributions and fund earnings, it is not yet mature enough to deliver for most a comfortable standard of living in retirement, and it does not deal well with the financial consequences of longevity for the large majority of members who are in defined contribution schemes.

However, compared to systems in most other countries, the Australian pensions system is sustainable, in that the respective burdens on governments, employers and individuals are manageable both now and in the future. It is comprehensive, in that all Australians benefit from an Age Pension from the government, which keeps individuals from poverty in retirement with near universal coverage of private pensions of employees and substantial coverage of the self employed. It is equitable, in that when all the elements of the system are looked at together, the amount of government assistance is broadly comparable across the income distribution. Finally, the Australian pension system helps to strengthen the financial system, in that assets in the pension system are invested in the real economy rather in notional securities issued by a central government.

References

Association of Superannuation Funds of Australia (ASFA). 2013. *ASFA Retirement Standard.* Sydney: Association of Superannuation Funds of Australia. http://www.superannuation.asn.au/resources/retirement-standard/ (accessed October 3, 2013.)

Australian Treasury. 2010. *Australia to 2050: Future Challenges.* Intergenerational report. Canberra: Australia.

Clare, Ross. 2012a. "The Equity of Government Assistance for Retirement Income in Australia." ASFA Research Paper. Sydney: Association of Superannuation Funds of Australia.

———. 2012b. *Equity and Superannuation—the Real Issues.* Sydney: Association of Superannuation Funds of Australia.

10
Social Security Reform in China

Tianhong Chen
Wuhan University

John A. Turner
Pension Policy Center

China has one-fifth of the world's population aged 60 and older (United Nations 2007). Thus, social security old-age benefits programs in China play an important role in the worldwide context of providing benefits for older persons.[1] Also adding to the importance of understanding China's retirement income system, China is undergoing a period of important changes in its provision of old-age benefits. At the start of 2009, less than 30 percent of its adult population was covered by a social security old-age benefits program, but in 2012 that had increased to 55 percent (*Economist* 2012). Chinese government data for the end of 2011 indicated that 241.1 million people were contributing to the new rural social security pension system, with 85.3 million people receiving benefits (Ministry of Human Resources and Social Security 2012). Another important development due to the one-child policy, and reflecting changes in the age distribution of workers compared to retired persons in China, is that in 2012 for the first time the Chinese labor force decreased, with decreases expected to continue for a number of years (Thai News Service 2013).

As in many countries around the world, until recently rural workers in China generally did not participate in a social security program providing old-age benefits. Traditionally, older persons worked as long as they were able. After that, they lived with their children or received financial support from their children, with the support in China traditionally coming primarily from their sons.

In countries such as China, however, where birth rates have fallen rapidly and where many adult children in rural areas are moving to

217

urban areas to work, the traditional support system for older persons is weakening. As evidence of this, one study finds that families in rural China with fewer children and with fewer sons tend to save more for their retirement (Ebenstein and Leung 2010). These changes increase the need for extending social security coverage to workers in rural areas.

Because most workers in middle- and lower-income countries generally do not participate in social security, extending social security or pension coverage to rural and informal sector workers is arguably the most important problem facing social security programs around the world (Gillion et al. 2000). Worldwide, only 26 percent of the working population is effectively covered by social security old-age benefits programs (ILO 2010). Extending coverage to rural areas and the informal sector is difficult, however, because generally these workers have low and variable cash incomes. For these reasons, they cannot make regular contributions and are limited in the amount they can contribute. At the same time, the transaction costs for contributors, and the transaction and administrative costs for the government, may be sufficiently high to make small contributions economically infeasible.

SOCIAL SECURITY OLD-AGE BENEFITS PROGRAMS IN CHINA

In China, all persons are registered as either urban or rural residents. This classification system (called the *hukuo* system), which is unique to China, is important in the provision of social security old-age benefits. When rural residents move to cities, they retain their registration as rural residents, which affects their access to social security programs in urban areas.

China has three major social security old-age benefits programs, covering three different groups of people: urban areas have two old-age benefits programs, and there is a separate program for rural workers. The central government is considering rules permitting transfer of contributions for workers between the three programs, so that workers who have contributed to more than one program can combine their contributions into one program and receive benefits solely from that program

(*China Daily* 2012). The current pension arrangements make it difficult for workers to move to different areas in China.

Urban Employees' Pension Program

The Urban Employees' Pension Program, established in 1997, is for employed workers in urban areas. It is a two-pillar mandatory program and the only one of the three major programs that is mandatory.

Coverage. In 2010, 36 percent of China's total workforce (urban and rural), or about 264 million workers, was participating in a social security pension plan. One of the reasons for the low coverage rate may be that workers in urban areas cannot afford the required contribution. Complicated procedures for enrolling and lack of trust in the systems may be other explanations (Zheng 2012). Another factor contributing to low coverage rates in urban areas is that rural workers are typically excluded (Oksanen 2012).

Contribution rate. The contribution rate for the Urban Employees' Pension Program is 28 percent, of which the employee contributes 8 percent to an individual account and the employer contributes 20 percent to the social account for the basic pension or social pension, which is a traditional pay-as-you-go defined benefit program.

By 2006, individual accounts programs were established in 10 provinces, but the extension to other provinces stagnated (Zheng 2012). However, government policy of the Ministry of Labor and Social Security at the end of 2005 mandated the extension of the program, with the 8 percent contribution rate, to all provinces, which now has occurred.

The government has not segregated the money in the individual accounts from other social security funds, and has spent much of that money, now in essence converting those accounts to notional accounts to which interest is credited to notional account balances (*Economist* 2012).

Benefits. The Urban Employees' Pension Program provides two benefits: one comes from the individual account, which depends on the contribution level of the individual and the rate of return received on the contribution; and the second comes from the social account, which is a pay-as-you-go defined benefit. All participants must contribute to this program for at least 15 years and arrive at the retirement age before they can apply for the old-age benefit from this program. The average benefit level of this program is 1,721 yuan per month by the end of the year 2012, which is adjusted according to the inflation rate.

Regional variation. The contribution rates of 8 percent plus 20 percent are set by the central government as guidelines, but the exact contribution rate for the social pension can be decided by local government, and can be higher or lower. The contribution rate of Guangzhou City is 12 percent for the social account. Guangzhou has a considerably lower contribution rate for the social account because many younger migrants live in the city, so population aging is not a serious problem. The contribution rate for the social account is 20 percent in Beijing and 22 percent in Shanghai. Shanghai faces serious population aging. The 8 percent contribution rate that workers make for the individual account does not vary across provinces because the account is linked to the individual participant and is not affected by the age structure in the province.

China has 33 provincial-level governments. Beijing, Shanghai, Chongqing, and Tianjin are four municipalities that are treated as provinces. Besides, two Special Administrative Regions—Hong Kong and Macao—are treated as provincial governments. Also, the contribution responsibility is divided among provincial, municipal, and county governments, and the exact proportion shared by different levels of local governments varies in different provinces.

The management of social security funds is fragmented, even within provinces. Only four provinces, two of which are Beijing and Shanghai, have pooled the social security funds. There are more than 2,000 social security funds managed by different government entities (Zheng 2012). The fragmentation of the system has historic origins. In 1949, soon after the founding of the People's Republic of China, a national pension system was established, but trade unions at the local level were given responsibility for administering it. In 1969, during the Cultural Revolution, trade unions were abolished, and state-owned enterprises were given responsibility for managing the pension system (Oksanen 2012).

Urban Residents' Pension Program

Coverage. The Urban Residents' Pension Program, started in 2011, is a voluntary program for urban residents who do not have jobs, are self-employed, work for small businesses, or are migrants from rural areas. It is similar to the National Rural Pension Plan, described later.

Contribution rate. Participants can choose the level of contributions they wish to make within a set range. The central government suggests a contribution range of 100–1,000 yuan per year, which is divided into 10 levels, in 100 yuan increments. But as the Urban Residents' Pension Program is managed by the county or municipal government, the range of contribution levels differs among areas.

Local governments subsidize the contributions of those urban residents who participate in the program through a matching contribution, which varies across provinces. The lowest matching contribution, set by the central government, is 30 yuan per participant per year. Thus, on the minimum contribution of 100 yuan a year, this provides a 30 percent match rate, which, of course, is lower for higher contributions. Local governments, however, can raise the match rate according to the financial ability of the government.

Benefits. The Urban Residents' Pension Program provides two benefits. One comes from the individual account, which depends on the contribution level of the individual, the government matching contribution, and the rate of return received on those contributions. The second benefit is entirely financed by the local governments and is not based on the contributions of participants, other than that they must contribute a minimum of 15 years in order to qualify for it. That benefit is 55 yuan per month, but local governments in high-income provinces can raise this benefit level according to the financial ability of the government.

The governments pay the cost of the noncontributory basic benefit. In the wealthier and eastern provinces of China, the central government subsidizes 50 percent, and the local governments pay the remaining 50 percent of the noncontributory benefit. In the poor middle and western provinces, the central government pays 100 percent of the benefit, and the local governments do not pay for the noncontributory benefit.

National Rural Pension Plan

Out of a population aged 60 and older of 150 million in China, 100 million live in rural areas (*China News* 2009). Thus, 14 percent of the world's population aged 60 and older is covered by China's National Rural Pension Plan.

Coverage

In 2008, only 12 percent of China's rural population was participating in a social security pension system (Oksanen 2012). The voluntary social security pension for rural residents that preceded the new National Rural Pension Plan had contribution and benefit levels that were low, and the program was not subsidized by the government.

Because most rural workers in China were not participating in a social security old-age benefits program, beginning in late 2009, China established the National Rural Pension Plan. It started by extending the program to more than 300 counties on a pilot basis and reached 23 percent of counties by the end of 2010 (Mu 2010). By the end of 2011 it was extended to 60 percent of counties, and it is expected to be in all counties by the end of 2012 (Yang 2012). The launch of the new program was preceded by a period during which different pension arrangements were tried on a pilot basis in different parts of the country to see which arrangement would work best (Cai et al. 2012).

All rural residents aged 16 and older who are not students and who are not enrolled in another pension plan can voluntarily participate in the rural plan. They can participate whether they work in a rural or urban area, whether they are employed or self-employed, and whether they work for pay or do not work for pay. The program is not earnings-related in that anyone meeting the age requirements can contribute to it regardless of earnings, and the amount of the individual's contributions is not related to his or her earnings.

Rural migrants to the city can participate in the Urban Employees' Pension Program if their employers contribute for them. If their employers do not contribute for them, they can choose to participate in the rural pension plan. Because of the high contribution rates, most employers are unwilling to make pension contributions for rural workers who migrate to urban areas. About one-third of the residents in urban areas are migrants from rural workers who do not have full rights to participate in the urban pension systems (Oksanen 2012).

Contributions

The central government has established minimum standards for contributions. The lowest minimum contribution is 100 yuan a year and the lowest maximum contribution is 500 yuan a year (about U.S.$80), with only 5 percent of participants contributing that amount (Dorfman et al. 2013).

While most small counties use the government minimum standards, variation above those standards is permitted and occurs in some places that have a higher standard of living. Wuhan and Shanghai are examples of regional variation in contribution levels. In Wuhan, the minimum contribution is 200 yuan a year and the maximum contribution is 1,200 yuan a year, while in Shanghai the minimum is 500 yuan a year and the maximum is 1,300 yuan a year. In both Wuhan and Shanghai, contributions are permissible between the minimum and maximum in 200 yuan increments. In some prosperous provinces, contributions of up to 2,500 yuan are allowed (Cai et al. 2012). These levels of contributions will be adjusted upward over time to reflect increases in income.

An important feature of this program is that the contribution rate is much lower than in the program for urban workers, where the rate is 28 percent of pay. The contributions to this program are made by individuals and government, with no contribution by employers.

Matching contributions

China provides a matching contribution to encourage rural residents to participate in the National Rural Pension Plan. Because rural residents do not pay income taxes, the lack of a tax incentive for rural residents to participate may explain in part the matching contribution. The subsidy, which is provided by the local government, is 30 yuan a year, where the minimum contribution by the participant is 100 yuan a year (about U.S.$16).

The matching contribution varies in different areas. For example, in Xian City, the matching amount varies from 30 yuan for a contribution of 100 or 200 yuan, to 40 yuan for a contribution of 300 yuan, to 45 yuan for a contribution of 400 yuan, and to 50 yuan for a contribution of 500 yuan. Thus, for contributions above 300 yuan there is an additional government match of 5 yuan for every additional 100 yuan contributed by the participant. In Guangzhou City, which is one of the most developed cities in China, the annual contribution levels (and its matching contribution) are divided into 120 (180) yuan; 360 (420) yuan; 600 (600) yuan, 840 (720) yuan; 1,080 (840) yuan; 1,320 (900) yuan; and 1,560 (960) yuan. The matching contribution is higher than the worker's contribution at the two lowest contribution levels. The subsidy level in Guangzhou is higher than in other cities.

Some commentators have argued that the matching contribution is low (Cai et al. 2012), but experience seems to indicate that it and the other incentives to participate may be adequate. Nearly half of participants make the minimum contribution (Dorfman et al. 2013), which generally provides the highest match rate. The government matching contribution is paid into the person's individual account.

Administrative rules for making contributions

Chinese residents who choose to participate in the rural pension plan have different contribution options, depending on where they live. In some areas, they must make the entire contribution for the year as a single payment in January. In Beijing, however, they can make the contribution between January 1 and December 20. They register to participate with the village government, which is at the lowest level of the hierarchy of government. They must contribute in cash. To be specific, they take cash to the government department in their village to make their annual contribution.

At the end of the contribution period, the village government aggregates all the contributions and sends them to the township government, which then sends the contributions of all the villages to the county government. The rural pension fund is generally managed by the county government, but in some cities, depending on local regulation, the municipal government manages the fund, which is deposited into banks. The central government intends for the funds to eventually be managed by the provincial governments (Cai et al. 2012).

Local governments pay the administrative expenses for the plan, which is a form of subsidy for the program. Those expenses thus are not taken out of the contributions, which would reduce the amount of benefits.

Benefits

While the National Rural Pension Plan is structured as one plan, it provides benefits to two different groups under different but related arrangements. The first is a contributory plan, to which participants must contribute in order to receive benefits when they reach age 60. The second is a noncontributory plan for people who are 60 and older. The relationship between the two parts of the rural plan is explained below.

Participants must contribute for 15 years in order to be eligible to receive benefits. For participants older than age 45 at the start of the system, to qualify for benefits they will need to contribute every year up to age 60 and then make a lump sum payment to cover the shortfall in years of contributions (Cai et al. 2012). It appears, however, that few workers are making lump sum contributions. Workers who are 60 and older can qualify to apply for the noncontributory benefit, which is currently 55 yuan per month in most of the counties in China.

The benefits for participants who have contributed a minimum of 15 years or who have contributed a lump sum equivalent to 15 years of payments have two components. The basic benefit currently is 55 yuan a month. This amount equals one-tenth of the average monthly wage in rural areas in 2011 (Wang and Qing 2012).

That benefit is payable at age 60 to both men and women in most of China. However, the benefit eligibility age varies to some extent, with, for example, women being able to receive the benefit at age 55 in Beijing. The benefit is not means tested, and workers are not required to stop working to receive it. By contrast, for the urban pension men can receive the benefit at age 60, while women can receive it at age 50, or if they are classified as cadres, meaning that they have a management position in their company, the age for benefit receipt is 55. These ages for benefit receipt also are mandatory retirement ages for most urban workers. A small percentage of urban workers, such as some university professors, are exempt from these requirements. In addition, workers in hazardous or dangerous occupations can qualify up to five years earlier than these ages. That exception for hazardous or dangerous occupations is not part of the rural pension system. One study finds an average retirement age in urban areas of 53 (Sin 2005). The benefit eligibility age in the rural pension system, and presumably actual retirement ages, are thus considerably higher than in the urban pension system.

Unlike most social security programs around the world, in China the social security benefit financing differs by region and also involves financing in part by local governments. The basic benefit is financed by the central government in the central and western parts of the country, but in the more prosperous eastern provinces it is financed half by the central government and half by the local governments (Lei, Zhang, and Zhao 2011). Localities can increase the benefit amount above 55 yuan a month if they have the financial resources to do so. The average benefit received by beneficiaries is 74 yuan a month (Yang 2012), which is not financed by the contributions of participants. This benefit represents the first time that the Chinese government has made a major financial commitment to a rural pension system (Shen and Williamson 2010).

In addition, a defined contribution benefit is provided based on the accumulation in the participant's individual account from the participant's contributions, government matching contributions, and accrued investment returns. That benefit is paid monthly and equals the individual account at age 60 divided by 139, which is the same factor used for calculating monthly pensions from the individual accounts in the urban plans. The divisor depends on the age at which the person collects benefits, with it being higher at lower ages. It is 195 for a woman retiring at age 50 and 170 for a woman retiring at age 55 in the urban pension system. Generally, men cannot collect retirement benefits at those ages. Individuals do not need to stop working to receive this benefit from the rural pension plan.

The benefit payment is not limited to the amount in the individual account, but it is guaranteed by the government for life and thus is paid as an annuity. If a person dies before receiving the full amount in his or her personal account, the spouse receives the remaining amount, and if the spouse is not surviving then the children. Otherwise, the system does not provide a benefit to a surviving spouse.

Noncontributory benefit

Persons aged 60 and older who have not qualified for another pension can receive the basic benefit of 55 yuan a month if all their children are contributing to the rural pension, regardless of whether the children are working. The benefits will be adjusted for inflation, but the exact adjustment mechanism has not yet been determined (Cai et al. 2012).

This requirement on the adult children is called "family binding." The incentive may work particularly well in China, which has a strong tradition of adult children taking care of their older parents. If the older persons do not have children, they automatically qualify. The central government requires that all the recipients' children contribute, but the enforcement is done at the local level. At the local level, however, the incentive to receive the central government subsidy for benefits for people aged 60 and older works against the strict enforcement of this requirement, so that some local governments may qualify all persons aged 60 and older.

Regional variations

China has a number of levels in the hierarchy of government. From lowest to highest, they are village, township, county or district, municipal, provincial, and central. The National Rural Pension Plan is sponsored by the central government and run by the county or municipal government, with oversight from the Ministry of Human Resources and Social Security.

The central government provides guidelines for the pension systems in China, but for the rural pension system, the details, including contribution rates, are determined at the level of the county or district government. It is called the county government in rural areas and the district government in urban areas. In some areas, the county or district government has established the system exactly according to the central government guidelines, while in other areas the systems vary. Thus, the systems may vary within provinces.

Combined Urban and Rural Programs

Some cities, such as Wuhan, did not establish the Urban Residents' Pension Program. Instead in 2011, Wuhan established a unified Pension Plan for Rural and Urban Residents. The plan covers those who live in urban areas and do not have jobs and all those in the rural areas. Neither group can get contributions from employers, but they do receive the government matching contribution. This is a reform trend for counties and cities to establish a unified pension program for both urban and rural residents who do not have formal jobs in China.

Government Employees' Pensions

Government employees and employees in government-owned enterprises in China are covered by a separate pension system, paid for out of general revenues. That system costs 0.7 percent of GDP per year. About 8 percent of covered participants are in that system. In addition to these programs, hundreds of thousands of plans have been established by local municipalities to meet the needs of migrant workers from rural areas or of particular industrial zones (Zheng 2012).

Hong Kong's Mandatory Provident Fund

Hong Kong has a separate old-age benefits system. All workers are required to join the Mandatory Provident Fund, which is a system of defined contribution plans. Employees earning between HK$6,500 (U.S.$839) and HK$25,000 (U.S.$3,226) monthly (in 2012) pay 5 percent of their earnings, with employers also paying 5 percent (U.S. Social Security Administration 2012).[2] The contributions go to a financial service provider chosen by the employer. As of November 2012, employees can choose the service provider for their contributions. Workers receive benefits as a lump sum. Because of savings accumulated through this program, Hong Kong has a high ratio of pension assets to GDP of 32.5 percent, which compares to a simple average for OECD countries of 33.9 percent (OECD 2012).

FINANCING ISSUES

Individual Account Benefits

Concerning the financing of the individual account benefit, the divisor of 139 for benefits received at age 60 is the key parameter in determining the generosity of the individual account benefit. Thus, in assessing the financing of those benefits, it is important to determine whether that divisor provides benefits that are adequately financed, or alternatively, whether the benefits are overly generous. When financial planners in the United States advise individual account holders about the sustainable amount that a retiree can withdraw from an account without overly risking that they will run out of money, they often advise that a retiree can withdraw 4 percent of the initial account balance, adjusted for inflation, each year (McKenzie and Turner 2012). The 4 percent amount is designed to provide an inflation-indexed withdrawal. That advice depends on the life expectancy of the individual and the expected rate of return received on the account. It would be a higher percentage for a shorter life expectancy and a higher expected rate of return. If the amount were used instead to purchase an annuity, which is a better comparison, it would be equivalent to a withdrawal of 5.7 percent, based on male annuity rates, no inflation adjustment of benefits, and the low interest rates available in 2013. The withdrawal rate would be lower than 5.7 percent for a benefit that was adjusted for inflation.

The divisor of 139 for monthly benefits is equivalent to withdrawing 8.6 percent of the initial account balance each year. Thus, it appears that the benefit divisor of 139 should be increased if the goal is to have a system that is financed primarily by the contributions of participants. That change would result in lower benefits, but it would be more consistent with a sustainable, self-funding pension system. By one analysis, county governments will be liable for 40 percent of the payments from the individual account pensions (Herd, Wu, and Koen 2010).

The Overall Expense of Pensions

In 2011, 61 percent of the revenues for the rural pension system overall came from government subsidies (Wang and Qing 2012). The individual pays for none of the basic benefit for parents and for none of his or her own basic benefit. The cost to the central government of providing the noncontributory benefit to all the 100 million rural persons currently aged 60 and older would be about 2 percent of the government budget (Shen and Williamson 2010). The government also subsidizes a substantial portion of the individual account benefit. This cost is borne by local governments. Overall, the individuals will only pay at most 18 percent of the cost of their pensions, with the government paying the rest (Herd, Wu, and Koen 2010).

The government is thus incurring what appear to be substantial unfunded liabilities for the social security pension systems (Reuters 2012). Most countries have pay-as-you-go social security systems with unfunded liabilities, thus unfunded liabilities are a common feature. China, however, differs from many countries in that it has a very high savings rate. Thus, there may be more justification for unfunded liabilities in China than in other countries. In addition, the central government has large nonpension reserves that could be used in the future to help pay for these liabilities (*Economist* 2012).

In comparison to programs in other countries, the total cost of the rural pension program in China is relatively low at 0.22 percent of GDP. This compares, for example, to 0.38 percent of GDP for a means-tested program in Chile (Herd, Wu, and Koen 2010). Thus, the program combines a relative low cost, due to low benefits, and a high degree of government subsidy, due to the relatively small amount contributed by participants.

Investment Policy Issues

In China, the rate of return on provincial urban pension funds has averaged 2 percent over the last 10 years, which is less than the rate of inflation over that period. However, in 2012 the national government announced a pilot program that would permit the 13 provinces that manage pension funds for individual accounts to invest in domestic equities. The council that manages the National Social Security Fund, which is China's public pension reserve fund, will act as the trustee and principal investor of each of these funds. The amount invested this way could be as much as 360 billion yuan (U.S.$57 billion), roughly 20 percent of the funds' combined total assets under management (U.S. Social Security Administration 2012).

The National Social Security Fund (NSFF) was established in 2000 to support China's future social security expenditures. The NSSF receives money from government allocations from a government lottery and from the sale of state-owned enterprises. It is a strategic reserve fund designed to help pay for future social security expenditures during future periods of rapid aging.

Since 2006, the NSSF has managed the investments of the individual account funds of nine provinces, municipalities, and autonomous regions. As of December 31, 2011, the NSSF had net assets of 838.6 billion yuan. Included in that, the value of the individual account funds managed by the NSSF is 65.8 billion yuan. Domestic fixed income investments accounted for 51 percent of the investments (National Council for Social Security Fund 2012). That percentage is relatively high for a fund of this type.

CONCLUSION

While social security old-age benefit programs around the world generally are uniform national programs, at least for the group of workers they cover, the three main programs in China have regional variations that make the program more complex, but that also relate to the regional differences in standard of living in the country. The financing of the programs varies across regions, with the central government providing all of the financing for the basic benefit in the central and western parts of the country, but half of the financing, with the local government providing the other half, in the more prosperous eastern provinces. The level of contributions by participants and the level of benefits they receive also vary across regions.

China has a program for rural workers that has features that may provide lessons for other countries wishing to extend pension coverage to the rural and informal sectors. It is a voluntary program, but by providing substantial government subsidies, it encourages coverage of workers who do not pay income taxes and thus have no tax incentive to participate. As a further incentive, old-age benefits are provided to the parents of participants who contribute when all the adult children in a family are participating in the program. Only a single contribution per year is required, and participants can choose from a range of contribution levels.

Notes

We have received helpful comments from Heikki Oksanen and David Rajnes. In this chapter, we follow the western convention of listing Chinese family names as the second name, with the given name the first name. The official name of China is the People's Republic of China.

1. The official name of Chinese currency is renminbi (RMB). The basic unit of the currency is yuan, which are the units used in this chapter. Hong Kong uses a different currency.
2. The dollar limits are adjusted upward over time.

References

Cai, Fang, John Giles, Philip O'Keefe, and Dewen Wang. 2012. *The Elderly and Old-age Support in Rural China: Challenges and Prospects.* Beijing: World Bank. http://issuu.com/world.bank.publications/docs/978082138685 9?mode=window&pageNumber=20 (accessed April 16, 2013).

China Daily. 2012. "Transfer of Pensions." November 28. http://www.china daily.com.cn/cndy/2012-11/28/content_15964931.htm (accessed April 16, 2013).

China News. 2009. "China Will Establish New Rural Pension Scheme." March 4.

Dorfman, Mark C., Dewen Wang, Philip O'Keefe, and Jie Cheng. 2013. "China's Pension Schemes for Urban and Rural Residents." In *Matching Contributions for Pensions: A Review of International Experience*, R. Hinz, R. Holzmann, D. Tuesta, and N. Takayama, eds. Washington, DC: World Bank, pp. 217–242.

Ebenstein, Avraham, and Steven Leung. 2010. "Son Preference and Access to Social Insurance: Evidence from China's Rural Pension Program." *Population and Development Review* 36(1): 47–70.

Economist. 2012. "Social Security with Chinese Characteristics." August 11. http://www.economist.com/node/21560259 (accessed April 16, 2013).

Gillion, Colin, John A. Turner, Clive Bailey, and Denis Latulippe. 2000. *Social Security Pensions: Development and Reform.* Geneva: International Labour Office.

Herd, Richard, Yu-Wei Hu, and Vincent Koen. 2010. "Providing Greater Old-Age Security in China." OECD Economics Department Working Paper No. 750. February 23. Paris: OECD. http://search.oecd.org/officialdocuments/display

documentpdf/?doclanguage=en&cote=eco/wkp(2010)6 (accessed April 16, 2013).

International Labour Organisation (ILO). 2010. "World Social Security Report 2010/11: Providing Coverage in Times of Crisis and Beyond." Geneva: ILO. http://www.ilo.org/gimi/gess/ShowTheme.do?tid=1985 (accessed April 16, 2013).

Lei, Xiaoyan, Chuanchuan Zhang, and Yaohui Zhao. 2011. "Incentive Problems in China's New Rural Pension Program." Beijing: Beijing University. http://www.iza.org/conference_files/CIER2011/lei_x6071.pdf (accessed April 16, 2013).

McKenzie, (Sandy) George, and John A. Turner. 2012. "Pitfalls Workers Face in Planning for Retirement." AARP Public Policy Institute Working Paper. Washington, DC: Association for the Advancement of Retired Persons.

Ministry of Human Resources and Social Security. 2012. "Statistics." Beijing: Ministry of Human Resources and Social Security.

Mu, Xuequan. 2010. "Chinese Farmers Turn to Old-age Pension for Financial Support during Golden Years." *EnglishNews*, December 21. http://news.xinhuanet.com/english2010/china/2010-12/21/c_13658874.htm (accessed April 16, 2013).

National Council for Social Security Fund. 2012. "About the National Council for Social Security Fund." Beijing: National Council for Social Security Fund. http://www.ssf.gov.cn/Eng_Introduction/201206/t20120620_5603.html (accessed April 16, 2013).

Oksanen, Heikki. 2012. "China: Pension Reform for an Aging Economy." In *Nonfinancial Defined Contribution Pension Schemes in a Changing Pension World Volume 1: Progress, Lessons and Implementation*, Robert Holzmann, Edward Palmer, and David Robalino, eds. Washington, DC: World Bank, pp. 213–255. https://openknowledge.worldbank.org/bitstream/handle/109 86/9378/705940PUB0EPI006792B09780821388488.pdf?sequence=1 (accessed April 16, 2013).

Organisation for Economic Co-operation and Development (OECD). 2012. *Pension Markets in Focus*. 9(September): 1–28. http://www.oecd.org/daf/financialmarketsinsuranceandpensions/privatepensions/PensionMarkets InFocus2012.pdf (accessed April 16, 2013).

Reuters. 2012. "China Pension Fund Gap to Top 80 Percent of 2011 GDP by 2050." December 13. http://www.reuters.com/article/2012/12/13/china -economy-pension-idUSL4N09N2QH20121213 (accessed April 16, 2013).

Shen, Ce, and John B. Williamson. 2010. "China's New Rural Pension Scheme: Can It Be Improved?" *International Journal of Sociology and Social Policy* 30(5/6): 239–250.

Sin, Y. 2005. "China: Pension Liabilities and Reform Options for Old-age Insurance." Working Paper No. 2005-1. Washington, DC: World Bank.

Thai News Service. 2013. "China: China's Demographic Dividend Disappearing." January 31.

United Nations (UN). 2007. "World Economic and Social Survey: In Search of New Development Finance." New York: United Nations. www.un.org/esa/policy/wess/ (accessed April 16, 2013).

U.S. Social Security Administration. 2012. "International Update—China." February. Washington, DC: U.S. Social Security Administration. http://www.ssa.gov/policy/docs/progdesc/intl_update/2012-02/index.html#china (accessed April 16, 2013).

Wang, Aileen, and Koh Gui Qing. 2012. "Analysis: China Slides Faster Into Pensions Black Hole." Reuters, October 1. http://www.reuters.com/article/2012/10/01/us-china-pensions-idUSBRE88T0JP20121001 (accessed April 16, 2013).

Yang, Zhao. 2012. "Age Pension for Rural Seniors Lags Behind." CRIEnglish. July 13. http://english.cri.cn/7146/2012/07/13/2702s711692.htm (accessed April 16, 2013).

Zheng, Bingwen. 2012. "China: An Innovative Hybrid Pension Design Proposal." In Nonfinancial Defined Contribution Pension Schemes in a Changing Pension World: Progress, Lessons and Implementation, Robert Holzmann, Edward Palmer, and David Robalino, eds. Washington, DC: World Bank, pp. 189–209. https://openknowledge.worldbank.org/bitstream/handle/10986/9378/705940PUB0EPI0067902B09780821388488.pdf?sequence=1 (accessed April 16, 2013).

11

Social Security and Pensions in East Africa

John A. Turner
Pension Policy Center

Five countries in East Africa have formed the East African Community (EAC)—Kenya, Tanzania, Uganda, Burundi, and Rwanda. These countries include both Anglophone and Francophone Africa, though English is the official language of the EAC. They have a total population of more than 140 million, which is more than one-tenth of the population of Africa. The EAC, headquartered in Arusha, Tanzania, was formed in 2000 with Kenya, Uganda, and Tanzania; Rwanda and Burundi joined in 2007. South Sudan, Sudan, Zambia, Malawi, and the Democratic Republic of the Congo have indicated an interest in joining. While the EAC is already an important regional organization, if these countries join, the EAC would include more than one-fifth of the population of Africa.

The EAC is seeking greater integration of the five countries in order to facilitate the development of a prosperous and peaceful East Africa. Integration goals include facilitating the movement of workers, capital, and commerce across countries, including developing a free trade zone. Facilitating the movement of workers raises issues of pension and social security portability across countries. It also involves harmonizing the social security and pension systems and laws in the five countries. The EAC has a committee responsible for these issues, the Capital Markets, Insurance and Pensions Committee.

In 2010, the EAC established the Common Market Protocol as a step toward greater economic integration, including the free movement of workers. The citizens of any of the five countries can work or live in any of the other countries and participate in the social security program of the new country of residence. The academic and professional qualifi-

235

cations of any country in the EAC are recognized in the other countries (Ministry of East African Community Affairs 2011).

The EAC countries have the stated goal of adopting a common currency, and in 2012 they are considering a policy that would set them on the path to having a common currency within 10 years. They eventually may even form a federation as a single country in order to facilitate their development through greater economies of scale and a larger free-trade area. The development of funded pensions can aid in the development of capital markets in the region, providing a source of funds for investments in government debt and corporate debt and equity.

This chapter discusses the pension and social security old-age benefit systems in the EAC, including discussing areas in need of reform. It first discusses mandatory social security systems, and then various aspects of employer-provided pensions, including pension regulators, the tax treatment of pensions, the types of pensions provided in the private sector, and pensions for public sector workers. It discusses attempts to extend coverage to more workers.

SOCIAL SECURITY

Overview

All the mandatory social security programs in the region are called the National Social Security Fund (NSSF) (Table 11.1). Social security pensions in East Africa cover only a small percentage of the workforce, mainly those in government employment. Tanzania, Uganda, Rwanda, and Burundi cover less than 10 percent of their populations, while Kenya

Table 11.1 Name of Primary Social Security Fund, 2012

Country	Name of plan
Burundi	National Social Security Fund
Kenya	National Social Security Fund
Rwanda	Social Security Fund of Rwanda
Tanzania	National Social Security Fund
Uganda	National Social Security Fund

covers 15 percent (Barya 2011). Lack of coverage is due in part to contribution evasion by employers and employees who are covered under the law but who do not contribute. Also, coverage for self-employed workers is generally voluntary, and workers in the informal sector generally are not covered (Table 11.2). Most people in old age depend on traditional arrangements through their families or clans.

Table 11.2 Workers Not Covered by Social Security, 2012

Country	Workers not covered
Burundi	Self employed
Kenya	Employers with less than five employees; persons earning less than Kshs1,000 a month
Rwanda	Self-employed
Tanzania	Self-employed; household workers
Uganda	Employers with less than five employees; persons aged 55 and older

Some programs for government employees have converted from noncontributory to contributory, meaning that government employees contribute toward their funding. Some programs have also moved from pay-as-you-go toward funding. The regulatory authority over the programs is in nearly all cases under the Ministry of Finance rather than the Ministry of Labor.

Countries in the region formerly under the influence of the British as colonies (Tanzania, Kenya) or protectorates (Uganda) have had provident funds, which are defined contribution plans that provide lump sum benefits (Table 11.3). As defined contribution plans, they are funded. Countries around the world with those systems have tended to move away from them and switch to social insurance pension systems,

Table 11.3 Type of Social Security Fund, 2012

Country	Type of social security fund
Burundi	Social insurance
Kenya	Provident fund
Rwanda	Social insurance
Tanzania	Social insurance
Uganda	Provident fund

which are defined benefit systems where benefits are based on a benefit formula. While Tanzania has converted its provident fund to a social insurance defined benefit pension, Kenya is planning to convert their provident funds to a defined contribution pension. Uganda is considering doing the same. Provident funds have the disadvantage that they do not provide a stream of benefits that protects the recipient against poverty during old age, thus providing no insurance against an unexpectedly long lifetime. A further problem with provident funds is that frequently the interest rate declared on the fund is less than the inflation rate, which, combined with high administrative costs, has resulted in low benefits (Gillion et al. 2000).

The social security systems of the region generally have retirement ages that are low by international standards (Table 11.4). Mandatory retirement at low ages in some countries is another problem. The countries need to adopt social security and pension programs that encourage work of skilled persons at older ages in order to make better use of their human resources.

Some of the social security programs in the region have high administrative expenses. Some funded systems managed by government agencies have made questionable investments, resulting in financial losses to the funds. Perhaps relating in part to those two problems, contribution evasion by employees and employers is also a major problem.

In some countries, public employees are covered under a plan that is different from private sector employees. Some countries have multiple programs for private sector employees (Table 11.5). Some countries have several different plans for different sectors of public employees, creating a need for reform that would harmonize the plans and provide equal treatment for all citizens. Preferential treatment of government employees is an issue in some countries. They have lower contribution

Table 11.4 Early Retirement Age for Social Security Old Age Benefits, 2012

Country	Early retirement age
Burundi	60
Kenya	50
Rwanda	55
Tanzania	Any age
Uganda	45

Table 11.5 National Social Security Fund or Multiple Funds, 2012

Country	Single or multiple funds
Burundi	Single
Kenya	Single
Rwanda	Single
Tanzania	Multiple
Uganda	Multiple

rates, a lower retirement age, and extremely generous benefits. Members of parliament and judges generally are covered by preferential pensions. In some countries, the generosity of the pensions for public service employees is further enhanced in that they are not subject to taxation.

Some countries in the region allow workers and employers to opt out of the mandatory social security program as long as they participate in an alternative program. It has been thought that having competitors for the national program would encourage greater efficiency and lower costs.

In order to encourage the mobility of workers across countries, social security systems need to provide portability so that workers can combine work in different countries in order to meet qualifying conditions to receive benefits (Table 11.6). In some countries, workers must work for a minimum of 15 years to qualify for benefits. A proposed law in Kenya in 2012 would enable workers working temporarily in other countries in the EAC to continue participating in the social security program in Kenya. It would also encourage the development of agreements with other EAC countries so that social security contributions in the other countries would be sent to Kenya for Kenyan workers who returned to Kenya when they retired (Mutegi 2012).

Table 11.6 Number of Years for Vesting in Social Security Fund, 2012

Country	Number of years
Burundi	15
Kenya	3
Rwanda	15
Tanzania	15

The EAC countries are members of several other regional organizations, which have overlapping interests and goals concerning pensions, and which may not include all of the EAC countries. These include the East and Central African Social Security Association (ECASSA), which was formed in 2007, and which also includes Zambia (ECASSA 2012). ECASSA, headquartered in Nairobi, Kenya, attempts to help the countries meet common challenges they face in their social security systems, including low coverage. It also encourages the development of multicountry agreements facilitating the transfer of social security credits across countries in the region.[1]

The remainder of this section discusses the social security and mandatory government-provided systems in each of the countries.

Kenya

Types of plans

Kenya has a provident fund for private sector employees that was established in 1965. In 2011, 4.6 million people were registered, of whom 1.2 million were active (EAC 2011). The total value of assets in this program exceeds the total value of funds in mandatory programs in the other four countries combined (Katto 2012). As of 2012, legislation converts this fund to a defined contribution pension fund.

Kenya has four different types of pension programs: 1) the NSSF, for private sector workers; 2) the Civil Service Pension Program, for government workers; 3) employer-provided occupational pensions, for private sector workers; and 4) individual pension programs, for private sector workers. The employer-provided occupational pensions account for 61 percent of total assets, the NSSF accounts for 38 percent, and individual pension programs account for 1 percent. The Civil Service Pension Program is unfunded. The accumulated assets in the funded programs equal 20 percent of GDP, exceeding the level in Germany, Italy, and Sweden in the early twenty-first century (Odundo 2004).

Financing

All private sector employers with at least five employees must register and pay contributions to the NSSF for their employees. These employers are responsible for assuring that all their employees are registered and that contributions are paid on their behalf. Other employers may voluntarily participate. Participation is voluntary for people who are self-employed. Data indicate that 10 percent of the population are paid employees (Machira 2011).

Both the employer and the employee contribute 5 percent of earnings, up to 200 shillings a month. Because of a low ceiling on earnings, most people contribute the maximum. However, a bill proposed in 2012 would raise the contribution of both employer and employee to 6 percent and convert the fund from a provident fund to a social security fund (*Daily Nation* 2012).

A major problem with the system has been a low ceiling on earnings, which has resulted in low contributions. In 2008, the low ceiling resulted in the maximum contribution equaling 1.3 percent of average pay. The ceiling is low because it is not adjusted for inflation and the growth of earnings. As of 2008, it had only been adjusted twice since 1965, in 1997 and 2001 (Raichura 2008).

Participants making mandatory contributions can increase their savings by also making voluntary contributions. The NSSF is encouraging employers to make contributions electronically, including through mobile phones. The NSSF, however, has had a problem correctly allocating contributions to the accounts of workers and as of 2008 had a large suspense account of unallocated contributions. The NSSF is responsible for collecting contributions, but an alternative approach would be collection through the tax collecting agency, the Kenya Revenue Authority (Raichura 2008).

In 2011, the NSSF transferred the management of 65 percent of its assets to external fund managers. Previously, the investment of all the funds had been managed by the government, where it had been subject to pressure to make investments that would benefit high government officials (Mchira and Ngigi 2012).

Benefits

As is typical of provident funds, the NSSF provides a single lump sum benefit rather than a pension benefit in the form of an annuity. Proposals for conversion to a social insurance system have been considered, but priority has been given to the development of the Retirement Benefits Authority, which regulates the activities of all private sector retirement benefit plans, and is discussed later in the chapter.

Benefits can be claimed at age 55 for persons who have stopped working (NSSF 2012). Workers are also eligible for a benefit at age 50, called the withdrawal benefit, if they have left regular paid employment. The social security program also provides a disability (invalidity) benefit at any age for full disability preventing work, and at age 50 for a partial disability. An emigration grant is available for people permanently emigrating from Kenya.

Benefits are low for several reasons. The low ceiling on contributions is one cause. The ceiling in 2011 was Ksh4,000 a month, or about U.S.$50. The ceiling should be raised and adjusted in line with inflation or the growth of earnings in order to assure that benefits are more adequate. In addition, the NSSF has had high administrative expenses relative to the low level of contributions it collects—they have exceeded 50 percent of contributions. Associated with this problem, some service providers to the NSSF have paid kickbacks to government officials in order to be chosen.

A minimum rate of return of 5 percent annually is guaranteed, so the fund can at times have an unfunded liability, even though it is a defined contribution plan (EAC 2011). Before 2009, the minimum guaranteed rate was 2.5 percent. That low rate provided a disincentive for participation in the fund (Raichura 2008). There is little connection between the crediting rate and the investment rate of return earned, with sometimes the crediting rate being higher, but frequently being lower, than the investment rate of return.

A pilot program is providing noncontributory benefits for people aged 65 and older because most people in that age group do not qualify for benefits based on their having made contributions while working.

Reform

One of the problems with implementing reforms relating to the NSSF is that it is under the Labour Ministry, while the Retirement Benefits Authority that regulates it is under the Finance Ministry (Odundo 2004).

As of 2012, legislation proposes converting the NSSF from a provident fund to an insurance fund. A defined contribution plan would be retained for the formal sector, while a defined benefit plan would be instituted for the informal sector. Contributions would be raised from 10 percent to 12 percent of pay, split evenly between the employer and employee. An important change is that there would be no ceiling on pay covered by the program, solving a problem with the current system, which has a low ceiling on pay. This program would also provide unemployment benefits, disability benefits, and maternity leave. The new program would provide annuity benefits rather than a single lump sum, as is provided in the current program.

Tanzania

Tanzania is composed of two distinct geographical and administrative areas. Tanzania mainland and Zanzibar, which is a nearby archipelago off the coast in the Indian Ocean, have two separate social security funds. Under the agreement forming the union between Tanganyika and Zanzibar, provision of social security benefits is not a union function (Barya 2011).

Types of plans

Tanzania mainland has a social insurance system for the private sector. It has about 460,000 active members (Mutero 2010). In 1997, that fund replaced the National Provident Fund, which had been established in 1964. The NSSF covers private sector employees, parastatal employees, and nonpensionable government employees. The NSSF has launched a campaign to encourage private sector workers to participate, particularly women and workers in the informal sector.

The NSSF and several other pension funds, including the Parastatal Pension Fund, are placed for administrative purposes under the Ministry of Labour and Youth Employment (Simbeye 2012). The Parastatal Pension Fund is for employees in government controlled enterprises, but it has also extended its coverage to private sector employees who wish to participate. It has two pension programs and about 100,000 active members (Mutero 2010). The Traditional Pension Program, a defined benefit program, is for employees of government owned enterprises. The Deposit Administration Program, a defined contribution program, is for other private sector workers (International Labour Organization 2012).

The NSSF and the Parastatal Pension Fund are the two largest publicly managed pension funds in Tanzania (Assad and Selemani, n.d.). Tanzania has six publicly managed mandatory pension funds. The other four are the Public Service Pension Fund, the Government Employees Provident Fund, the Local Authorities Pensions Fund, and the Zanzibar Social Security Fund (Ngotezi 2010). With the exception of the Government Employees Provident Fund, all the funds are defined benefit plans. The Local Authorities Pension Fund was converted from a provident fund in 2005. It has about 70,000 active members (Mutero 2010).

Except for the Zanzibar Social Security Fund, all funds are under the supervision of the Social Security Regulatory Authority, which is under the Ministry of Finance. The Ministry of Labour and Employment provides general supervision over the NSSF (International Organisation of Pension Supervisors [IOPS] 2011b).

The Government Employees Provident Fund enrolls people who work for the government on contracts, who then switch to the Public Service Pension Fund if they become permanent employees. Their contributions are transferred from the Government Employees Provident Fund to the Public Service Pension Fund when they make that change. These programs cover about 5 percent of the labor force (IOPS 2011b). Special noncontributory (the participant does not contribute) systems have been established for the military and for political leaders (IOPS 2011b). In order to encourage competition across programs, workers can choose to participate in any of the six government-managed pension programs.

Financing

In Tanzania, the total (employer plus employee) contribution rate for social security is 20 percent, of which the employee cannot contribute more than 10 percent. This contribution rate is considerably higher than for the other countries in the region (Table 11.7). The employee and employer contribution rate varies across plans. The provident fund that preceded the NSSF had a contribution rate of 20 percent, but it was decided that a rate of 10 percent for a funded pension system would be adequate. Rather than reduce the contribution rate, Tanzania decided to retain the provident fund at a lower contribution rate and then phase it out as other social security benefits were introduced (Gillion et al. 2000).

For the NSSF, both the employer and employee contribute 10 percent of earnings, but this contribution also funds medical benefits

Table 11.7 Social Security Contribution Rates, 2012 (%)

Country	Total	Employee	Employer
Burundi	10	4	6
Kenya	10	5	5
Rwanda	6	3	3
Tanzania	20	10	10
Uganda	6	3	3

and other nonretirement benefits. Self-employed persons who voluntarily join the NSSF contribute 20 percent of their declared earnings. This high contribution rate discourages self-employed persons from participating. It also discourages the provision of employer-provided pensions. Employees in the Parastatal Pension Fund also contribute 10 percent of their earnings. However, government employees receive preferential treatment. Participants to the Public Service Pension Fund and the Local Authorities Pension Fund only contribute 5 percent of their earnings (IOPS 2011b).The NSSF invests its money in projects and investments in Tanzania, primarily in interest-bearing investments, such as government and corporate bonds, money market investments, and loans (NSSF, Tanzania 2010a).

Benefits

For the NSSF, benefits can be claimed at age 55 with 180 months (15 years) of contributions. However, workers can collect their benefits before retirement age—they can claim benefits at any age as long as the person has not worked for six months. In 2012, the Social Security Regulatory Authority (SSRA) proposed ending this provision, called withdrawal benefits. Public opposition to ending withdrawal benefits forced the SSRA to withdraw its proposal. Compulsory retirement occurs at age 60 (NSSF, Tanzania 2010b).

Old-age pension benefits from the NSSF are paid in two parts. An initial lump sum benefit equals 24 multiplied by the monthly benefit. In addition, monthly benefits are paid. Benefits received between ages 55 and 59 are reduced by 0.5 percent for every year before age 60. This reduction is far less than what would be actuarially fair, which would be more like 6 percent, providing an incentive to take benefits at earlier ages. Thus, the NSSF discourages work in paid employment at older ages.

Zanzibar

The Zanzibar Social Security Fund was established in 1998, which was the last social security system established in the region. The Zanzibar Social Security Fund covers both public and private sector employees. As of 2006, it covered about 35,000 workers (EAC 2011). Employees contribute 5 percent and employers contribute 10 percent of earnings. Thus, the contribution rate for the Zanzibar Social Security Fund is less than the rate for the Social Security Fund of Tanzania. Workers can receive retirement benefits at age 60, which is the mandatory retirement age, but workers leaving employment can receive benefits at age 55.

Uganda

Types of plans

Uganda has a provident fund that was established in 1967. It covers all private sector employees working for employers with five or more employees. Membership is voluntary for employers with less than five employees. Workers between the ages of 16 and 55 participate. As of 2011, the NSSF had about 500,000 registered members and 400,000 active contributors, and covers about 3.5 percent of the working population (Katto 2012). Civil servants are covered under the Public Service Pension Program, while members of the military are covered under the Uganda Post Defense Forces program.

Financing

For the NSSF, the employer contributes 10 percent of earnings and the employee contributes 5 percent, with no ceiling on earnings (Wafuja 2011). Contribution evasion is widespread, with most eligible employers and employees not contributing. To deal with this problem, in 2011 the NSSF offered defaulters a temporary amnesty period, during which they could pay contributions they owed without having to pay the 10 percent interest on late payments (Wafuja 2011).

The NSSF has misused funds it is entrusted for investing. For example, it has purchased property from a government minister at an inflated price (Barya 2011). In addition, it has fraudulently paid large amounts to "ghost" beneficiaries, with the money actually being paid to high government officials. In 2012, the Ugandan government temporarily suspended payment of benefits while it attempted to resolve the issue. In 2012, the NSSF was considering loaning U.S.$400 million, or about one-third of its funds, to the government to help pay for the construction of roads (Reuters 2012).

Benefits

Benefits from the NSSF can be claimed at age 55 as a lump sum payment, whether or not the person has stopped working, or at age 50 if the person has been out of employment for at least a year. The NSSF also provides a disability benefit, a survivors' benefit, and an emigration benefit for persons permanently leaving the country (NSSF, Uganda 2012).

Each year interest is credited to each worker's account, based on the rate of return received on the national fund. Benefits are based on the amount contributed by the worker and the worker's employer to the fund and the interest rate credited to the fund. In 2011, the NSSF cut the crediting rate from 7 percent to 6 percent, in part because of a lawsuit against the fund for cancellation of a building contract. In that year, the inflation rate was 28 percent, so the real value of the future benefits for workers declined by more than 20 percent (Ojambo 2011). The NSSF has provided a negative rate of real return (subtracting the inflation rate) in most years since its founding.

A pilot program funded by the World Bank is providing non-contributory benefits to persons aged 70 and older in some provinces.

Reform

The NSSF is being converted from a provident fund that only provided lump sum payments to a pension plan that will either be a defined benefit plan or a defined contribution plan, with that decision currently pending.

In order to encourage greater competition in the provision of retirement benefits, plans are in the works to allow other programs to compete, allowing workers to opt out of the NSSF and participate in another program (Kiwanuka 2012). During a phase-in period, workers will be required to make a reduced contribution to the NSSF. It was thought that this policy would reduce costs and increase efficiency.

Rwanda

Types of plans

Rwanda's social insurance system, founded in 1956, is called the Social Security Fund of Rwanda and is a funded defined benefit program. The Rwanda Social Security Board was formed by the merger of the Rwanda Medical Insurance and the Social Security Fund of Rwanda. It covers all public and private sector employees (IOPS 2011a).

Financing

The employer and the employee both contribute 3 percent. Contributions also provide insurance coverage against occupational injuries. Self-employed persons can be voluntarily covered, and they pay 6 percent of earnings. In 2011, it had 300,000 active members (EAC 2011), or about 5 percent of the employed workforce (National Bank of Rwanda 2008).

In Rwanda, self-employed groups can contribute to the social security fund as a federation. An example is the Rwanda Federation of Motorcyclists' Cooperatives, which promotes the use of motorcycles as taxis. Its 10,000 members send contributions to the federation each month, 8 percent of which goes toward social security (Kamndaya 2011).

Benefits

Benefits can be claimed at age 55 if the person has ceased working and has at least 15 years of contributions. A bill in 2012 in Parliament proposed raising the age to 60 (Karuhanga 2012). For people who have worked at least 15 years, the retirement benefit is 30 percent of the average of the final 3 or 5 years of work, whichever average is higher, plus 2 percent for every year of work beyond 15 years. Thus, for someone who had worked and contributed for 16 years, the benefit would be 32 percent of the average of the final 3 or 5 years of work (Rwanda Social Security Board 2012).

Burundi

Types of plans

Burundi's social insurance system was established in 1962 under the Minister of Public Functions, Work and Social Security. It covers both private and public sector employees.

Financing

The employer contributes 6 percent of earnings and the employee contributes 4 percent, for a total of 10 percent, up from 6.5 percent in 2010. The total contribution rate for military personnel is 14.6 percent, up from a rate of 9.5 percent in 2010. The contribution rates were raised because an actuarial study indicated that the previous contribution rates were not adequate to pay for the benefits promised (EAC 2011). Civil servants and judges have a special system.

Benefits

Benefits can be claimed at age 60. Early benefits are available at age 55 for workers "prematurely aged," and benefits can be claimed at age 45 for workers in arduous occupations. Monthly benefits equal 30 percent of the average of the last 3 or 5 years of monthly earnings, whichever is higher, plus 2 percent of average monthly earnings for every 12-month period of coverage exceeding 180 months (15 years). Benefits in payment are adjusted according to changes in the cost of living, depending on the finances of the system (U.S. Social Security Administration 2011).

PENSION REGULATORS

This section considers the pension regulators in each of the five countries (Table 11.8). The pension regulators cover private sector pensions and may cover some pensions in the public sector. Pension regulators and regulations have been established to protect the interest of workers.

Table 11.8 Name of Retirement Benefits Program Regulatory Authority, 2012

Country	Name of regulator	Year took effect	Oversight ministry
Burundi	National Social Protection Commission	2013	President of Burundi
Kenya	Retirement Benefits Authority	2000	Ministry of Finance
Rwanda	National Bank of Rwanda	—	Ministry of Finance
Tanzania	Social Security Regulatory Authority	2008	Ministry of Finance
Uganda	Uganda Retirement Benefits Authority	2013	Ministry of Finance

Kenya

The pension regulator in Kenya, the Retirement Benefits Authority (RBA), is under the Ministry of Finance. It is managed by a board of five members from the private sector appointed by the Minister of Finance, as well as the Commissioner of Insurance, the Chief Executive of the Capital Markets Authority, and a representative of the Minister of Finance. Thus, a majority of its board members are from the private sector, giving it some autonomy from government influence (Odundo 2004).

The RBA expenses are paid for in part by a tax on pension assets. The RBA uses a risk-based approach to supervising the pension industry, based on the size and risk associated with each pension fund. It regulates the NSSF and private sector pension funds but not pension funds for civil servants. The NSSF is the only government-managed pension fund that it regulates. Before the RBA became operational in 2000, pensions were regulated solely under trust and income tax laws.

In 2011, Kenya developed a trustee training program for trustees of pension plans. Previously, trustees often had no special background that qualified them for that responsibility.

The Kenyan Auditor General also plays a role in the governance of pensions for public sector workers. It must verify and approve payment of benefits.

Tanzania

Tanzania has a pension regulator, established in 2008, the Social Security Regulatory Authority (SSRA), under the Ministry of Finance, which became operational in 2010. It shares regulatory authority with the Bank of Tanzania, which, in cooperation with the Social Security Regulatory Authority, is responsibile for investment issues relating to pensions. Together they are preparing investment guidelines for the pension funds (Simbeye 2012).

Uganda

Uganda is in the process of establishing a pension regulator, the Uganda Retirement Benefits Authority, which is under the Ministry of Finance. The law establishing this agency was passed in 2011, with the agency expected to become operational in 2013. This agency will regulate employer-provided pensions in both the private and public sectors. It will require all pension programs to register.

Rwanda

Rwanda has a pension regulator, the National Bank of Rwanda, which is under the Ministry of Finance. Its Social Security is under the Rwanda Social Security Board. The Rwanda Social Security Board has a director of pensions.

Burundi

Burundi in 2012 passed legislation establishing a pension regulator, the National Institute of Social Security and Professional Risks. It is not yet fully operational.

PRIVATE SECTOR PENSIONS

Most private sector workers with pensions in East Africa are covered under defined contribution plans, and until recently, most government workers had defined benefit plans (Mushi 2012). The only country in the region with a substantial number of pensions provided by private sector entities is Kenya (Katto 2012). Most of the pensions in the region for private sector workers are government-managed pensions. For this reason, most of the assets in pension programs in Tanzania, Uganda, and Rwanda are held by government-managed programs (Mutero 2010). The same holds true for Burundi.

The pensions receive favorable tax treatment according to either the EET tax regime, which refers to exempt (tax deductible) contributions, exempt investment earnings and taxed benefits, or the TTE tax regime (Uganda), which refers to taxed contributions, exempt investment earnings, and exempt benefits (Table 11.9). However, many low-income workers do not pay any income tax, effectively making the tax regime for pensions for them EEE, which stands for contributions being exempt from taxation, investment earnings being exempt from taxation, and retirement benefits being exempt from taxation.

Funded pensions tend to invest primarily in government securities, with all five countries having government debt markets. They also invest in real estate. In the EAC, with the exception of Kenya, opportunities for investing domestically in stock are limited. Burundi does not have a stock exchange. The stock exchange in Rwanda listed two stocks at the end of 2010 (Yabara 2012). The Nairobi Stock Exchange is the largest in the region. The Dar es Salaam Stock Exchange (Tanzania) has 15 listed companies, and the Uganda Stock Exchange has 10 listed companies. The Kenya, Rwanda, and Uganda stock exchanges have signed a memorandum of understanding, permitting cross listing of stocks. The Uganda National Social Security Fund owns 80 percent of the Uganda stock market. Kenya permits a maximum of 15 percent of a pension portfolio to be invested in other countries. Some of the

Table 11.9 Tax Regime for Retirement Benefit Programs, 2012

Country	Tax regime
Burundi	EET
Kenya	EET
Rwanda	EET
Tanzania	EET
Uganda	TTE

other countries have not permitted investments outside the country, thus prohibiting investment in other EAC countries (Mutero 2010), but that is changing as part of the move toward a common market.

Pension funds in Kenya held 26 percent of their assets in stocks in the East African Community in 2011, almost all of which was in the Nairobi Stock Exchange (RBA 2012a). Reflecting the relative importance of pension funds in the different countries, pension funds hold 2 percent of government bonds in Rwanda and 4 percent in Burundi, compared to 27 percent in Kenya, 23 percent in Tanzania, and 15 percent in Uganda (Yabara 2012). Pension funds in Kenya are subject to regulations as to the maximum percentage of their portfolios that can be invested in different asset classes.

Kenya

Kenya has an EET tax regime, but that characterization is a simplification of the actual tax regime. Investment earnings are not taxed while accruing. However, a Retirement Benefits Levy is charged on the assets of pension funds, varying from 0.2 percent of assets for funds up to Ksh500 million (Kenyan shillings) to 0.05 percent of assets for funds with more than 5 trillion shillings (RBA 2012b). Tax-exempt contributions are capped at Ksh20,000 a month. Lump sum payments of Ksh600,000 are tax free. Further, benefits received at age 65 and older are tax free, and benefits received at younger ages are tax free up to a limit (IOPS 2009). Tax-exempt benefits after age 65 are designed to encourage workers to postpone receipt of benefits.

Employers may establish defined benefit or defined contribution plans. About 90 percent of private sector pension plans are defined contribution plans (Raichura 2008). Employers have shifted from defined benefit toward defined contribution programs over the past decade (RBA 2012a). All pension programs and providers are required to register with the RBA. The RBA Web site in 2012 listed 1,216 registered pension programs and 22 individual pension plan providers (RBA 2012c). Retirement benefits vest after one year of work (Raichura 2008). Defined benefit programs are required to have an actuarial valuation every three years.

Anyone who wants to save for retirement can establish an Individual Retirement Benefit program (IRB). Prior to 2003, IRBs in Kenya did not receive any special tax preference. Since then, workers can make tax-deductible contributions up to a limit, receive tax-free investment earnings, and receive tax-free benefits for 10 years, up to a limit per year. Most IRBs are provided through insurance companies. In 2005, Kenya established an Insurance Policy Compensation fund to protect members of IRBs in the case of the insolvency of insurance companies. The fund is financed based on a levy of 0.25 percent of premiums charged both on policyholders and on the insurance companies. The motivation for the fund is to reduce the risk and instill confidence in Kenyans in saving for retirement this way (RBA 2007). As of 2009, Individual Retirement Benefit programs covered less than 1 percent of the workforce (IOPS 2009). Membership grew rapidly from 2010 to 2011, however, increasing from 25,000 to 41,000 (RBA 2012a).

An estimated 15 percent of Kenya's labor force is covered under some form of retirement benefits program (RBA 2007). To deal with low coverage and issues of low financial literacy, the RBA, in conjunction with the Kenyan Institute of Education, has undertaken a public education campaign starting in 2009 concerning the importance of saving for retirement. It has held roadshow events and had an advertising campaign, and it is working on a financial education curriculum for schools. The RBA has taken a holistic approach to financial education, combining it with education on health and mental health. Initially, the program targeted workers aged 50 and older but has expanded to include younger workers. It is attempting to change Kenya to a savings culture rather than a consumption culture.

In addition, the Mbao Jua Kali Pension Plan is an innovative program organized by the RBA that targets informal sector workers but is open to anyone. It is a voluntary program where workers register by paying Ksh100 and can pay a minimum of Ksh20 a day toward their retirement. (Ksh20 equal roughly U.S.$0.25.) It was started in June 2011 and by 2012 had 37,000 members. *Mbao* is Swahili slang for 20 shillings, or one Kenyan pound. *Jua kali* means hot sun in Swahili and is the term used to refer to workers in the informal sector. It refers to the working conditions in the informal sector, which is about 80 percent of the labor force (Raichura 2008). Participants can pay by *M-Pesa*, which is a mobile phone money transfer system (in Swahili, *M* stands for mobile and *pesa* stands for money).

The main mobile money service provider, Safaricom, charges the individual Ksh2 and the pension plan Ksh3 for money transfers, so in essence there is a 2 percent fee to the worker for a transfer of Ksh100 but a 10 percent fee for a transfer of Ksh20. Payments can also be made through an alternative provider, Airtel Money. Previously, without this technology, it was not feasible to have a pension program with such low contributions because of the high transactions costs, which are fixed costs, relative to the transactions. This system is relatively new but appears to be a promising innovation. Its success in providing meaningful benefits will depend in part on participants eventually being able to make larger contributions than the minimum required.

Starting in 2009, to encourage participation in pension plans and the development of a market for mortgages, the government allowed pension program participants to use up to 60 percent of their defined contribution pension accounts as security for mortgages. This amount can also be used to guarantee a loan for renovating a home. Mortgage lending in Kenya generally requires a down payment of 10 percent of the purchase price of the house. However, with pension-backed mortgages, lenders can lend up to 115 percent of the purchase price, with the borrower using the amount above 100 percent to pay for closing costs. This program provides an immediate, tangible benefit to workers for participating in a pension plan or social security. The house is the first form of guarantee of the mortgage. If an individual loses his job and defaults on his mortgage, but the value of his house exceeds the amount remaining on the mortgage, the house is sold and the individual does not lose any of his pension.

While the mortgage program undoubtedly will encourage the growth of the mortgage market, and may encourage participation in pensions, in part to be used for this purpose, the success of this program as an aspect of retirement income policy will depend partially on how many people lose their pensions if they have to default on their mortgages. That in turn will depend on the qualifying conditions to receive a mortgage. If mortgages are extended to people who do not fully qualify, and thus have a greater risk of default, this may become more of a problem in the future, particularly if housing prices fall. A similar program in South Africa has had difficulty assuring that the loans were not diverted for other purposes (Mutero 2010).

Kenya has relaxed the preservation of benefits rule so that participants can withdraw up to 50 percent of the employer contributions to their defined contribution pension plans, and up to 100 percent of their own contributions, at any age before retirement. In addition, they can withdraw up to 50 percent of the accrued value in a defined benefit plan (RBA 2011).

Tanzania

Tanzania has an EET tax regime. The high contribution rate of 20 percent to the mandatory social security fund may be a factor discouraging the development of employer-provided pensions in the private sector. A study in 2012 indicates that there are a small number of employer-provided pensions in the private sector, perhaps about a dozen, primarily for multinational companies (Kiwanuka 2012).

To encourage greater efficiency in fund management, government-managed pension funds are competing with the National Social Security Fund as substitute programs for workers. The Government Employees Provident Fund is seeking to enroll self-employed workers in the private sector in its Voluntary Savings Retirement Program. As of 2011, it had enrolled about 3,000 persons. The Parastatal Pension Fund has also extended its coverage to encourage voluntary enrollment by private sector employees and the self-employed, as well as workers in the informal labor sector (Kamndaya 2011). The Local Authorities Pension Fund is for employees of local governments, but is also seeking self-employed members to voluntarily join.

Uganda

Uganda has a TTE tax regime, where both contributions and investment earnings are taxed, but benefits are not taxed. The tax exemption of pension benefits is written into the Ugandan Constitution, making it particularly difficult to change. Investment earnings are only taxed on investments in fixed income securities, such as government bonds. Investment income from other assets, such as real estate and stock, is not taxed. Anyone earning less than about U.S.$90 a month is exempt from tax. The elderly do not pay any tax because of an age exemption.

As of 2011, the NSSF was the main provider of retirement benefits in the private sector (International Social Security Association 2011), but Uganda has some private sector pensions. These are primarily defined contribution plans, but they can be defined benefit plans. One estimate puts the number of programs at more than 50 (Mutero 2010). These programs have mandatory vesting of benefits after one year of participation (Kiwanuka 2012).

Rwanda

Rwanda has an EET tax regime. Employer and employee contributions and investment earnings are taxed at 30 percent, while benefits are tax free (IOPS 2011a). Pensions are generally managed by insurance companies. There are an estimated 40 private sector pension programs (Mutero 2010).

Individuals can voluntarily establish personal pension funds, which are generally managed by insurance companies. For personal pensions, contributions are tax free. Investment earnings are taxed, and benefits are tax free (IOPS 2011a).

Burundi

Burundi has an EET tax regime and a few private sector defined contribution plans. As of 2012, it is considering a law to regulate employer-provided pensions.

PUBLIC SERVICE PENSIONS

As of 2012, the pensions for government employees in the EAC are defined benefit plans (Table 11.10). These plans generally predate the NSSF. Some of them provide benefits that are overly generous by international standards and that contain other generous features, such as commutation to lump sums on favorable terms. Particularly considering that government sector work is generally not physically arduous, the plans tend to provide early retirement benefits at young ages (Table 11.11). Another generous feature is that they generally are calculated on the single year of highest pay. Calculation using such a short period creates the possibility of a person receiving a pay increase in the final year for the purpose of raising his pension. Further, even more generous pensions are sometimes received by members of parliament, judges, and other high officials, sometimes after only limited periods of service. The EAC, however, does not provide a pension for EAC secretariat employees, but instead provides a lump sum payment when they end their service, based on their salary and years of service.

Kenya

Public sector employees as of 2012 were covered by the Public Service Pension Program, which is an unfunded defined benefit plan administered by the Pensions Department in the Ministry of Finance.

In 2013, all defined benefit plans for which the Kenyan government has a liability, a total of 40 programs, will be converted to defined contribution plans to reduce the risk to the government. Worker contributions will be required. Workers aged 45 and older will remain in the old defined benefit programs. People younger than age 45 will be completely transferred to the new defined contribution program, with a contribution made to that program by the government to compensate them for the benefits already accrued under the old program. The government will manage the investments of the defined contribution program. Individual choice of investments will not be an option. According to the bill being considered at the end of 2012, the government would contribute 15.5 percent of salary for civil servants, and employees would contribute 7.5 percent (Republic of Kenya 2012).

Starting in 2009, the normal retirement age for the Public Service Pension Program was raised from age 55 to 60, but early retirement

Table 11.10 Pensions for Government Sector Employees, 2012

Country	Type
Burundi	Contributory defined benefit
Kenya	Defined benefit, converting to defined contribution
Rwanda	Contributory defined benefit
Tanzania	Contributory funded defined benefit, multiple plans
Uganda	Unfunded noncontributory defined benefit

Table 11.11   Early Retirement Age for Government Sector Employees, 2012

Country	Type
Kenya	50
Tanzania	55
Uganda	45 with 10 years' service, less than 45 with 20 years

is still available at age 50 for workers with 10 years of service (Were 2009). Women can retire on grounds of marriage at any age with 5 years of work. As of 2008, the program had about 406,000 active members. A separate program applies for the armed forces.

The Public Service Pension Program provides generous benefits, which are based on 2.5 percent multiplied by years of service multiplied by final base pay. Up to 25 percent of the benefit can be taken as a lump sum, which is calculated at a very generous rate (20:1). One aspect of the benefit calculation that is not generous is that there are not regular enhancements for benefits in payment to take into account inflation (Raichura 2008). By comparison, the U.S. Civil Service Retirement System benefit is calculated as 1.5 percent for the first 5 years, plus 1.75 percent for the second 5 years, plus 2 percent for years beyond 10 years, multiplied by the high 3 years of average pay (U.S. Office of Personnel Management 2012). The pension benefits are paid through banking accounts, though for a number of retirees without banking accounts they are paid through the Post Office Savings Bank (Raichura 2008).

LAPTRUST is a funded contributory defined benefit plan for employees of local government that was started in 1929. It had 25,800 active members in 2011. Employees contribute 12 percent of pay while employers contribute 15 percent. Perhaps in part because of the high contribution rates, many of the 175 local government agencies are in arrears on their payments. LAPTRUST has registered a defined contribution program in line with the requirement that all defined benefit programs that are a liability to the national government convert to defined contribution programs, so as to reduce the risk to the national government finances (Kiwanuka 2012). The defined benefit program closed to new members starting August 2012.

Tanzania

The Public Service Pensions Fund, under the Ministry of Finance, covers central government employees, who contribute 5 percent of their salary. It has about 250,000 members (Mutero 2010). Starting in 1999, the unfunded defined benefit program was converted to a funded program. The program was created in 1954, predating the National Provident Fund, which was started in 1964. Benefits can be claimed at age 55, with mandatory retirement at age 60 (Public Service Pensions Fund 2012).

As with other government pensions in the region, the Public Service Pensions Fund provides generous benefits. The basic benefit is calculated as total months worked multiplied by final annual salary multiplied by $1/(540)$ (Public Service Pensions Fund 2012). The final factor is equivalent to 2.2 percent multiplied by years of service. The Political Service Retirement Benefits Act of 1999 established a special pension fund for members of parliament and other elected officials, who receive preferential pensions (Barya 2011).

Local government employees are covered under the Local Authorities Pensions Fund. In addition to providing generous benefits, those benefits are tax exempt (Public Service Retirement Benefits Act 1999).

Certain high government officials receive even more generous pensions. Judges, the Director General of Intelligence, the Inspector General of Police, and other high officials receive pensions that are 80 percent of final pay, and these can be received after short periods of service. In addition, these officials are given a car and sufficient money to pay for a driver for four years, all of which are tax free. These generous pensions create a major conflict of interest for high public officials when it comes to the reform of civil service pensions.

The Chief Justice receives an even more favorable pension, that being equal to 80 percent of the salary not of himself but of the current incumbent holding that office, plus a lump sum payment equal to 50 percent of the salary he received while holding that office (Public Service Retirement Benefits Act 1999). By comparison, Supreme Court Justices in the United States receive 100 percent of their final salary, provided they have served at least 10 years and that the sum of their age and years of Supreme Court service is at least 80 (Longley 2012).

In Zanzibar, public service employees are covered under a separate system, which began in 1990, predating the country's social security program (Zanzibar Social Security Fund 2009).

Uganda

Preferential pensions are provided to government employees. Employees of the police, army, prisons, civil service, or government teaching service are exempt from contributing to the NSSF because they have their own pension systems. Members of parliament and their staffs are covered under the Parliamentary Pensions Act of 2007 (Barya 2011). Judges have particularly favorable pensions and are eligible for a pension after one year of service (Barya 2011).

The pensions for government employees are unfunded defined benefit plans. The Public Service Pension Program, managed by the Ministry of Public Service, covers most civil servants. As of 2012, it has about 269,000 participants. The Armed Forces pension has about 45,000 participants (Katto 2012). It was established in 1939, predating the Public Service Pension Program, which was established in 1946. An earlier program was established in 1939 for public service employees, but it excluded African employees and only covered colonial Europeans (Inter Ministerial Task Force 2012).

Covered workers do not contribute to the Public Service Pension Program, with the funds coming from general government revenue. A reform proposal in 2012 would make the program contributory. The minimum qualifying age for benefits is 45 with continuous service of 10 years, with compulsory retirement at age 60 (Barya 2011). Workers with 20 years of contributions can retire at any age. There are no penalties for early retirement. Female employees are eligible for a special pension if they retire because of marriage (Pensions Act 1946).

As well as having generous provisions for early retirement, the Public Service Pension Program has a generous benefit formula, calculated as 2.4 percent of final gross pay multiplied by the number of years of service, with the maximum capped at 87 percent of gross pay (after 36.25 years of work). They vest after 10 years of work. The pensions are indexed to wages, which is generally more generous than price indexation (Nyakundi 2009). Pensions are paid either in Uganda shillings or U.S. dollars and are paid for a maximum of 15 years.

Pensions are not being paid to some retirees, however, because of a lack of sufficient funds to provide such generous benefits, creating a problem of arrears. The Pensions Act has a provision that public servants cannot contest in courts (Pensions Act 1946). According to Kiwanuka (2012), the unfunded liability for this program is an astounding 63 percent of GDP.

The generosity of this system can be compared to that of the Civil Service Retirement System for federal government workers in the United States. In that system, maximum benefits of 80 percent of the average of the highest three years of earnings are received after 42 years of work, with these benefits being indexed to prices once in payment. The Civil Service Retirement System was closed to new entrants in 1980, and a less generous pension system has since replaced it. The pensions for civil servants in Uganda are thus substantially more generous than for civil servants in the United States.

The Public Service Pension Program and other plans for civil servants and other government employees are run by the Ministry of Public Service. The Public Service Pension Program covers about 2.8 percent of the workforce, which is larger than the 2.3 percent covered by the private sector program, the National Social Security Fund (Barya 2011). In addition, the military is covered under the Armed Forces Pension Program. Until 1994, local government employees had their own program, which was a provident fund, but since then they are covered under the Public Service Pension Program (Nyakundi 2009). Because many local governments do not have much money, the central government pays for their pension expenses.

Rwanda

The National Social Security Fund in Rwanda covers all private sector employees and all public sector employees, including the military.

Burundi

Civil servants and judges in Burundi are not covered by the National Social Security Fund, but are instead covered by special programs. Pensions for civil servants are noncontributory, but as of 2012 they are being restructured to require employee contributions.

CONCLUSION

This chapter has surveyed the social security and pension systems in the five countries of the East African Community. It has described pensions for both private and public sector workers. As well as describing the basic features of the systems, it has focused on areas of innovation and also on areas in need of reform. Extending coverage to workers in the informal sector is a major challenge in all of these countries. Kenya and Rwanda have innovative programs to extend coverage to workers in the informal sector by facilitating the regular collection of contributions of small amounts. Regulating pensions to help protect the interests of participants is another issue, and now all of the countries have in place pension regulators. Some of the countries have pensions for government employees that are overly generous by international standards.

Some of the countries discourage the provision of private sector pensions by high mandatory contribution rates for social security, but Kenya has low mandatory contribution rates and has successfully developed a pension sector with more than 1,000 pension plans.

Notes

I have received valuable comments from David Rajnes.

1. The EAC countries are also members of the East African Trade Union Confederation (EATUC), which is an organization of labor unions, with Burundi having observer status, and the East African Development Bank. In addition, the government officials involved in the retirement systems of these countries work with, and are influenced to some extent by, other international organizations, such as the World Bank, the International Labour Organization, the International Monetary Fund, the International Organisation of Pension Supervisors, the African Development Bank, and by private sector nongovernment organizations such as the Gates Foundation and the Financial Services Volunteer Corps.

References

Assad, Mussa J., and Athmani Selemani. n.d. "Pensions Funds Performance in Tanzania: Insights from Comparison of the National Social Securities Fund and Parastatals Pension Fund." *Business Management Review* 10(2). http://www.udbs.udsm.ac.tz/publications/articles/Abstracts/BMR102_3.pdf (accessed April 29, 2013).

Barya, John-Jean. 2011. *Social Security and Social Protection in the East African Community.* Kampala, Uganda: Fountain Publishers. http://www.kituochakatiba.org/index2.php?option=com_docman&task=doc_view&gid=1304&Itemid=36 (accessed April 29, 2013).

Daily Nation. 2012. "Atwoli Backs Proposed Pension Plan." August 23. http://www.nation.co.ke/News/Atwoli+backs+proposed++pension+plan+/-/1056/1484440/-/13hmi6m/-/index.html (accessed April 29, 2013).

East African Community (EAC). 2011. "Technical Meeting of Social Security Experts to Discuss the Way Forward on the Co-ordination of Benefits within the EAC Common Market." Paper presented at a conference June 15–17, held in Arusha, Tanzania.

East and Central African Social Security Association (ECASSA). 2012. "Background." Nairobi: ECASSA. http://www.ecassa.org/index.php/2012-07-24-04-32-24/background (accessed April 29, 2013).

Gillion, Colin, John Turner, Clive Bailey, and Denis Latulippe. 2000. *Social Security Pensions: Development and Reform.* Geneva: International Labour Office.

Inter Ministerial Task Force (Uganda). 2012. *Report of the Inter-Ministerial Task Force on the Reform of the Public Service Pension Scheme.* Kampala, Uganda: Ministry of Public Service.

International Labour Organization. 2012. "Tanzania: Parastatal Pension Fund." Geneva: International Labour Organization. http://www.ilo.org/dyn/ilossi/ssimain.viewProgramp_lang=en&p_program_id=268&p_geoaid=834 (accessed April 29, 2013).

International Organisation of Pension Supervisors (IOPS). 2009. "Country Profiles: Kenya." Paris: IOPS.

———. 2011a. "Country Profiles—Rwanda." Paris: IOPS.

———. 2011b. "Country Profiles—Tanzania." Paris: IOPS.

International Social Security Association. 2011. "Uganda: Retirement Benefit Authority Established." Geneva: International Social Security Association. http://www.issa.int/Observatory/Country-Profiles/Regions/Africa/Uganda/Reforms/Retirement-Benefit-Authority-established (accessed April 29, 2013).

Kamndaya, Samuel. 2011. "Pension Funds in Bid to Widen Coverage." *Citizen*, January 27. http://thecitizen.co.tz/magazines/31-business-week/7670 -pension-funds-in-bid-to-widen-coverage.html (accessed April 29, 2013).

Karuhanga, James. 2012. "MPs Query Pension Policy." *New Times,* July 12. http://allafrica.com/stories/201207131121.html (accessed April 29, 2013).

Katto, Japheth. 2012. "Sharing the East African Experience: The Case of Uganda." Paper presented at the World Bank Contractual Savings Conference, held in Washington, DC, January 9–11. http://siteresources.world-bank.org/FINANCIALSECTOR/Resources/session13.pdf (accessed April 29, 2013).

Kiwanuka, Patricia. 2012. "Consultancy Services of the Pension Advisor for the EAC Financial Sector Development and Regionalization." August. Arusha, Tanzania: East African Community Secretariat.

Longley, Robert. 2012. "U.S. Supreme Court Retirement Benefits: A Full Salary for Life." *About.com.* http://usgovinfo.about.com/od/uscourtsystem/a /scotusretire.htm (accessed April 29, 2013).

Machira, Polycarp. 2011. "Regulator to Improve Social Security." *Citizen*, January 2. http://www.thecitizen.co.tz/business/13-local-business/6873 -regulator-to-improve-social-security.html (accessed April 29, 2013).

Mchira, Moses, and George Ngigi. 2012. "Kenya: Government Targets Larger Share of Workers' Salaries for NSSF Deductions." *Business Daily*, February 2. http://allafrica.com/stories/201202030739.html (accessed April 29, 2013).

Ministry of East African Community Affairs. 2011. "Workers on the Move in the East African Community." Kampala, Uganda: Ministry of East African Community Affairs.

Mushi, Ansgar Africanus. 2012. "Pensions Developments in East Africa." Paper presented at the World Bank Contractual Savings Conference, held in Washington, DC, January 9–11. http://siteresources.worldbank.org /FINANCIALSECTOR/Resources/session13.pdf (accessed April 29, 2013).

Mutegi, Mugambi. 2012. "Bill Allows Workers to Transfer Benefits from EAC Nations." *Business Daily*, September 4. http://www.business dailyafrica.com/Bill-allows-workers-to-transfer-benefits-from-EAC -nations/-/539546/1496456/-/a0lvcg/-/index.html (accessed April 29, 2013).

Mutero, James. 2010. *Mobilising Pension Assets for Housing Finance Needs in Africa: Experience and Prospects in East Africa.* Report to the FinMark Trust. Parkview, South Africa: Centre for Affordable Housing Finance in Africa. http://www.housingfinanceafrica.org/wp-content/uploads/2010/12/Pension _assets_and_housing_Eastern_Africa.pdf (accessed April 29, 2013).

National Bank of Rwanda. 2008. "National Workshop on Regulatory and Policy Framework for Pension Programs and Products in Rwanda." Kigali, Rwanda: National Bank of Rwanda.

National Social Security Fund (NSSF), Kenya. 2012. *NSSF Benefits and Grants*. Nairobi: National Social Security Fund, Kenya. http://www.nssf.or.ke/benefits-and-grants (accessed April 29, 2013).

National Social Security Fund (NSSF), Tanzania. 2010a. *Allotment of Investible Fund*. Dar es Salaam: National Social Security Fund, Tanzania. http://www.nssf.or.tz/index.php?option=com_content&view=article&id=132&Itemid=224 (accessed April 29, 2013).

———. 2010b. *Old Age Pension*. Dar es Salaam: National Social Security Fund, Tanzania. http://www.nssf.or.tz/index.php?option=com_content&view=article&id=194&Itemid=198 (accessed April 29, 2013).

National Social Security Fund, Uganda. 2012. *National Social Security Fund*. Kampala: National Social Security Fund, Uganda. http://www.nssfug.org/ (accessed April 29, 2013).

Ngotezi, Alfred. 2010. "Caution as We Regulate Social Security Funds in Tanzania." *DailyNews*, August 15. http://www.dailynews.co.tz/columnist/?n=13528&cat=columnist (accessed April 29, 2013).

Nyakundi, David B. 2009. "A Description of the Pension System in Uganda: Need for Reform." London: Retirement Benefits Authority. http://dx.doi.org/10.2139/ssrn.1508364 (accessed April 29, 2013).

Odundo, Edward. 2004. "Supervision of a Public Pension Fund: Experience and Challenges in Kenya." In *Public Pension Fund Management: Governance, Accountability and Investment Policies*, Alberto R. Musalem and Robert J. Palacios, eds. Washington, DC: World Bank, pp. 281–287.

Ojambo, Fred. 2011. "Uganda's Pension Fund Reduces Interest Rate, Monitor Reports." *Bloomberg*, October 4. http://www.bloomberg.com/news/2011-10-04/uganda-s-pension-fund-reduces-interest-rate-monitor-reports.html (accessed April 29, 2013).

Pensions Act (Uganda). 1946. http://www.publicservice.go.ug/public/Pensions%20Act%20Chapter%20286.pdf (accessed April 29, 2013).

Public Service Pensions Fund. 2012. *Old Age Benefits*. Dodoma, Tanzania: Public Service Pensions Fund. http://www.pspf-tz.org/en/index.php?page=14 (accessed April 29, 2013).

Public Service Retirement Benefits Act (Tanzania). 1999. http://www.ulii.org/ug/legislation/consolidated-act/286 (accessed June 26, 2013).

Raichura, Sundeep K. 2008. "Analytical Review of the Pension System in Kenya." Paris: Organisation for Economic Co-operation and Development. http://www.oecd.org/insurance/privatepensions/41564693.pdf (accessed April 29, 2013).

Republic of Kenya, Ministry of Planning. 2012. *Kenya Social Protection Sector Review: Executive Report.* June. Nairobi: Vision2030. http://www .vision2030.go.ke/cms/vds/SP_Executive_Report_FINAL1.pdf (accessed April 29, 2013).

Retirement Benefits Authority (RBA). 2007. "Individual Retirement Benefits Programs in Kenya." June. Nairobi: RBA. http://www.rba.go.ke/ publications/research-papers/category/5-research-reports-2006-2007 (accessed April 29, 2013).

_____. 2011. "Mbao Pension Plan." *The Pensioner*, September. Nairobi: RBA. http://www.rba.go.ke/home/the-pensioner (accessed April 29, 2013).

_____. 2012a. "Relatively New Individual Retirement Benefits Programs Sector Records Massive Growth." *The Pensioner*, March. Nairobi: RBA. http: //www.rba.go.ke/home/the-pensioner (accessed April 29, 2013).

_____. 2012b. "Retirement Benefits Levy." Nairobi: RBA. http://www.rba .go.ke/retirement-benefits-programs/the-retirement-benefits-levy (accessed April 29, 2013).

_____. 2012c. "Supervision Framework." Nairobi: RBA. http://www.rba .go.ke/regulatory-framework/supervision-framework (accessed April 29, 2013).

Reuters. 2012. "Uganda Eyes $400 mln Loan from State Pension Fund." June 8. http://af.reuters.com/article/investingNews/idAFJOE85701B20120608 (accessed April 29, 2013).

Rwanda Social Security Board. 2012. *Pension Benefits.* Kigali, Rwanda: Social Security Board. http://www.csr.gov.rw/content/pension-benefits (accessed April 29, 2013).

Simbeye, Finnegan Wa. 2012. "Tanzania: Pension Funds Regulator in Strong Financial Position." *Tanzania Daily News*, April 24. http://allafrica.com /stories/201204240177.html (accessed April 29, 2013).

U.S. Office of Personnel Management. 2012. *Computation.*Washington, DC: U.S. Office of Personnel Management. http://www.opm.gov/retire/pre/csrs/ computation.asp (accessed April 29, 2013).

U.S. Social Security Administration. 2011. "Social Security Programs throughout the World: Africa, 2011." Washington, DC: U.S. Social Security Administration. http://www.socialsecurity.gov/policy/docs/progdesc /ssptw/2010-2011/africa/ssptw11africa.pdf (accessed April 29, 2013).

Wafuja, Walter. 2011. "NSSF Recovers Shs8 billion from Defaulters." *Daily Monitor*, May 4. http://www.monitor.co.ug/Business/-/688322/1155906 /-/3u1s15/-/index.html (accessed April 29, 2013).

Were, Monica. 2009. *The Concept of Retirement Age: A Commentary.* London: Kenya Retirement Benefits Authority. http://www.rba.go.ke/publications

/research-papers/category/3-research-reports-2008-2009   (accessed April 29, 2013).

Yabara, Masafumi. 2012. "Capital Market Integration: Progress Ahead of the East African Community Monetary Union." IMF Working Paper, January. Washington, DC: International Monetary Fund. http://www.imf.org /external/pubs/ft/wp/2012/wp1218.pdf (accessed April 29, 2013).

Zanzibar Social Security Fund. 2009. *Zanzibar Social Security Fund*. Zanzibar: Zanzibar Social Security Fund. http://www.zssf.org/ (accessed April 29, 2013).

12

The Efficiency of Defined Contribution Pension Plans in the Americas

Denise Gómez-Hernández
Autonomous University of Querétaro

Alberto M. Ramírez de Jurado Frías
Conference of Consulting Actuaries, American Academy of Actuaries, and Colegio Actuarial Mexicano

Defined contribution pension plans are widespread among the Americas. Pension actuaries use the pension replacement rate as a benchmark to measure how much a worker's preretirement income is replaced by its pension. Although this measure is intended to make the system efficient, the postretirement challenge for workers is to be able to purchase at least the basic market basket. Income projections used in pension replacement benchmark rates do not capture this because workers' incomes are not efficiently linked to macroeconomic variables in Latin America. This chapter proposes the use of macroeconomic variables such as the Consumer Price Index and the basic market basket to develop a benchmark indicator of basic income replacement as an alternative to the replacement rate. This indicator is calculated along with the replacement rate by country and compared to illustrate the efficiency level of their current defined contribution plans.

REPLACEMENT RATES

A pension is intended to replace a worker's income after his working lifetime. Because of this replacement objective, the pension serves the same purpose as the worker's preretirement salary, that is, to purchase goods like the basic market basket, health care, housing, entertainment, and other needs or goods. Upon retirement, the pension amount is often the only source of income for retirees; this is the main reason why the pension amount is compared with the salary, defined as the Traditional Replacement Rate (TRR), which is the ratio of the pension amount and salary upon retirement

$$TRR_t = \frac{f_t}{\ddot{a}_y^{(12)} S_t} \,,$$

where f_t is the amount in the fund at the end of the accumulation period, (t) is the worker's individual account under the defined contribution plan, $\ddot{a}$ is the annuity factor used to convert a lump sum to an annuity, and S_t is the projected salary for the accumulation period (t). The traditional replacement rate is affected by the contribution rate to the pension plan, the fees charged, the rate of return received, and the starting salary.

In the Americas—North, Central, and South—the race between inflation and salary is often lost by the salary, that is, salaries are often adjusted by employers at a rate below the inflation increase. Therefore, the salary is not an item that is necessarily linked to macroeconomic variables. For this reason, the authors believe the current replacement rate approach underestimates the future effectiveness of pension income due to price increases in the set of goods.

Three aspects are affected when salary and macroeconomic variables are unlinked:

1) country-wise comparison between different geographies, economies, and currencies,

2) determination of money purchase levels for goods upon in and out of work lifetime periods, and

3) notion of pension plan efficiency and retiree satisfaction levels.

The authors identified the basic market basket variable as a candidate to benchmark a defined contribution plan, particularly because this is a standard measurement performed by most if not all of the central banks in the Americas. The minimum satisfaction level or replacement rate under this measure is when the pension amount is sufficient to purchase the basic market basket.

LITERATURE REVIEW

Since the implementation and growth of defined contribution plans, many authors have tried to model and project the final amount in the individual accounts at retirement. Vigna and Haberman (2001) analyze the financial risk in defined contribution plans using dynamic programming through a model that incorporates a regime of fixed and variable income. The main conclusion of this research is the sensitivity of the projected amounts in the fund to the returns during the accumulation period.

Gómez-Hernández, Vidal, and Enrique (2009) compare the competitiveness of the defined contribution plans in Mexico, Chile, and Argentina. They conclude that in Argentina and Chile, the pension obtained is greater than in Mexico mainly because of high commissions in Mexico. Ramírez de Jurado Frías (2010) proposed a revised model for Vigna and Haberman (2001) and implemented it to analyze the Mexican regulatory framework, showing various curves for projected accumulated amounts of the individual accounts at retirement.

In the latest G20 report for pensions (OECD 2011), the OECD uses two benchmarks to measure pension entitlements: the replacement rate and pension wealth. It also provides comparisons of replacement rates between various OECD members and G20 countries.

METHODOLOGY

We calculated the working life contributions and investment returns until age 65 for a worker with $0 initial account balance and entry age of 25. The accumulative model uses the current regulatory framework in various countries of the Americas with defined contribution plans.

We selected a group of nine countries with defined contribution pension plans in the Americas. The selected countries may provide a fair representation of the current situation from the perspective of the benchmark indicator of basic income replacement. The nine countries are Canada, the United States, Mexico, Costa Rica, El Salvador, Colombia, Brazil, and Chile; thus, North, Central, and South America are each represented by three countries. For details about the selected countries—population size, mortality, and annuity factors—refer to Appendix 12A.

The basic market baskets were then projected to retirement age (65) by country using the consumer price index. The projected income or final projected salary at age 65 is compared to the projected basic market basket at age 65 for an arbitrary and fixed annual salary increase assumption of 2 percent real per annum. The Basic Satisfaction Level (BASAL) is then calculated as the ratio of the accumulated fund at retirement, converted into an annual benefit by the annuity factor and divided by the basic market basket at age of retirement. (In medicine, *basal* commonly refers to the minimal level that is necessary for health or life.) These BASAL values are then used to compare by country the efficiency of the defined contribution systems.

MODEL

The BASAL postretirement is defined as the ratio

$$BASAL_t = \frac{f_t}{\ddot{a}_y^{(12)} P_t} ,$$

where f_t is the accumulated fund for accumulation period (t) of the worker's individual account under the defined contribution plan and P_t is the projected basic market basket for the accumulation period (t). The accumulation period t is the difference between the entry age (x) and retirement age (y).

The accumulated fund at retirement age (t) of the worker f_t is also defined as

$$f_{i+1} = f_i\left[(1-y_i)e^{\mu i} + y_i e^{\lambda i}\right]e^{-\delta i} + S_i(c-\beta)(1+s)\left[(1-y_i)e^{\frac{\mu i}{2}} + y_i e^{\frac{\lambda i}{2}}\right]e^{\frac{-\delta i}{2}},$$

where f_i is the accumulated fund value under the defined contribution plan during year i or period $[i, i + 1]$, the factor c is the contribution percentage over the pre-retirement salary S_i at year i, β is the commission charged on the value of the contributions (known also as commission on entry fee and death and disability insurance fee), the factor s is the real salary increase, y_i is the percentage allocated to fix return instruments during the period $[i, i + 1]$ and $(1 - y_i)$ the percentage allocated to variable return instruments during the same period $[i, i + 1]$, μ_i is the force of interest for fix return instruments and λ_i the force of interest for variable return instruments and δ_i are the commissions on rates of return (or assets under management) charged.

The projected basic market basket cost at retirement age (t) of the worker PB_t is given by

$$PB_{i+1} = B_i(1 + j)^{y - x},$$

where PB_i is the projected basic market basket value during year i or period $[i, i + 1]$, B_i is the annualized basic market basket value at the year i, and is an average of the rates at which the historical values of B_i increased (or decreased).

DATA DESCRIPTION

Information was collected from original and secondary sources. Below is a brief description of the data. In order to model the accumulation of contributions and returns, the authors relied on data from the International Association of Supervisors of Pension Funds (AIOS). Data were collected on rates of return, contributions, commissions, investment portfolios, and salaries. Other data for countries not included in the AIOS report was collected from the original country source. The mortality factors used to calculate the annuities came from the documentation issued by the regulators or the country legislation relative to their pension plans. Basic market basket or basket of goods costs came from the central banks or minister of statistics from the respective countries. Other inputs, parameters, or assumptions used in this chapter have been set by the authors and are documented in Appendix 12B.

RESULTS

Figure 12.1 shows the benchmark comparison for BASAL and TRR rates. These are compared side by side to illustrate their differences, although these values are not entirely comparable as they use a different basis in their calculations; that is, BASAL uses the basic market basket and TRR uses projected salaries. The x-axis shows the country names segmented by regions in the Americas, whereas the y-axis shows the ratio between the final accumulated fund amount value converted into an annualized pension and the basis or item (basic market basket or salary).

Figure 12.1 Benchmark Comparison for BASAL and Replacement Rate

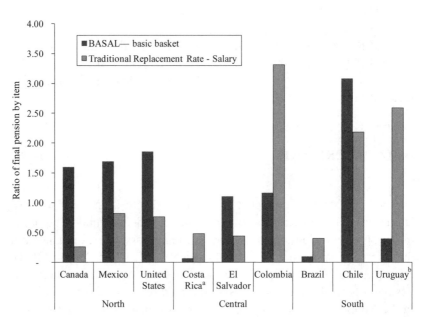

[a] The Costa Rica pension system relies on pension fund managers added to a public system. In this chapter only the pension fund manager system was taken into account to obtain the results.

[b] The Uruguay pension system relies on a private system administrated by the Uruguay Central Bank plus a public pension system. In this article only the UCB fund was taken into account to obtain the results.

SOURCE: Authors' calculations.

ANALYSIS

Comparing the BASAL levels in Figure 12.1, we conclude that Costa Rica holds the lowest BASAL from all the countries with 0.07, followed by Brazil with 0.10 and Uruguay with 0.40. The low BASAL in Costa Rica and Brazil indicates that workers in these countries will not have enough resources at retirement to buy 1.0 basic market basket if they rely solely on the basic pension system. In other words, an average worker in Costa Rica and Brazil can expect to buy 0.07 and 0.10 basic market baskets, respectively, at retirement with his or her pension. The reason for this is because Costa Rica charges two kinds of fees: an entry fee and a high percentage of charge on returns. This reduces considerably the amount accumulated at retirement by the worker. Another key factor is that in Costa Rica only 3.85 percent of salary is contributed to the pension fund. Additionally, the high 10-year average basic market basket inflation for Costa Rica and Brazil (11.8 and 17.1, respectively) reduces the purchasing power over the accumulation period; salary growth is assumed to be 2.00 percent real annually.

On the other side we have Chile, which holds the highest BASAL followed by United States. The reason for this high level of BASAL is because Chile only charges one kind of fee (an entry fee with no charge on returns), reducing considerably the total amount charged at the end of the cumulative period. Another difference with respect to Costa Rica (the lowest BASAL) is that the contribution percentage of the salary is higher in Chile: 10.0 percent.

In North America there are small differences in the values obtained for the BASAL: Mexico, 1.69; United States, 1.86; and Canada, 1.60. This suggests that upon retirement age the workers from this region will be able to buy more than 1.50 basic market baskets with their monthly pensions. The annual salary increase rates in these countries are similar to the increase rates seen in the 10-year average basic market basket inflation, so these results were expected.

The results are consistent with Gómez-Hernández and Stewart (2008), who find that El Salvador has the lowest 40-year weighted charge (fee) ratio of the 21 countries analyzed, and Costa Rica one of the highest. The results for the TRR benchmark suggest Colombia has the highest TRR at 3.31 and Canada the lowest with 0.26. This low value of TRR would appear to be a problem for the Canadian workers. However, the Canada Pension Plan is designed to provide a 0.25 TRR upon workers retirement, and Canadian workers rely on other complementary pensions to increase their retirement incomes, as well as receiving benefits from the old-age security program, which is a social security benefits program that is financed out of general revenues. For Colombians, the 3.31 TRR value, which is the result of a relatively high contribution rate and the highest rates of return of any country considered, seems appealing, but this value cannot tell Colombian workers how much purchasing power they will have with a monthly pension 3.31 higher than their latest preretirement salary. In fact, Canada has higher purchasing power with a BASAL of 1.60 versus 1.17 for Colombia (Table 12.1).

Comparing the results between BASAL and the TRR benchmarks, the difference in values is evident. Colombia has the highest value of TRR 3.31 but a BASAL of 1.17. Chile has the highest value of BASAL 3.08 and TRR of 2.18. In Colombia, the TRR value is misleading, as it would suggest that retirees have done a good job saving for retirement; they are receiving 3.31 times their salary when converting their individual retirement savings into a monthly pension, while in reality Colombian workers would be able to buy only 1.17 basic market baskets. For Chile, the BASAL and TRR do not appear to be critically different, still TRR cannot reflect the final salary purchasing power at retirement.

CONCLUSION

For future research, it would be relevant to consider the use of a benchmark like BASAL to tie the future workers' incomes upon retirement with macroeconomic variables. A standardized methodology tied to the macroeconomic environment would help the contributory systems to benchmark, identify, quantify, and address potential issues concerning purchasing power at retirement age.

Appendix 12A

The Americas are composed of 35 sovereign states. We make an arbitrary region segmentation into North, Central, and South America and select an arbitrary assortment of nine countries that provide defined benefit contribution pension schemes to the working class.

With the selected countries, we intend to show, compare, and determine the defined contribution systems efficiency when it comes to replacing income upon workers retirement. Although arbitrary, the selected countries provide a reasonable representation of the benchmark indicator of basic income replacement.

Table 12A.1 Summary of Population Size, Mortality Tables, and Annuity Factors

Region/country	Total population in millions	Percent of people aged 65 and older	Mortality table name	Annuity factor
North				
Canada	33	14.80	ICA2020	14.11
Mexico	110	6.20	EMSS 97	11.87
United States	312	13.30	2008 PY IRC 430 Static	13.70
Central				
Costa Rica	3	5.60	SP-2005	13.08
El Salvador	7	5.20	SP-2005	13.08
Colombia	47	6.70	Ren ISS 80-89	11.87
South				
Brazil	190	6.50	AT 83	13.92
Chile	17	9.40	MI-2006	11.95
Uruguay	3	13.50	MI-2006	11.95

SOURCE: Prepared by the authors from data collected from various sources.

Appendix 12B

Table 12B.1 Historical Annual Basic Market Basket Prices ($, U.S.)

	North			Central			South		
Year	Canada	Mexico	United States	Costa Rica	El Salvador	Colombia	Brazil	Chile	Uruguay
2001	4,418	1,183	6,612	n/a	881	1,759	n/a	3,321	3,025
2002	4,517	1,244	6,716	n/a	866	1,867	n/a	3,403	3,159
2003	4,644	1,291	6,870	n/a	866	1,965	n/a	3,499	4,008
2004	4,730	1,362	7,052	411	877	2,055	1,232	3,536	4,441
2005	4,834	1,415	7,291	474	912	2,137	687	3,644	4,683
2006	4,929	1,465	7,527	545	936	2,220	1,259	3,768	4,969
2007	5,037	1,510	7,741	608	996	2,329	1,582	3,934	5,324
2008	5,154	1,555	8,038	740	1,085	2,482	1,004	4,276	5,726
2009	5,168	1,602	8,010	909	1,195	2,653	1,578	4,340	6,276
2010	5,263	1,645	8,141	894	1,103	2,845	2,512	4,406	6,725
2011	5,416	1,727	8,398	967	1,227	3,062	4,048	4,476	7,213
2012	5,580	1,752	8,544	985	1,214	3,308	6,609	4,550	7,881

SOURCE: Prepared by the authors from data collected from various sources. The authors collected historical Consumer Price Index (CPI) data and determined the average increase rate over a 10-year period. Additionally collected average basic market basket household costs per country and applied CPI to roll back/forward the basic market basket. Certain underlying assumptions were made to have data consistency, for example Chilean ministry of social development only provides basic market basket per individual, so original cost was multiplied by five to reflect the household annual basket.

Table 12B.2 Average Monthly Salary ($, U.S.)

Region/country	Year							
	2003	2004	2005	2006	2007	2008	2009	2010
North								
Canada	2,560	2,633	2,745	2,822	2,940	3,031	3,110	3,215
United States	2,299	2,295	2,330	2,375	2,349	2,275	2,247	2,207
Mexico	451	483	545	543	578	492	548	607
Central								
Costa Rica	438	448	459	479	556	567	441	461
El Salvador	313	298	452	459	474	518	522	560
Colombia	245	300	334	364	458	480	486	538
South								
Brazil	665	656	666	693	715	739	762	791
Chile	539	614	681	685	794	685	877	1,012
Uruguay	348	379	471	511	634	632	912	987

SOURCE: 2010 AIOS Bulletin. Data for Mexico, Canada, Brazil, and the United States come from various sources.

Table 12B.3 Pension Funds Composition, December 2010 (%)

Region/country	Fix rate	Variable rate
North		
Canada	33.2	66.8
United States	38.0	62.0
Mexico	58.9	41.1
Central		
Costa Rica	62.4	37.6
El Salvador	84.7	15.3
Colombia	39.9	60.1
South		
Brazil	49.0	51.0
Chile	11.7	88.3
Uruguay	83.9	16.1

SOURCE: 2010 AIOS Bulletin. Data for Mexico, Canada, Brazil, and the United States come from various sources.

Table 12B.4 Pension Fund Annual Returns (%)

Region/country	Average annual return
North	
Canada	6.2
United States	8.0
Mexico	10.2
Central	
Costa Rica	15.1
El Salvador	4.0
Colombia	12.6
South	
Brazil	6.0
Chile	9.2
Uruguay	9.2

SOURCE: 2010 AIOS Bulletin. Data for Mexico, Colombia, Chile, Canada, Brazil, and the United States come from various sources. Percentages shown for Colombia, Mexico, and Chile are the weighted average of the target or risk portfolio returns for each of those countries.

Table 12B.5 Fees and Contributions, December 2009

	Fees			Contributions		
	Salary percent	Death and disability insurances	Net fees	Contribution	Fee over contributions	Total
Region/country	(1)	(2)	(3) = (1) − (2)	(4)	(5) = [3(4) + (3)]	(6) = (1)/(4) + (1)
North						
Canada	—	—	1.32	4.95	—	—
United States	—	—	0.78	8.20	—	—
Mexico	—	—	1.81	8.50	—	—
Central						
Costa Rica[a]	—	—	0.40	3.85	0.09	—
El Salvador	2.70	1.20	1.50	10.30	0.13	0.21
Colombia[b]	3.00	1.41	1.59	11.50	0.12	0.21
South						
Brazil	—	—	2.00	8.00	—	—
Chile	3.37	1.87	1.50	10.00	0.13	0.25
Uruguay[c]	2.62	1.01	1.62	14.94	0.11	0.16

NOTE: — = not applicable or not necessary input for purpose of BASAL or traditional replacement rate calculation.

[a] Fee per transaction. Death and disability coverage is provided by public plan but its cost is included in the aging contribution period.

[b] Additional fees apply for rollover and voluntary contributions.

[c] Additionally, a custodial fee applied to balance. The average rate as of December 2007 was 0.0002%.

SOURCE: 2010 AIOS Bulletin with original footnotes translated into English. Data for Mexico, Colombia, Chile, Canada, Brazil, and the United States come from different sources.

References

Gómez-Hernández, Denise, and Fiona Stewart. 2008. "Comparison of Costs and Fees in Countries with Private Defined Contribution Pension Systems." Working Paper No. 6. Paris: International Organisation of Pension Supervisors.

Gómez-Hernández, Denise, Kato Vidal, and Leonardo Enrique. 2009. *Competitividad del Sistema de Pensiones Mexicano. Mercados y Negocios* (8): 25–37. Jalisco, Mexico: Universidad de Guadalajara, Centro Universitario de Ciencius Economico Administrativas.

Organisation for Economic Co-operation and Development (OECD). 2011. *Pensions at a Glance 2011: Retirement-income Systems in OECD and G20 Countries.* Paris: OECD. http://dx.doi.org/10.1787/pension_glance-2011-en (accessed July 12, 2012).

Ramírez de Jurado Frías, Alberto M. 2010. "Metodología para la Proyección del Monto Constitutivo de la Cuenta Individual dentro del Sistema de Ahorro para el Retiro en México." *Revista Actuari@* online magazine. http://revista-actuario.com/weff/ (accessed May 21, 2013).

Vigna, E., and S. Haberman. 2001. "Optimal Investment Strategy for Defined Contribution Pension Schemes." *Insurance: Mathematics and Economics* (28)2: 233–262.

Part 4

Reform Issues

13
Pension Fund Governance

Adam Samborski
Poznań School of Banking

This chapter analyzes the formal institutions of corporate governance for pension plans. It applies this analysis to open pension funds, which are mandatory individual account plans, operating in Poland. Each pension fund has a specific institutional arrangement, which determines to a large extent its effectiveness. Such an arrangement sets the pension fund under the influence of many stakeholders. The primary objective of regulations in the governance area of pension funds becomes a minimization of potential agency problems—conflicts of interest that may arise between the pension participants and those responsible for the fund's management.

PRINCIPAL–AGENT PROBLEM

In agency theory, agency relationships are understood as contracts under which a principal engages a third party (agent) to perform certain actions on their behalf in dealing with a second party, which is the provider of the service. The essence of agency theory can be reduced to two basic assumptions. First, expectations and objectives of principal and agent are various and remain in conflict (difference of interests, different objective function). Second, it is very difficult and expensive for the principal to check the agent's work. In agency theory the basic concept is the agency relationships (Szczepański 2010).

In pension arrangements, the plan participant is the principal, the plan sponsor is the agent, and the financial institution managing the pension funds is the second party. This implies the need for the principal to delegate certain powers to the agent to make certain decisions.

Then an agency relationship arises, which can be a public contract (formal, explicit) or an implicit contract (informal). The purpose of the contract is to ensure such actions of the agent so that he/she strives to maximize the principal's benefits. However, between the agent and the principal there is an asymmetry of information. This can lead to the agency problem, which usually occurs in two situations: hidden action of the agent, and hidden information or hidden knowledge possessed by the agent (Mesjasz 2002). In the first situation, the agent takes action, the course or outcome of which cannot be observed by the principal, resulting in the risk of moral hazard (the inclination of someone who is imperfectly checked to take part in behavior which may be dishonest or undesirable). In the second situation, the agent has information about environment variables, which the principal does not have before or after the conclusion of the contract. Ex ante asymmetry can lead to adverse selection, with the party having the superior information benefiting at the expense of the party with inferior information (Mesjasz 2002).

Agency problems can be prevented by concluding a complete contract, which will take into account all possible aspects and options of future situations. However, drawing up a complete contract is not feasible. Thus, we are dealing with incomplete contracts between principals and agents (Mesjasz 2002).

Agency problems can be limited in three ways:

1) reduction of information asymmetry,

2) seek harmonization between the principal's and the agent's objectives, and

3) building trust.

There are two options for reducing information asymmetry: screening (the principal keeps track of the agent in the corporation) and signaling (the agent gives specific signals to the principal, such as reports). Second, the interests of the principal and the agent can be harmonized by introducing incentive schemes (such as managerial options). Third, the agency problem can be reduced by agents building reputational capital that they want to maintain (Brink 2007).

Shaping the behavior of the agent in such a direction that his or her actions diverge from the principal interest as little as possible requires incurring certain costs, including drawing up contracts, monitoring and controlling the conduct of the agent by the principal, ensuring the interests of the principal, and residual loss (Aluchna 2002).

AGENCY PROBLEMS IN PRIVATE PENSION FUNDS AND WAYS TO LIMIT IT

Three levels of retirement provision can be distinguished under pension plans. The first two are mandatory and consist of redistributive and saving parts. The third, however, is voluntary: individual or occupational. The first level, redistributive, includes programs to ensure the minimum subsistence level for pensioners. The second level, savings, is designed to provide pensioners with a target retirement standard of living comparable to that when they were economically active. Within these levels, the programs are further classified by source (public, private), or the way to determine the pension benefits (Samborski 2011).

The following discussion addresses the second level—more precisely, private pension plans and funds—and the third level of pension provision. (The discussion does not apply to pension plans financed using book reserves, as in Germany.)

Assuming that the pension fund, like any organization, is a nexus of contracts, one can identify different expectations of pension funds stakeholders, but also areas of potential conflicts (Hess and Impavido 2004). Pension fund governance is, therefore, a mirror image of corporate governance in joint stock companies, which consists of a set of relations between the company's management, supervisory board, shareholders, and other stakeholders (OECD 2002). Pension fund governance, as well as corporate governance, deals with the posting of property rights by the principal to the agent, and consequently relies on the professional skills and management effectiveness of the agent (World Bank 2007). Private pension plans operate on the basis of the agency relationship between the plan members and beneficiaries, and the persons or entities involved in administering or funding it (such as a plan administrator or a plan sponsor). Governance under such plans includes all of the relationships between the entities and persons involved in the operation of a retirement plan, and it provides the structure through which the objectives of the retirement plan are established and the means to meet those objectives (OECD 2002).

Pension fund governance deals with issues of pension fund control and seeks to answer two basic questions: 1) in whose interests should checks on pension funds be carried out, and 2) who should monitor and control the pension funds on behalf of their members? The basic principles of corporate governance are applicable here: transparency, accountability, fairness, and responsibility (World Bank 2007).

Nonetheless, pension fund governance is much more complex than corporate governance because of the larger number of parties directly involved in pension fund operations. Therefore, all the rules of corporate governance do not apply here. Pension fund members do not generally exercise control through voting on fund administration, asset management companies, and their employees. It is difficult for fund members to dismiss a body managing the fund if it fulfills its duties improperly. In such cases the only solution for fund members is to change the fund or make claims for damages (World Bank 2007).

Governance in private pension plans and funds includes managerial control of the organization and means of regulation, including liability of management, and how it is monitored. The primary objective of regulation in pension funds governance is to reduce the potential agency problems or conflicts of interest that may arise between fund members and those responsible for managing the fund, which could negatively affect the security of retirement savings (Stewart and Yermo 2008). From this perspective, pension fund governance comes down to two issues: to protect the rights and interests of pension funds members, and to ensure the safety of sources of funding for future retirement benefits (World Bank 2007). It is worth considering, however, whether pension fund governance should be limited to minimizing the agency problems occurring between pension fund members and the entity responsible for managing the fund.

The pension fund can be considered as a nexus or network of explicit and implicit contracts between all entities in the relationship with it. Hence, pension fund governance cannot be confined only to deal with agency problems; its aim should be understood broadly to ensure good performance of the pension fund while maintaining low costs for all stakeholders (Stewart and Yermo 2008). Good governance, therefore, should be correlated with high rates of return on investment and low cost of capital (World Bank 2007).

Good governance of pension funds has a lot of benefits, which include building trust between all stakeholders, and reducing the need for specific regulations or facilitating supervision. It is also conducive to improving the efficiency of corporate governance in portfolio companies. The better managed the pension fund, the greater the opportunity to multiply the value of investments through the policy of active shareholders. Good governance in the pension fund must take into account the risk. The more sophisticated the investment strategies, the stricter and stronger the pension plan supervision must be (Stewart and Yermo 2008). The basis of pension fund operations should be, therefore, trust and development of long-term relationships with all stakeholders.

In pursuing these objectives, it is worth looking at the Guidelines for Pension Fund Governance elaborated by the OECD. The guidelines contained in them may be useful in the implementation of strategies for building trust and developing long-term relationships with all stakeholders. These guidelines are divided into two groups: governance structure and governance mechanisms.

Governance structure should provide the appropriate division of operational and supervisory responsibilities, and define the responsibilities and abilities of those entrusted to pension fund responsibilities (OECD 2002). Thus, it includes the following eight points:

1) Identification of responsibilities. There should be a clear identification and separation of operational and oversight responsibilities in the governance of a pension fund.

2) Governing body. Every pension fund should have a governing body vested with the power to administer the pension fund and which is ultimately responsible for ensuring the adherence to the terms of the arrangement and the protection of the best interest of plan members and beneficiaries.

3) Accountability. The governing body should be accountable to the pension plan members and beneficiaries, its supervisory board (where relevant), and the competent authorities.

4) Suitability. Membership in the governing body should be subject to minimum suitability (or nonsuitability) standards in order to ensure a high level of integrity, competence, experience, and professionalism in the governance of the pension fund.

5) Delegation and expert advice. The governing body may rely on the support of subcommittees and may delegate functions to internal staff of the pension entity or external service providers.

6) Auditor. An auditor, independent of the pension entity, the governing body, and the plan sponsor, should be appointed by the appropriate body or authority to carry out a periodic audit consistent with the needs of the arrangement.

7) Actuary. An actuary should be appointed by the appropriate body or authority for all defined benefit plans financed via pension funds.

8) Custodian. Custody of the pension fund assets may be carried out by the pension entity, the financial institution that manages the pension fund, or by an independent custodian (OECD 2009).

Pension funds should have appropriate control mechanisms, communication, and incentives to encourage good decision making, proper and timely implementation, and regular reviews and assessments (OECD 2002). The mechanisms of governance include the following:

- Risk-based internal controls. There should be adequate internal controls in place to ensure that all persons and entities with operational and oversight responsibilities act in accordance with the objectives set out in the pension entity's bylaws, statutes, contract, or trust instrument, or in documents associated with any of these, and that they comply with the law.

- Reporting. Reporting channels between all the persons and entities involved in the governance of the pension fund should be established in order to ensure the effective and timely transmission of relevant and accurate information.

- Disclosure. The governing body should disclose relevant information to all parties involved (notably pension plan members and beneficiaries, plan sponsors, supervisory authorities, and auditors,) in a clear, accurate, and timely fashion (OECD 2009).

ADDRESSING THE AGENCY PROBLEM IN PENSION FUNDS IN LIGHT OF POLISH EXPERIENCE

This analysis of governance solutions in pension funds in Poland is limited to open pension funds (see Figure 13.1), which are manda-

Figure 13.1 Structure of the Pension System in Poland

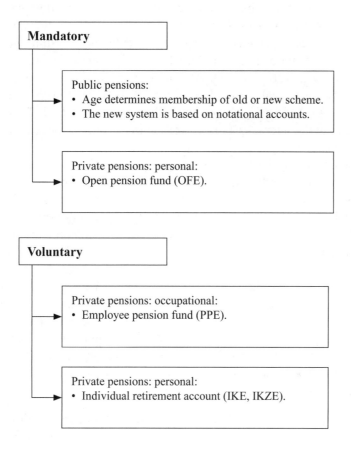

SOURCE: IOPS (2009).

tory individual account pension plans. Through the pension funds, part of the employee's earnings (collected by the Social Insurance Institution—it also manages the public pension plan) is invested in individual accounts. These accounts are managed by one of several funds. Employees buy from their fund a retirement annuity, which, when they retire, will serve as a source of retirement income. The amount of annuity depends on the amount of cash accumulated during one's career and the effectiveness of their investment.

Open pension funds can be created only by a general pension society (hereafter Society) acting as a joint stock company. The dominant shareholders of general pension societies are financial institutions, including international insurance companies, Polish financial institutions, and various consortia of Polish and international financial institutions (Kerner and Reinhardt 2010). The duration of the fund is unlimited. The fund acquires a legal personality upon being entered in the register of funds, then the fund authority becomes the Society. The basic document governing the internal affairs prevailing in the fund is the Articles of Association.

The objectives of the company are solely devoted to the creation and management of funds and their representation to third parties. The general society creates and manages (for a fee) only one open fund. The share capital of the company cannot be raised by public subscription. A purchase or acquisition of company's shares requires an approval of a supervisory authority, which is the Financial Supervision Commission.

The governing bodies of the Society are the Management Board, the Supervisory Board, and the general meeting. The Management Board of the Society cannot have fewer than three members, and it may also have an audit committee. Unless the Articles of Association provide otherwise, the general society board members are appointed and dismissed by the general meeting. The member of the Management Board must be a person who meets the following requirements:

- has full legal capacity;
- has not been convicted of an offense against property, credibility of documents, business transactions, trading in money and securities, tax offense;
- has higher education;
- holds a work experience of no less than seven years; and
- gives guarantee of the due performance as the board member.

At least one-third of the board should hold a university degree in law, economics, or be included in the list of investment advisors.

The Supervisory Board member of the Society must be a person who meets the requirements for the management board members in the first two points and gives guarantee of due performance as a member of the Supervisory Board. At least half of the Society Supervisory Board members should have a degree in law or economics. Moreover, at least half of the members of the general pension society are appointed from outside of shareholders of the Society and other related entities. The Society is responsible to the members of the fund for any damage caused by failure to perform or improper performance of their duties in managing the fund and its representation. The membership of the open fund follows the conclusion of the contract with the fund (Act of 28 August 1997).

The pension society receives from the pension fund a fee levied in the form of a percentage deduction from the amount of premiums (contributions) paid, not more than 3.5 percent, except that the deduction is made before the conversion of contributions into accounting units. In addition, the pension society charges a fee at the rate specified in the Articles of Association. This rate cannot exceed the amount calculated according to the scale specified by law. The rates of management fees decrease with each increase in fund assets exceeding the successive assets thresholds by the fund. Costs related to transactions of purchase or sale of fund assets and costs associated with the storage of assets by the depositary are covered by the fund assets. In addition, pension societies incur a fee for the contributions transfer and the costs of supervision and the Insurance Ombudsman. There is also the cost of the guarantee fund that insures the pension funds (Sołdek 2011).

The pension fund invests its assets in accordance with the law, seeking to achieve a maximum degree of safety and profitability of the investments made. The legislature defines the investment limits.

The open fund, which has received contributions for at least 36 months, determines each year at the end of March and September the rate of return for the last 36 months and reports it to the supervisory body. On this basis, the supervisory body calculates the weighted average rate of return of all open-end funds and releases that information to the public. The weighted average rate of return is the basis for calculating the minimum required rate of return that applies for all open pension funds. When the rate of return of an open pension fund for the period of 36 months is smaller than the minimum required rate of return, a deficit arises in an open fund, which sponsors of the open fund will pay.

The fund is obliged to choose a depositary, to whom, by an agreement, it entrusts the storage of its assets. A depositary can only be a bank. The agreement with the depositary for the fund assets storage should specify in detail the duties of a depositary and the fund.

The open fund is obliged to publish a prospectus once a year in a national daily newspaper dedicated to the fund announcements and advertising. The fund's prospectus should contain its Articles of Association, information on the fund's investment performance, and approved annual financial statements of the fund. The Society and the fund provide periodic reports to the supervisory authority and current information on their activities and financial position (Act of 28 August 1997).

CONCLUSION

The basic sources of conflicts of interest in the pension funds occur in the relationships between fund members and the management entity on the amount of fees charged by the Society.

The pension fund is a legal entity. The managing body of the fund is the pension society established as a joint stock company. Such a solution entails reducing the efficiency of the management authority focused on the best interests of pension plan members. Pension funds have been established in the majority of cases by the general pension societies in which dominant shareholders are financial institutions. As a result, financial institutions easily introduce their candidates to the supervisory boards of societies. It may turn out that the financial institution controls both the Supervisory Board and the Management Board. Therefore, it is proposed to take steps aimed at increasing the independence of supervisory boards in general pension societies.

Furthermore, the low level of society's economic awareness and the low interest in retirement issues encourage societies to undertake expensive marketing campaigns to attract as many members as possible. Such campaigns usually lead not to improved investment performance of the fund but to higher administrative costs and fees incurred by fund members. Hence, I propose a statutory reduction of fees that pension societies charge, and linking their pay to the results of open pension funds investment. In addition, greater emphasis should be laid on financial education relating to the pension system operating principles in the Polish society.

A wider analysis of detailed internal regulations in the area of governance would be advisable, both in open pension funds and in general pension societies. The problem, however, is that such legal solutions have not been made public. This remark does not apply to principles of corporate governance in investment operations of open funds and their Articles of Association, which are publicly available. To explain the reasons for varying the rate of development of individual pension funds, the institutional analysis should be applied not only to formal institutions of corporate governance, but also informal institutions. The results of such analyses would allow for studying the issue of improving the efficiency of Polish pension funds investment from a different perspective.

References

Act of 28 August 1997. Law on the Organization and Operation of Pension Funds. Based on Journal of Laws of 2010, No. 34, Item 189, with subsequent amendments.

Aluchna, Maria. 2002. "Koszty agencji jako determinanta efektywności nadzoru korporacyjnego." In *Strategiczne obszary nadzoru korporacyjnego zewnętrznego i wewnętrznego,* Stanislaw Rudolf, ed. Łódź, Poland: University of Łódź, pp. 75–85.

Brink, Alexander. 2007. "A Normative Theory of the Firm. Specific Investments as Legitimation for Residual Claims: Considerations on Ethical Integration from the Perspective of Governance Theory." Paper presented at the Conference of the German Association of Economists, held at the University of Freiburg, March 1–3. http://www.wipo.uni-freiburg.de/conferences/vfs-tagung (accessed August 26, 2013).

Hess, David, and Gregorio Impavido. 2004. "Governance of Public Pension Funds: Lessons from Corporate Governance and International Evidence." In *Public Pension Fund Management. Governance, Accountability and Investment Policies*, Alberto R. Musalem and Robert J. Palacios, eds. Washington, DC: World Bank, pp. 49–90.

International Organization of Pension Supervisors (IOPS). 2009. *Country Profiles—Poland.* Paris: IOPS. http://www.oecd.org/site/iops/research/44873983.pdf (accessed September 30, 2012).

Kerner, Andrew, and Eric Reinhardt. 2010. *Wpływ polityki inwestycyjnej OFE na ład korporacyjny w Polsce*. Sprawne państwo.Warsaw: Ernst & Young Polska Sp. z o.o.

Mesjasz, Czesław. 2002. "Kontrakty niekompletne jako podstawa teoretyczna nadzoru korporacyjnego." In *Strategiczne obszary nadzoru korporacyjnego zewnętrznego i wewnętrznego*, Stanisław Rudolf, ed. Łódź, Poland: University of Łódź, pp. 53–66.

Organisation for Economic Co-operation and Development (OECD). 2002. *Guidelines for Pension Fund Governance*. Paris: OECD. http://www.oecd.org/insurance/privatepensions/2767694.pdf (accessed September 30, 2012).

————. 2009. *OECD Guidelines for Pension Fund Governance*. Paris: OECD. http://www.oecd.org/insurance/privatepensions/34799965.pdf (accessed September 30, 2012).

Samborski, Adam. 2011. "Determinanty zmian w systemach emerytalnych – ujęcie globalne." *Polityka Społeczna*. Numer specjalny: Problemy zabezpieczenia emerytalnego w Polsce i na świecie. Część I: pp. 31–35.

Sołdek, Andrzej. 2011. "Wpływ opłat na wielkość oszczędności gromadzonych w regulowanych i dobrowolnych systemach emerytalnych." *Polityka Społeczna*. Numer specjalny: Problemy zabezpieczenia emerytalnego w Polsce i na świecie. Część I: pp. 38 – 43.

Stewart, Fiona, and Juan Yermo. 2008. "Pension Fund Governance: Challenges and Potential Solutions." OECD Working Papers on Insurance and Private Pensions. No. 18. Paris: OECD. doi:10.1787/24140225631 (accessed August 26, 2013).

Szczepański, Marek. 2010. *Stymulatory i bariery rozwoju zakładowych systemów emerytalnych na przykładzie Polski*. Poznań: Wydawnictwo Politechniki Poznańskiej.

World Bank. 2007. *Czech Republic. Pilot Diagnostic Review of Governance of the Private Pension Fund Sector*. Washington, DC: World Bank.

14

Financial Literacy, Education, and Advice

John A. Turner
Pension Policy Center

Dana M. Muir
Stephen M. Ross School of Business, University of Michigan

Social security privatization with individual accounts and employer-provided defined contribution systems shift responsibility for investment decisions to individual workers. With social security privatization, workers usually have some choice as to how the money in their individual accounts is invested. The choices workers make can have an important effect on their levels of retirement income. By comparison, in traditional social security and pension systems, fewer burdens for decision-making responsibility are placed on individual workers. Instead, decisions regarding financial management of investments are made by financial professionals. A further distinction is that in traditional defined benefit plans workers do not bear financial market risk, while in privatized defined contribution plans workers do bear this risk. This raises the issue of how to communicate to workers who are financially unsophisticated to the possible consequences of financial market risk.

Proponents of social security privatization and defined contribution systems argue that workers are capable of learning about financial markets and investments and making good financial decisions. Traditional economics, which assumes well-informed, rational decision makers, supports that position. Behavioral economics, however, focuses on the difficulties that many workers have making financial decisions. Many workers are not interested in, and some are not capable of, learning the financial information needed to adequately manage an individual account. In addition, the market for financial services is more complex and less transparent than most other markets for goods and services (Rajnes 2003).

In part because of problems clients have encountered when they seek financial advice, trust in financial services is at a low level. A recent survey in the EU finds that many people mistrust pension and investment services, ranking 50th among the services surveyed and ranking lower in trust than the market for used cars or for gambling (KPMG 2011).

In this chapter, we discuss financial literacy and financial advice as weak links in social security privatization and employer-provided defined contribution systems. They cause programs to take on added expenses to try to reduce the effects of worker investment errors and bad advice. Widespread financial education has become a necessary part of social security privatization.

We begin by discussing the lack of financial literacy and some of the types of errors that workers make in managing individual account pensions. We document that lack of financial literacy is widespread in a number of countries. We then discuss in turn financial education and financial advice as possible responses. Financial education is often seen to have limited success, in part because of a lack of interest by workers. This discussion is followed by commentary on problems that have arisen with financial advice, including legal issues that arise when advisers do not have a fiduciary duty to act in the best interest of their clients. We explain how the structure and level of advisory fees may result in conflicts of interest that may affect the quality of advice provided to individuals. Then we explain how laws and regulations are evolving in different countries in response to the conflicts of interest. We offer conclusions in a final section.

ERRORS INVESTORS MAKE

Making investment decisions is a complex process that requires an understanding of risk diversification as well as knowledge about different types of investments. A recent U.S. survey finds that 34 percent of investors were "overwhelmed" by the options facing them (Cornfield

2012). Another study finds that only 31 percent of U.S. workers are confident in their ability to manage their investments during retirement (Yakoboski 2005). A Canadian study finds that workers rated choosing the right investment for their individual account pension plan (RRSP plan in Canada) as more stressful than seeing the dentist (*Canadian Press* 2005).

While traditional economic theory assumes that investors do not make systematic errors, increasingly economic theory, using insights from behavioral economics, suggests otherwise (Turner 2003). Pension participants make at least three types of investment errors: 1) insufficient diversification of their investment portfolios, 2) inappropriate level of risk holdings in their investment portfolios, and 3) inappropriate portfolio adjustments, for example, in response to a market downturn.

With insufficient diversification, participants in some individual account systems purchase investment funds that are too narrowly focused on a particular segment of the investment market. For example, one study of U.S. defined contribution plan participants finds that most held either no equities (48 percent) or only equities (22 percent) in their portfolios, rather than diversifying (Agnew, Balduzzi, and Sundén 2003). Thus, with inappropriate levels of risk holdings, some investors hold investment portfolios that are either too conservative or too risky. With inappropriate portfolio adjustments, some investors tend to chase returns, purchasing the mutual funds that have risen and selling those that have fallen in value. A further error may be lack of sensitivity to fees, causing pension participants to spend too much in fees (Hastings, Mitchell, and Chyn 2011).

Sweden has attempted to provide investment information to the participants of its privatized social security system. Survey results concerning the mandatory individual account system in Sweden, where workers can choose from more than 600 mutual funds (Turner 2004), suggest that some participants may have been confused about their participation in the investment process. While 18 percent actually chose their investments (rather than taking the default), 34 percent thought they had (Betson 2001). Another Swedish survey indicated that of those Swedes who made a choice, 73 percent could not name all the funds they had invested in, and 41 percent could not name any of them (Jarvenpaa 2001).

A World Bank survey of the privatized social security systems in Latin America finds that workers and retirees encountered problems in making a number of decisions required of them by those systems (Devesa-Carpio and Vidal-Meliá 2002). These decisions extend beyond simply making investment decisions regarding the composition of their investment portfolios. They had difficulty choosing a pension fund management company, deciding whether to make additional contributions, whether to switch into the privatized system (when that choice was open to them), what form to receive benefits (phased withdrawal, annuity), and choosing a life insurance company to provide an annuity.

The errors participants make can be due to their lack of information when making investment decisions. Lack of information can include lack of knowledge about investing and lack of information about stock markets. Pension participants may lack information for financial decision making because of both the amount of information they have assimilated and the amount available to them. As a result of government or employer attempts to overcome the lack of information, some workers may suffer from the opposite problem—information overload (Agnew and Szykman 2004). They may have too much information, which also causes difficulties for workers when attempting to make investment decisions.

FINANCIAL LITERACY

A major reason why pension participants make investment errors may be a lack of financial literacy. Many do not have basic financial knowledge, lacking an understanding of financial terms and how financial markets work. For example, studies generally show that people do not know what happens to bond prices when interest rates rise (Lusardi 2006). In another survey in the United States, only a third of respondents correctly answered three questions about inflation, interest rates, and risk diversification (Lusardi and Mitchell 2006). Many people may not understand commonly used financial market jargon, such as "equity." A survey of pension participants finds that 10 percent did not know what the word *fund* meant (Russell 2012).

Causes of Financial Illiteracy

Numeracy is an aspect of financial literacy; it is the ability to apply simple mathematical concepts. One example of a lack of numeracy is exponential growth bias, which results in a lack of understanding of compound interest. Studies have shown that many people have a tendency to do linear (straight line) projections of growth of account balances, rather than exponential (upward curved) projections that are the result of compound interest. For this reason, they underestimate the benefits of saving because they underestimate its future value (Stango and Zinman 2009).

Literacy is a basic skill needed for financial literacy. A study in the United Kingdom finds that one-fifth of young persons aged 16–19 have low levels of literacy (17 percent) and numeracy (22 percent), making it difficult for them to function in the labor market (Shepherd 2010). These people would also have difficulty dealing with issues relating to investments. Data from the World Bank indicate that small minorities of people are illiterate in some countries that have privatized their social security systems. For example, the literacy rate in El Salvador is 84 percent, in Peru it is 90 percent, and in Mexico it is 93 percent. These rates are high compared to some poor African countries, such as Ethiopia (World Bank 2012). In the United States, the state of Alabama has an adult literacy rate of 85 percent (National Center for Educational Statistics 2012).

Prevalence of Financial Illiteracy

In some countries with generous traditional social security systems, financial literacy is not a major policy issue. Countries where the retirement system relies on defined contribution plans, either as part of privatized social security or as voluntary plans, place a greater burden of financial literacy on their workers. A study of financial literacy in 28 countries finds that, according to its measure, the leading countries for financial literacy are Brazil, Mexico, Australia, United States, and Canada (Ribeiro 2012). Nearly all of these countries place heavy reliance on defined contribution plans.

Even in countries that rank relatively high in financial literacy, many people lack basic financial knowledge. For example, a study in Canada finds that 16 percent participating in an employer-provided pension plan did not know whether the plan was an individual account (defined contribution) or traditional pension (defined benefit) plan (Schellenberg and Ostrovsky 2008). A study in the United States finds that fewer than one-third of young adults had basic knowledge about risk diversification, interest rates, and inflation (Lusardi, Mitchell, and Curto 2010). In the United States, studies document that many workers lack basic financial knowledge (e.g., Lusardi and Mitchell 2006; McCarthy and Turner 2000). For example, surveys have found that many people do not know that they are paying fees for the management of the investments in their defined contribution plans (Turner and Korczyk 2004). Studies have indicated that a lack of financial literacy is prevalent in many countries. International research demonstrates that many workers lack financial literacy in Germany, the Netherlands, Sweden, Japan, Italy, New Zealand, and the United States (Lusardi and Mitchell 2011).

Gender plays a role in the lack of financial literacy—women on average are less financially literate than men (Lusardi and Mitchell 2011). Reasons for this could include a division of labor in some households, where men take responsibility for financial decisions, or it could be that women are less confident in dealing with numbers. The groups who are the least financially literate also are those who are the most financially vulnerable—minorities, women, and people with low levels of education and income (Hastings, Mitchell, and Chyn 2011). Thus, those most in need of financial skills to deal with a privatized social security system are the least well-equipped, making them even more vulnerable.

Chile is a leader of the social security privatization movement, having privatized its social security system in 1981. In Chile, according to the 2009 Social Protection Survey, 94 percent of respondents indicated that they did not know anything about the pension options that existed (IOPS 2011). This lack of knowledge existed even though the pension system had been in existence for more than 25 years. A study in Chile finds that workers with lower levels of financial literacy and lower education and income tend to rely on their employers, coworkers, and friends more than on cost fundamentals in choosing a pension fund (Hastings, Mitchell, and Chyn 2011). As a result, they may make poor fund choices that adversely affect their retirement security.

One problem for people with low levels of financial literacy is that people tend to think they know more than they do. For example, in an

Australian survey, 67 percent indicated that they understood compound interest, but only 28 percent were able to determine the correct answer to a problem involving that concept (OECD 2006). Before governments can successfully provide financial education, they need to convince workers that they need it.

FINANCIAL EDUCATION

Growth

The growth in financial education provided by governments and employers in a number of countries is a direct result of the increasing importance of defined contribution plans as voluntary or mandatory parts of retirement income systems. Financial education can cover such topics as investment terminology, asset allocation, risk tolerance, and retirement goal setting (Olsen and Whitman 2007). The cost of financial education becomes one of the costs of social security privatization, though it often is not included in studies that compare the advantages of privatized to traditional social security programs and compute the rates of return in privatized systems. Using financial education to address the lack of financial literacy of pension participants is not a quick fix; it needs to be a long-term and sustained effort, which can be quite costly (Ashcroft and Stewart 2010).

Several international organizations, such as the OECD and the International Organisation of Pension Supervisors (IOPS 2011), have taken an interest in financial education for pension participants in individual account pension systems. In 2008, the OECD created the International Network on Financial Education.

A survey by IOPS (2011) found that 16 out of 19 financial supervisors of pension systems provided some type of financial education. The pension supervisors not providing financial education tend to be fairly young, with intentions of providing financial education in the future. In Chile, the pension supervisory authority has a specific budget set aside for financial education (Ashcroft and Stewart 2010). Chile has launched several initiatives to encourage financial literacy, and in Mexico, the pension supervisory authority has undertaken a comprehensive program of financial education (IOPS 2011). This program has provided financial education not only to workers and those nearing retirement, but also to school children. In the United States, 13 out of the 50 states require that children in secondary (high) school are required to take a class in personal finance (Malcolm 2012).

In 2009, more than 20 U.S. federal government agencies had programs aimed at improving financial literacy (U.S. Government Accountability Office 2011). One of the often overlooked aspects of these programs is their cost, as they are funded with general government tax revenues.

Along with financial education, there has been an increased focus on the content of periodic statements provided to pension participants, which is part of an effort to improve communication. These statements are being used to attempt to improve the financial literacy of participants and their understanding of their pension plans. However, there is little consensus as to what information, beyond basic account information, should be provided and how. In particular, there is no consensus as to whether projections of possible future account balances should be included and how they should be calculated so as to indicate the possible effects of financial market risk. Communicating to pension participants about risk is a difficult and unresolved aspect of financial education (Antolin and Harrison 2012).

Effectiveness

In the United States, financial education often occurs at the workplace. Evidence suggests that financial education programs have had some success in helping people who participate in them make better decisions concerning saving for retirement (Hathaway and Kahtiwada 2008). Studies of workplace financial education programs have shown improved financial literacy after taking the programs (Clark, Morrill, and Allen 2012). These results, however, may be affected to some extent by selection bias in that positive results are found for programs for people who voluntarily participate because of their interest in learning about the subject. Some studies show limited effects of financial education, which may be in part because the financial education provided was of limited duration, such as a one-time presentation. Also, some people have difficulty following through on their intentions for making changes following financial education (Lusardi 2006).

Studies indicate that many people are not interested in financial education. One U.S. survey finds that 56 percent of employees did not review the educational material provided by their pension plans. In that survey, 52 percent said that they do not have the time, interest, or knowledge to manage their 401(k) plan adequately (Gray 2012). These results indicate that provision of information alone is insufficient to deal with problems of financial literacy.

The effectiveness of financial education may depend in part on details as to how it is presented, with behavioral economics providing insights as to effective methods. A study of Chilean workers (Hastings, Mitchell, and Chyn 2011) finds that framing investment information relating to investment choices as gains rather than losses had a large effect on the way the information was perceived, particularly by people with lower levels of education.

TRANSPARENCY

An alternative to dealing with problems of financial literacy is to make financial products more transparent in their features and costs. Often, pension participants and other investors do not understand the fees they are paying (Turner and Korczyk 2004). A lack of understanding about fees may in part be the result of a lack of transparency. In addition, attempts can be made to standardize financial products, simplify them, and limit their possible features so as to facilitate comparability across financial products (Inderst and Ottaviani 2012). A further approach is to standardize disclosure, to make it easier for clients to compare costs and risks across financial products. In addition, attempts have been made to assure that disclosures are made in "plain English," that is, that they are written in language that is comprehensible by people with low levels of education.

DEFAULTS

Transparency and financial education, however, rarely are sufficient to deal with the problems many participants face when given
the responsibility for managing their investments (Ashcroft and Stewart 2010). One way of dealing with the lack of interest in and lack of
knowledge of about financial market issues of some participants in
privatized social security systems is to establish defaults that provide
reasonable outcomes for workers opting out of the decision-making
process. Studies have shown that defaults can have a major impact on
pension participants in some circumstances (Choi et al. 2002; Madrian
and Shea 2001). Sweden has a default investment in its mandatory individual account system for people not choosing an investment (Turner
2004). Australia has also established a system of investment defaults
for its mandatory individual account system (Muir 2012).

Defaults are a form of implicit advice, incorporating decision-
making outcomes that experts view as desirable. With defaults, individuals who lack interest or knowledge in making financial decisions rely
on the default investments to be a reasonable option. In addition, others
who are knowledgeable may accept the default as a form of advice.

FINANCIAL INCENTIVES

The traditional policy approach to affect people's behavior is
through financial incentives. Individuals do have financial incentives
to overcome financial illiteracy and make effective investment decisions, because doing so would presumably improve their investment
decisions and ultimately the amount of money they had accumulated
at retirement. However, it seems that the incentives are not sufficient to
have much effect on behavior. This may be due in part to the lack of a
clear connection between achieving financial literacy and the financial
rewards from doing so.

BANNING SOME PRODUCTS OR PRACTICES

Another approach to protecting unsophisticated investors is to ban certain financial products or practices. For example, in the United States, financial advisers are not permitted to charge fees based on the performance of the clients' portfolios, except for wealthy clients who are presumably sophisticated investors. Similarly, in the United States participants in defined contribution plans and Individual Retirement Accounts are prohibited from making certain investments, such as using their pension funds to purchase a home, short selling, or investing in collectibles, such as art work.

FINANCIAL ADVICE

Because of a lack of interest and engagement among some workers, there has been limited success with financial education. Therefore, attention has also focused on providing financial advice. While financial education provides general information about investments and financial markets, financial advice provides specific suggestions as to what investments to make. The use of advisers allows for specialization and economies of scale in the acquisition of financial skills and knowledge. With advisers, not everyone needs to become an expert. Financial expertise can be a specialized skill rather than one that is generally held. However, workers with low financial literacy may be vulnerable to exploitation through bad advice when the adviser can profit by steering clients to more expensive options.

Financial advisers can assist clients in several ways. They can provide financial advice, financial education, decision support, and marketing information, and they can manage the individual's investments. Decision support is education targeted to help a client reach a decision. Marketing information may appear to the client to be unbiased advice but is designed to sell a product. Many advisers assist their clients in carrying out their advice. If they provide financial management, they make investment decisions and carry them out, generally without involving the individual investor in the decision (Turner and Muir 2012).

Problems with Financial Advice

Workers seeking financial advice concerning investment decisions may encounter problems relating to the advice they receive, including the use of jargon and confusing terminology relating to fees, lack of knowledge about the client's goals and risk tolerance, lack of disclosure about fees, conflicts of interest of financial advisers that affect the quality of advice, lack of fiduciary protection against conflicts of interest, and a problem called "hat switching." With hat switching, a financial adviser has different levels of responsibility to the client depending on the circumstances. For example, under some circumstances in the United States advisers are required to provide advice in the best interest of their clients, while in other circumstances they are only required to provide advice that is suitable for their clients. For a financial adviser to provide quality advice, he must have some knowledge of the goals and risk tolerance of the client. This issue is sometimes formalized in "know your client requirements" that establish minimum standards for advisers concerning information they obtain from their clients.

Financial advisers have conflicts of interest when they have a financial stake in the advice that they provide. For example, that occurs if the adviser receives greater compensation when he recommends investments with higher fees for the recipient of the advice. If the adviser is also a salesperson, he will probably advise purchasing the financial products he sells rather than other products.

Information that financial advisers provide to participants can be tainted by conflicts of interest that the advisers have. Mutual funds, for example, often provide information about investing, but rarely does that information include the advice to determine how much the person is paying in fees, and to look for low-cost providers and funds. Lack of knowledge about fees charged can lead to participants paying higher fees than if they were better informed.

Part of the problem arising from conflicts of interest is that financial advisers do not have a fiduciary duty to their clients in some countries. For example, in the United States stockbrokers generally do not have a fiduciary duty to their clients when they advise them. Financial advisers have a clear information advantage over their clients that they can exploit for their gain when they do not have a fiduciary duty to act in the best interest of their clients. This may result in agency costs, which clients incur when an agent does not act in the best interest of the client. Agency costs can include the client paying higher fees, taking on greater risk, and having too much trading of their portfolio (churning). A lack of both educational standards for advisers and uniform certification requirements, combined with insufficient regulation of conflicts of interest, prevent financial advisers from achieving the quality expected of an advice professional.

An audit study in the United States has documented a number of problems with the financial advice that clients receive (Mullainathan, Noeth, and Schoar 2012). The study finds that advisers push for actively managed portfolios with high fees, even if clients start with well-diversified portfolios with low fees, and that financial advisers tend to profit from investor errors. For example, some investors sell during downturns and buy during upturns, known as "chasing returns." Rather than "debiasing" their clients, some advisers support that strategy, presumably because it involves greater sales commissions for themselves, even though it results in worse outcomes for their clients.

Australia has recognized the importance of pension participants receiving quality financial advice in its system of mandatory individual accounts. It recently commissioned a study where it rated the quality of financial advice that people received. Out of 64 cases reviewed, only two people received what was considered to be high-quality financial advice. The majority (37 people) received adequate advice, while a significant minority (25 people) received poor quality advice. People receiving poor advice received advice that was inappropriate for their situation. Forty-two percent of people do not trust financial advisers and would not follow their recommendations (Kell 2012). Most people are not capable of judging whether the advice they are receiving is good. In the Australian study, most people who received poor advice thought that they had received good advice (Kell 2012). People may have difficulty assessing the quality of advice they receive. Nonetheless, according to a survey by the Investor Protection Trust, about 20 percent of adults aged 65 or older in the United States report having "been taken advantage of financially in terms of an inappropriate investment, unreasonably high fees for financial services, or outright fraud" (Infogroup/ORC 2010).

A study conducted in Singapore concerning the quality of financial advice received by "mystery shoppers," people who took part in the study, finds that frequently financial advisers did not obtain enough information from their clients to make suitable recommendations (Monetary Authority of Singapore 2012). For example, less than half asked about the clients' risk preferences. The study also finds that fees were not disclosed or discussed in nearly half of the cases. In 28 percent of the cases, the advice was judged to be suitable by independent financial experts, in 40 percent the advice might be suitable, and in 28 percent the advice was not suitable for the clients' needs.

Financial advice can provide a valuable service to clients. However, a U.S. survey finds that 83 percent of those surveyed indicated that they would be interested in receiving professional assistance in managing their 401(k) plans, but only 10 percent took advantage of that option when it was offered (Gray 2012).

Effects of Financial Advice

Several studies have examined the effects of advice. Hung and Yoong (2012) examine survey data relating to defined contribution plan participants to study whether advice resulted in improved results. They find little evidence of improved results. In an experiment, they find some evidence that unsolicited advice was ineffective, but when participants actively solicited advice the advice resulted in improved outcomes. Employees with low levels of financial literacy were more likely to solicit advice and to benefit from the advice.

Because of conflicts of interest, recipients of advice may actually have worse outcomes than those not receiving advice. A study in Germany of bank customers who used a financial adviser compensated through commissions finds that the portfolios of those customers who used a financial adviser had lower rates of return net of costs (Hackenthal, Haliassos, and Japelli 2011). Similarly, a U.S. study finds that mutual funds recommended by financial advisers underperformed other mutual funds on a risk-adjusted basis, taking into account fees (Bergstresser, Chalmers, and Tufano 2009).

Financial Advice Reforms

A number of countries are considering the issues of the quality of financial advice and its cost, and are considering reforms that would increase consumer protection.

United States. The U.S. Department of Labor is working on proposed regulations to improve the quality of advice to pension plan participants. Proposals have been made to extend fiduciary standards that apply to investment advisers and brokers.

United Kingdom. In order to improve the quality of advice, the UK has made it illegal for advisers to receive commissions for selling products to clients. Advisers who sell products tend to recommend the products they sell, which may not be the best products for particular clients. Instead, advisers will be required to charge their clients fees for their services, which will reduce conflicts of interest. It will have the further advantage that the compensation advisers receive will be more transparent. This reform is being made because the receipt of commissions has been viewed as a root cause of the pension misselling scandal in the UK. Previously, financial advisers receiving commissions for making recommendations concerning pensions to clients had an obligation to make recommendations in the best interest of the client, but it had become clear that because of commissions that approach was not working.

One criticism of banning commissions is that a single fee paid at the time of the advice may be too expensive for some clients, effectively preventing them from receiving advice. If the upfront fees are too expensive for a client to pay at one time, advisers in the UK are permitted to spread the fee charged over a period of time (BBC 2010).

An additional new requirement in the UK is that advisers will be required to tell their clients if their advice is independent, meaning that they provide advice over a full range of investment options, or if it is restricted, meaning that the advice they provide is only over a limited range of investments options, such as the options provided by the company they work for (Osborne 2010).

In addition, as of the end of 2012, a new agency in the UK, the Financial Conduct Authority, will be responsible for protecting consumers in financial markets. A regulatory issue this agency will face is the trade-off between protecting some consumers from detriment by not permitting certain risky investment products, while limiting the choice of others.

Australia. Australia is implementing legislation to improve the quality of advice (Kell 2012). To address problems associated with financial advice, Australia has instituted the Future of Financial Advice (FoFA) reform, which takes effect in July 2013. By eliminating commissions for advisers, the reform eliminates the problem of "hat switching," which occurs when an adviser receives fees for advice but also receives commissions depending on what he advises that the client purchases. In addition, advisers have a statutory requirement to act in the best interest of their clients, which is commonly considered to be a fiduciary duty. Thus, when they recommend a financial product, they will have the duty to recommend the product that is in the best interest of their client, not the one that is merely suitable. Also, the reform attempts to improve the transparency of fees. When advisers provide ongoing advice, they will be required to renew their fee agreements with clients every two years. In addition, the reforms attempt to facilitate the provision of "scaled" advice, which would be advice on a limited set of issues, rather than a full-scale review of their financial situation.

The Netherlands. The Netherlands Minister of Finance is considering legislation to improve the quality of advice, including requiring that every adviser have a college degree, that there be more emphasis on continuing education for financial advisers, and that examination questions for advisers' certification correspond more to the actual situations for which they provide advice (Schlingmann, Schutte, and Somsen 2012).

Singapore. Singapore is considering reforms of the way financial advice is provided. The Singapore regulator has already introduced limits on fees (KPMG 2011).

India. India has banned load fees charged on purchases of investment products (KPMG 2011).

While a number of countries are taking steps to increase the availability of unbiased financial advice to pension participants, the question remains whether implementing costly reforms will help participants in terms of improving pension outcomes.

LEGAL ISSUES

As the foregoing discussion indicates, countries around the world face similar issues when structuring a legal framework intended to increase access to financial advice while also ensuring that advice is not degraded by conflicts of interest, fraud, or misrepresentation of the adviser's qualifications. Examples also exist to illustrate the potential legal issues that result when a population is not financially literate.

Misselling in the United Kingdom

In the late 1980s, UK citizens were permitted to choose more in-dividualized pensions, known as personal pensions, where they could select the pension provider rather than participate in the public pension scheme or a scheme offered by their employers. Insurance companies and financial advisers aggressively sold personal pensions without complying with the regulations that required them to understand the risk preferences and financial positions of their customers. A study commissioned after the misselling came to the attention of regulators, who concluded that the lack of regulatory compliance was widespread (Muir 2009).

The misselling caused many employees who bought personal pensions to be worse off than if they would have stayed in their employers' occupational scheme. At least at the time, the benefits formulas of occupational schemes tended to result in higher benefits than the investment returns on the personal pensions. Also, only employees (not employers) contributed to personal pensions. In comparison, employers typically did contribute to occupational schemes. So, the employees who were sold personal pensions forfeited their employers' contributions and received lower returns on the money they personally contributed (Muir 2009).

Some experts held both the financial services industry and the regulatory system to blame for the misselling scandal. The financial services industry provided compensation incentives for their sales forces to market personal pensions. This illustrates the potential effects of conflicts of interest, particularly when a new market opens up because of a rapid shift in a country's retirement funding paradigm. At the same time, regulators had little experience with the products being sold and the marketing techniques being used because of the shift in the paradigm to increase employee choice (Muir 2009).

Australia's Attention to Defaults

Australia does not have any history of shifting its government-run social insurance scheme to a privatization model. However, there is a sense in which there is a shadow privatization scheme in existence. Australia's government-run system, known as the Age Pension, is a pay-as-you-go pension program that is both means and asset tested. Australia also has a mandatory employment-based system, known as the Superannuation Guarantee (SG System), which requires employers to contribute 9 percent of most income for most employees to an individual account (Muir 2011). Because the Age Pension is means and asset tested, retirees with higher SG System account balances are less likely to qualify for the Age Pension. Thus, there is a sense in which the SG System is a privatized Age Pension for those fortunate enough to accumulate substantial account balances.

In 2010, a panel constituted by the Australian government to study the SG System released its report, which has come to be known as the *Cooper Report*. The two-part report addresses many perceived deficiencies in the SG System and made recommendations for improvement. The panel's findings on the importance of defaults are of particular interest here. The panel determined that having a financially literate population as a long-term goal would be useful. But, critical to the *Cooper Report*'s recommendation is its finding that shorter-term issues could not be resolved through education and financial literacy. Instead, it based its recommendation for a low-cost, more heavily regulated default system on the principle that not all members of the SG System are able or want to be involved in investment selection. Australia is currently in the process of moving toward the "MySuper" default product recommended in the *Cooper Report* (Muir 2011).

Regulation of Investment Advice in the United States

The United States has not moved to privatize Social Security, although as noted earlier such privatization has been considered. The issues of financial literacy and financial advice, however, have become more important as the population ages, as the United States becomes increasingly reliant on a defined contribution paradigm, and as the twin problems of high unemployment and a volatile stock market challenge retirement wealth creation.

A detailed discussion of the U.S. regulatory structure that applies to mutual funds, investment advice, brokers, and related financial services industry entities is beyond the scope of this chapter. At its essence, the complexities derive from two sources. The first is the state government and federal government dichotomy. Each state has some regulatory power over financial services industry entities that are active in the state. The federal government effectively has regulatory authority over all financial services entities. In some instances a state or multiple states may impose higher standards than imposed by the federal regulators. In others, the federal regulations may be more strict than those of the states. The second set of complexities results from the way regulatory power is allocated within a state and particularly at the federal level. The primary division of power at the federal level is between the Securities and Exchange Commission (SEC) and Employee Benefits Security Administration (EBSA). The SEC's mandate is to focus on investor protection. EBSA is charged with overseeing the regulation of private-sector employer-based retirement plans, including defined contribution plans (Turner and Muir 2012).

Over the past two years, the most controversial regulatory issue of import for this chapter has been whether the SEC or EBSA will apply fiduciary obligations to a larger set of financial services entities and individuals. EBSA proposed regulations to accomplish that in 2010 and—after congressional hearings, widespread publicity, and significant industry concern—withdrew the proposed regulations in 2011. Reportedly efforts continue to revise the proposed regulations for reissue. In response to a legislative requirement, the SEC staff studied the differing levels of client obligation discussed above, from fiduciary to suitability, as well as the hat-switching problem. In a report issued in 2011, the SEC staff recommended adoption of a single federal fiduciary standard that would apply to brokers as well as investment advisers. The costs and benefits of such an approach remain under study (Turner and Muir 2012).

CONCLUSION

An aspect of social security privatization and employer-provided defined contribution systems that raises their costs is that they place greater responsibility on workers for making financial decisions. They shift financial decision-making from professionals to individual workers. Proponents of privatization and defined contribution systems argue that workers should be capable of making these decisions, while opponents argue that many workers lack interest in acquiring the necessary knowledge. Studies have documented widespread financial illiteracy in many countries, with this issue being more important in countries with privatized social security systems. While lack of literacy and numeracy are causes of lack of financial literacy, financial literacy rates are considerably lower than literacy rates. Furthermore, financial illiteracy is most prevalent among people who are already economically vulnerable—women, minorities, and those with less education and income. The requirements for financial literacy placed on them by privatized social security systems only increase their economic vulnerability.

Financial education has been the focus of efforts to deal with financial illiteracy, but studies have documented that it often has limited success, perhaps because many workers are not interested. Some programs of financial education may have been ineffective because they have been of limited duration. In addition, some workers have had difficulty following through on changes that they intended to implement following financial education. Thus, while some programs have succeeded in improving financial knowledge, they have done less well in changing financial behavior.

The limited effectiveness of financial education shifts the focus in some countries to issues of financial advice. Workers seeking financial advice, however, have encountered a number of problems, the most significant of which perhaps is conflicts of interest that financial advisers may have, combined with not having a fiduciary duty to act in the best interest of their clients. Conflicts of interest arise because of the ways that the compensation of advisers is determined. For example, a financial adviser may receive higher compensation when he recommends a financial product that charges higher fees to the recipient of the advice. Studies in several countries have documented that many clients are receiving financial advice that is not appropriate for their needs. The level of fees charged is another issue. Frequently, fees are not disclosed or are not disclosed in a manner that is salient to the client. Because of the problems with the quality and cost of financial advice, a number of countries are considering reforms of the ways that financial advice is provided.

Note

We have received valuable comments and assistance from David Rajnes.

References

Agnew, Julie, Pierluigi Balduzzi, and Annika Sundén. 2003. "Portfolio Choice and Trading in a Large 401(k) Plan. *American Economic Review* 93(1): 193–215.

Agnew, Julie, and Lisa R. Szykman. 2004. "Asset Allocation and Information Overload: The Influence of Information Display, Asset Choice and Investor Experience." CRR Working Paper No. 2004-15. Boston: Center for Retirement Research at Boston College.

Antolin, Pablo, and Debbie Harrison. 2012. "Annual DC Pension Statements and the Communications Challenge." OECD Working Papers on Finance, Pensions and Insurance No. 19. Paris: Organisation for Economic Co-operation and Development.

Ashcroft, John, and Fiona Stewart. 2010. "Managing and Supervising Risks in Defined Contribution Systems." IOPS Working Paper No. 12. Paris: International Organisation of Pension Supervisors. http://www.iopsweb.org/dataoecd/48/1/46126017.pdf (accessed May 1, 2013).

Bergstresser, Daniel, John M. R. Chalmers, and Peter Tufano. 2009. "Assessing the Costs and Benefits of Brokers in the Mutual Fund Industry." *Review of Financial Studies* 22(10): 4129–4156.

Betson, Fennell. 2001. "One in Five Swedes Makes Active PPM Choice." Investments & Pensions Europe. London: IPE. http://www.ipe.com/article.asp?article=11880 (accessed May 1, 2013).

British Broadcasting Corporation (BBC). 2010. "Financial Advisers' Commission to be Banned from 2012." *BBC News*. http://news.bbc.co.uk/2/hi/business/8589042.stm (accessed May 1, 2013).

Canadian Press. 2005. "Retirement Saving, Financial Planning More Stress-

ful Than Seeing Dentist: RBC." *Canadian Press*, February 21. http://www
.canada.com/finance/rrsp/archives.html (accessed October 12, 2005).

Choi, James J., David Laibson, Brigitte Madrian, and Andrew Metrick. 2002.
"Defined Contribution Pensions: Plan Rules, Participant Choices, and the
Path of Least Resistance." In *Tax Policy and the Economy*, Vol. 16, James
Poterba, ed. Cambridge, MA: MIT Press, pp. 67–113.

Clark, Robert L., Melinda Sandler Morrill, and Steven G. Allen. 2012. "Effectiveness of Employer-Provided Financial Information: Hiring to Retiring."
American Economic Review: Papers and Proceedings 102(3): 314–318.

Cornfield, Jill. 2012. "Many Investors Need Help Navigating the World of Investments." planadviser.com. May 8. http://www.planadviser.com/Many_
Investors_Need_Help_Navigating_the_World_of_Investments.aspx (accessed May 1, 2013).

Devesa-Carpio J., and C. Vidal-Meliá. 2002. *The Reformed Pension Systems
in Latin America*. World Bank Social Protection Discussion Paper No.
0209. Washington, DC: World Bank. http://siteresources.worldbank.org
/SOCIALPROTECTION/Resources/SP-Discussion-papers/Pensions
-DP/0209.pdf (accessed May 1, 2013).

Gray, Dave. 2012. "401(k) Plans: Bridging the Gap between Sponsors and
Participants." Bridgeville, PA: fi360, Inc. http://www.fi360.com/main/pdf/
Gray_2012_slides.pdf (accessed May 1, 2013).

Hackenthal, Andres, M. Haliassos, and T. Japelli. 2011. "Financial Advisers: A
Case of Babysitters." CSEF Working Paper No. 219. Naples: University of
Italy, Naples; Center for Studies in Economics and Finance.

Hastings, Justine, Olivia S. Mitchell, and Eric Chyn. 2011. "Financial Literacy
and Pension Fund Fees." *Trends and Issues*. New York: TIAA-CREF Institute. http://www.tiaa-cref.org/ucm/groups/content/@ap_ucm_p_tcp_docs/
documents/document/tiaa02029455.pdf (accessed May 1, 2013).

Hathaway, Ian, and Sameer Kahtiwada. 2008. "Do Financial Education
Programs Work?" Federal Reserve Bank of Cleveland. Working Paper
No. 08-03. Cleveland: Federal Reserve Bank of Cleveland. http://www
.clevelandfed.org/research/workpaper/2008/wp0803.pdf (accessed May 1,
2013).

Hung, Angela, and Joanne Yoong. 2012. "Asking for Help: Survey and Experi-
mental Evidence on Financial Advice and Behavior Change." Paper presented at the 2012 conference The Market for Retirement Financial Advice,
held at the Wharton School, University of Pennsylvania, May 3–4.

Inderst, Roman, and Marco Ottaviani. 2012. "Financial Advice." *Journal of
Economic Literature* 50(2): 494–512.

Infogroup/ORC. 2010. *Elder Investment Fraud and Financial Exploitation: A
Survey Conducted for Investor Protection Trust*. Washington, DC: The In-

vestor Protection Trust. http://www.investorprotection.org/downloads/pdf/
learn/research/EIFFE_Press_Release.pdf (accessed March 20, 2012).

International Organisation of Pension Supervisors (IOPS). 2011. "Pension Supervisory Authorities and Financial Education: Lessons Learnt." IOPS Information Paper No. 1. Paris: IOPS. http://www.iopsweb.org/dataoecd/3/41/
49009719.pdf (accessed May 1, 2013).

Jarvenpaa, Perttu. 2001. "Swedes Fear Pension Loss on Retirement." London:
Investment & Pensions Europe, I&PE Newsline, April 25. http://www.ipe
-newsline.com/article.asp?article=1240 (accessed May 1, 2013).

Kell, Peter. 2012. "The Future of Financial Advice Post FOFA." Victoria, Australia: Australian Securities & Investments Commission. http://www.asic
.gov.au/asic/pdflib.nsf/LookupByFileName/Future-of-advice-post-FoFA
.pdf/$file/Future-of-advice-post-FoFA.pdf (accessed May 1, 2013).

KPMG. 2011. "Evolving Investment Management Regulation." Various lo-
cations: KPMG.   http://www.kpmg.com/Global/en/IssuesAndInsights
/ArticlesPublications/Documents/evolving-investment-management
-regulationv4.pdf (accessed May 1, 2013).

Lusardi, Annamaria. 2006. "Financial Literacy and Financial Education: Review and Policy Implications." NFI Policy Brief 2006-PB-11. Terre Haute,
IN: Indiana State University, Networks Financial Institute. http://papers
.ssrn.com/sol3/papers.cfm?abstract_id=923437 (accessed May 1, 2013).

Lusardi, Annamaria, and Olivia S. Mitchell. 2006. "Financial Literacy and
Planning: Implications for Retirement Wellbeing." Pension Research Coun-
cil Working Paper No. 1. Philadelphia, PA: University of Pennsylvania,
Wharton School of Business, Pension Research Council.

———. 2011. "Financial Literacy around the World: Introduction and Overview." Financialliteracyfocus.org. http://www.financialliteracyfocus.org/
files/FLatDocs/Lusardi_Mitchell_Overview.pdf.

Lusardi, Annamaria, Olivia S. Mitchell, and Vilsa Curto. 2010. "Financial Lit-
eracy among the Young: Evidence and Implications for Consumer Policy."
Hanover, NH: Dartmouth. http://www.dartmouth.edu/~alusardi/Papers
/Financial_literacy_young.pdf (accessed May 1, 2013).

Madrian, Brigitte C., and Dennis Shea. 2001. "The Power of Suggestion: In-
ertia in 401(k) Participation and Savings Behavior." *Quarterly Journal of
Economics* 116(4): 1149–1187.

Malcolm, Hadley. 2012. "Millennials Struggle with Financial Literacy."
USA Today, April 24. http://www.usatoday.com/money/perfi/basics/story/
2012-04-23/millenials-financial-knowledge/54494856/1 (accessed May 1,
2013).

McCarthy, David M., and John A. Turner. 2000. "Pension Education: Does It
Help? Does It Matter?" *Benefits Quarterly* 16(1): 64–72.

Monetary Authority of Singapore. 2012. "MAS Releases Results of Mystery Shopping Survey Conducted on Financial Advisory Process of Banks and Insurers." Singapore: Monetary Authority of Singapore. http://www.mas .gov.sg/News-and-Publications/Press-Releases/2012/MAS-Releases -Results-of-Mystery-Shopping-Survey.aspx (accessed May 1, 2013).

Muir, Dana M. 2009. "Regulation and Personal Pensions." In *Personal Provision of Retirement Income*, Jim Stewart and Gerard Hughes, eds. Cheltenham, UK: Edward Elgar, pp. 229–252.

———. 2011. "Building Value in the Australian Defined Contribution System: A Values Perspective." *Comparative Labor Law & Policy Journal* 33(49): 93–136.

———. 2012. "Default Settings in Defined Contribution Plans: A Comparative Approach to Fiduciary Obligation and the Role of Markets." Paper presented at Employee Benefits in an Era of Retrenchment, held at Washington University Law School, St. Louis, MO, March 29.

Mullainathan, Sendhil, Markus Noeth, and Antionette Schoar. 2012. "The Market for Financial Advice: An Audit Study." NBER Working Paper No. 17929. Cambridge, MA: National Bureau of Economic Research. http:// www.nber.org/papers/w17929.pdf (accessed May 1, 2013).

National Center for Educational Statistics. 2012. "State and County Estimates of Low Literacy." Washington, DC: NCES. http://nces.ed.gov/naal /estimates/StateEstimates.aspx (accessed May 1, 2013).

Olsen, Anya, and Kevin Whitman. 2007. "Effective Retirement Savings Programs: Design Features and Financial Education." *Social Security Bulletin* 67(3): 53–72. http://www.socialsecurity.gov/policy/docs/ssb/v67n3/ v67n3p53.pdf (accessed May 1, 2013).

Organisation for Economic Co-operation and Development (OECD). 2006. "The Importance of Financial Education." *Policy Brief*, July. http://www .oecd.org/dataoecd/8/32/37087833.pdf (accessed May 1, 2013).

Osborne, Hilary. 2010. "Financial Advisers' Commission to Cease, Says FSA." *The Guardian.* http://www.guardian.co.uk/money/2010/mar/26/financial -advisers-commission-ban (accessed May 1, 2013).

Rajnes, David. 2003. "International Evidence: Development and Delivery of Financial/Investment Information to the Public." Unpublished paper. Washington, DC: Social Security Administration.

Ribeiro, Ana Gonazlez. 2012. "The Most Financially Literate Countries." *Investopedia*, June 25. http://in.finance.yahoo.com/news/most-financially -literate-countries-211036210.html (accessed May 1, 2013).

Russell, Corie. 2012. "Plan Sponsors Should Steer Clear of Investment 'Jargon'." *PlanSponsor*, July 18. http://www.plansponsor.com/Plan_Sponsors_ Should_Steer_Clear_of_Investment_Jargon.aspx (accessed May 1, 2013).

Schellenberg, Grant, and Yuri Ostrovsky. 2008. "The Retirement Puzzle: Sorting the Pieces." Ottawa, ON: Statistics Canada. http://www.statcan.gc.ca/pub/11 -008-x/2008002/article/10667-eng.htm#a7 (accessed May 1, 2013).

Schlingmann, Francine, Joost Schutte, and Marnix Somsen. 2012. "Government Outlines Plans to Improve Quality of Advice." Netherlands: De Brauw Blackstone Westbroek. http://www.lexology.com/library/detail .aspx?g=eedde15b-19d4-4208-874f-eaf5d0f29b6b (accessed May 1, 2013).

Shepherd, Jessica. 2010. "Poor Literacy and Math Skills Leave Teenagers Ill-Equipped." *The Guardian*, May 7. http://www.guardian.co.uk/education/ 2010/may/07/poor-literacy-numeracy (accessed May 1, 2013).

Stango, Victor, and Jonathan Zinman. 2009. "Exponential Growth Bias and Household Finance." *Journal of Finance* 64(6): 2807–2849. http: //onlinelibrary.wiley.com/doi/10.1111/j.1540-6261.2009.01518.x/abstract (accessed May 1, 2013).

Turner, John A. 2003. "Errors Workers Make in Managing 401(k) Investments." *Benefits Quarterly* 19(4): 75–82.

———. 2004. "Individual Accounts: Lessons from Sweden." *International Social Security Review* 57(1): 65–84.

Turner, John A., and Sophie Korczyk. 2004. "Pension Participant Knowledge about Plan Fees." *AARP Data Digest* 105. http://assets.aarp.org/rgcenter/ post-import/dd105_fees.pdf (accessed May 1, 2013).

Turner, John A. and Dana M. Muir. 2012. "The Market for Financial Advisers." Paper presented at the 2012 conference The Market for Financial Advice, held at the Wharton School, University of Pennsylvania, May 3–4.

U.S. Government Accountability Office. 2011. "Financial Literacy: A Federal Certification Process for Providers Would Pose Challenges." GAO-11-614. Washington, DC: GAO.

World Bank. 2012. "Literacy Rate, Adult Total." Washington, DC: World Bank. http://data.worldbank.org/indicator/SE.ADT.LITR.ZS (accessed May 1, 2013).

Yakoboski, Paul. 2005. "Annuitization: What Individuals Say, What Individuals Do." TIAA-CREF Institute Issue Brief. New York: TIAA-CREF.

Authors

Tomasz Brzęczek has a PhD in economics, and is a researcher and lecturer at Faculty of Management Engineering at Poznań University of Technology. He focuses on operations research in microeconomics and finance.

Tianhong Chen is a PhD candidate at the Center for Social Security Studies, Wuhan University, China.

Ross Clare is director of research at the Association of Superannuation Funds of Australia, and previously worked at the Australian Treasury and a government research agency. He has degrees in law and economics from the Australian National University.

Denise Gómez-Hernández is professor at Autonomous University of Querètaro. She is a member of the SNI Level 1 and head-leader of a researching group in finance and economics.

Gerard Hughes is an adjunct professor in the School of Business, Trinity College Dublin. Formerly he was a research professor at the Economic and Social Research Institute in Dublin. He is a founder member of the European Network for Research on Supplementary Pensions and is a member of the Trinity College Pension Policy Research Group.

Magdalena Mosionek-Schweda is assistant professor at the University of Gdansk (Poland), the Faculty of Economics, Department of International Financial Markets. Her research focus is international finance, with an emphasis on capital markets and stock exchanges.

Dana M. Muir is an Arthur F. Thurnau Professor of Business Law, Stephen M. Ross School of Business at the University of Michigan and a Fellow of the American College of Employee Benefits Counsel.

Maria Clara Murteira is assistant professor of economics at the Faculty of Economics, University of Coimbra, Portugal. She has a PhD in economics. Her main research areas are the Economics of the Welfare State, Social Security and Pension Policy.

David Rajnes works as a social science research analyst with the U.S. Social Security Administration in Washington, D.C.

Alberto M. Ramírez de Jurado Frías is consulting actuary and president of Colegio Actuarial Mexicano in México, member of the Conference of Consulting Actuaries, and member of the American Academy of Actuaries in the United States.

Adam Samborski is professor at the University of Economics in Katowice, and the Poznań School of Banking. He specializes in corporate governance, pension fund governance, corporate finance, and capital markets.

Gabriella Sjögren Lindquist is associate professor of economics and deputy director at the Swedish Institute for Social Research at Stockholm University. Her main research interests are pensions, social security insurances, collectively bargained and other private supplementary insurances, work injuries, and income inequality.

Marek Szczepański is chair of Economic Sciences in the Faculty of Management Engineering at Poznań University of Technology.

John A. Turner is director of the Pension Policy Center. He has a PhD in economics from the University of Chicago, and has published numerous articles concerning retirement income policy.

Eskil Wadensjö is professor of labor economics at the Swedish Institute for Social Research, Stockholm University, and director of the Stockholm University Linnaeus Center for Integration Studies. His main research areas are social and labor market policy and international migration and integration.

Maciej Żukowski is professor of economics at the Poznań University of Economics in Poland and since 2008 Vice-Rector for Research and International Relations. His research, mainly in comparative perspective, concerns public policy, mainly social security, labor market, international migration, education and European integration.

Index

The italic letters *f*, *n*, or *t* following a page number indicate that the subject information of the entry heading is within a figure, note, or table, respectively, on that page. Double letters, e.g., *nn*, indicate more than one such feature.

About the Institute

The W.E. Upjohn Institute for Employment Research is a nonprofit research organization devoted to finding and promoting solutions to employment-related problems at the national, state, and local levels. It is an activity of the W.E. Upjohn Unemployment Trustee Corporation, which was established in 1932 to administer a fund set aside by Dr. W.E. Upjohn, founder of The Upjohn Company, to seek ways to counteract the loss of employment income during economic downturns.

The Institute is funded largely by income from the W.E. Upjohn Unemployment Trust, supplemented by outside grants, contracts, and sales of publications. Activities of the Institute comprise the following elements: 1) a research program conducted by a resident staff of professional social scientists; 2) a competitive grant program, which expands and complements the internal research program by providing financial support to researchers outside the Institute; 3) a publications program, which provides the major vehicle for disseminating the research of staff and grantees, as well as other selected works in the field; and 4) an Employment Management Services division, which manages most of the publicly funded employment and training programs in the local area.

The broad objectives of the Institute's research, grant, and publication programs are to 1) promote scholarship and experimentation on issues of public and private employment and unemployment policy, and 2) make knowledge and scholarship relevant and useful to policymakers in their pursuit of solutions to employment and unemployment problems.

Current areas of concentration for these programs include causes, consequences, and measures to alleviate unemployment; social insurance and income maintenance programs; compensation; workforce quality; work arrangements; family labor issues; labor-management relations; and regional economic development and local labor markets.